Dr Magnesium Mg^{2+}

Lee-Michael Keegan

ISBN 978-1-3999-8871-1

Cover Design: Andy Magee

T.E.K, a Royal Marine to the very end, little did you know, I owed you so much.

To my parents for the aspiration, my wife for the perspiration, and my kids for the motivation.

Contents

Preface

So, who am I? And why should you be interested in the tortuous journey, the emotional rollercoaster of dizzying highs and gut-wrenching lows, that has been my career in Medicine?

I suppose the first thing to state is that I am not your usual doctor. I did not take the traditional route into this profession, there was no top private school or high-flying educational achievement for me. I did not follow in my parents' footsteps, along the well-trodden family path. To be honest, I barely attended the last year of my comprehensive secondary school education, and Medicine was so far removed from my life plan at this point that I couldn't have seen it loitering on my distant horizon, even with the aid of a decent pair of binoculars. It was not a consideration for a lad like me. I don't say this as part of some social crusade but to illustrate that I've experienced a different life to most of my colleagues, and therefore, I offer a perspective more similar to that of our patients. To this day, I still find myself wondering how the bloody hell it all happened, how I found myself accepted onto a medical degree at the grand old age of thirty.

My story began in the late seventies, in Speke, a deprived borough of the proud and unashamedly working-class city of Liverpool, in north-west England. Many of my city's folk had fallen victim to the heroin or "scag" epidemic that plagued our city throughout the eighties, and as a result, it was a tough area in which to grow up, the kind of place that provided you with two choices: fight or become a victim.

I always chose to fight. Luckily, my parents were fighters too, and they managed to move me and my two brothers out of the rough-and-tumble of Speke, settling us into the much more sedate and affluent suburb of Aigburth before we suffered any irreversible damage. From there, I managed to scrape my way through the awkward teen years without completely destroying what little promise I had left. I completed the minimum schooling I could legally get away with and left at the tender age of sixteen with barely a qualification to my name and was essentially forced onto a government-backed youth training scheme (YTS) in plastering for the princely return of £29 per week.

Deciding I wanted to see a bit more of the world, I joined the RAF Regiment as an immature eighteen-year-old, which eventually honed my scrappy rebellious temperament into a tough and steely determination whilst providing me with the discipline I so badly needed, and gave me my first experience of death in a professional capacity. I served the minimum term I could get away with, just like school, before performing a complete one-eighty by turning down a lucrative close protection opportunity in favour of studying Art and Design at Liverpool Community College, where I met my wonderful wife and started our family. We eventually both earned a place on the prestigious Fine Arts degree course at Liverpool John Moores University, and true to character, I dropped out in second year, this time to start up a landscaping company, which I developed and ran for around five years, before performing another complete one-eighty and enrolling on an Access to Medicine course back at Liverpool Community College. As you can no doubt appreciate, all of this meant I was coming at my medical career from a very different perspective to my colleagues.

I began this book in 2015, initially intending it as a lecture or presentation piece. My idea was to give the final-year medical students a glimpse of what to expect in the upcoming first year of Foundation, wedging a few witty anecdotes in amongst the heart-wrenchingly depressing experiences these poor unsuspecting fuckers were about to live through. At that time, I was a relatively new doctor who had taken a beating from my first year of Foundation and was still battered and bruised from the whole experience. I wanted to help in some way – after all, isn't that what we doctors are supposed to do? – by giving the next cohort a heads-up and preparing them for what may lie in store.

But as I entered the second year of Foundation, the landscape around us doctors shifted significantly as the Conservative government attempted to force a new contract upon us. This led to unprecedented events, culminating in the junior doctors' strikes of 2015/16, which had a devastating effect on my career after I steadfastly refused to sign the contract. As a result, I was cast adrift on a sea of uncertainty, eventually landing on the well-trodden path of the career locum.

The first doctors' strike in the history of the NHS was quickly followed by the devastating change to the IR35 tax laws. Next came a little issue with our European neighbours, labelled "Brexit" by the UK tabloid media, which was an unmitigated disaster for the staffing levels of our hospitals. And hot on the Union-Jack-emblazoned heels of Brexit was the most high-profile pandemic since the Black Death toured the globe way back in the 1340s: COVID-19.

To say that I have worked through interesting and controversial times is perhaps somewhat of an understatement. It has certainly made the experiences covered in this book eventful and memorable, and I count it as a genuine honour to have both lived through them and written about them. It all culminates in a brutally honest account of life as an acute medical doctor, and I have pulled no punches. I hope this book achieves its aims of not only being entertaining, but also giving insight into the job we do, the often unbearable physical and emotional strain we put ourselves through to try and help our patients in the best way we can, and the effect so much regular proximity to loss can have on our own humanity. A friend described this book as Adam Kay's excellent *This is Going to Hurt* on crack, and I genuinely don't believe I could top that.

Anyway, only nine years later than planned, I finally got there in the end. I hope you enjoy this journey as much as I have.

*

Out of respect for the patients and families involved in this book, as well as my own family, and current and ex-colleagues, I have avoided using real names/initials or even mentioning the specific hospitals in which I have worked, although there will be some pretty significant hints along the way, and a few rather witty aliases, even if I do say so myself.

A list of Useful Terminology (relevant to this book) can be found at the back of the book.

Sergeant Bastard

I stepped down from the stuffy train carriage onto Wendover railway station's cool and refreshing platform, on that bright morning in late May 1996. I was still slightly intoxicated from my father's fortieth birthday celebrations which had started off civilised enough the previous evening but had somehow descended into a drunken send-off that had lasted well into the early hours of the morning – an unwise decision that I was now regretting.

I was completely alone as the train pulled away, the rusted old bridge, perilously spanning the track, directly above my head. The small station was surrounded by tall pines, and I found myself enveloped by an almost deafening silence, the rather eerie and strange atmosphere bringing to mind the popular eighties television series *Twin Peaks*.

I was apprehensive, nervous, and wondering what the hell I had signed up for when I heard a vehicle engine approaching in the distance. I walked through the deserted station and out to the front just as a battered olive-green and black Land Rover pulled up, rattling viciously and coughing out dark clouds of smoke from its rear end. A tall, wiry, stern-looking man with a moustache, bordering on the Hitler style, stepped out and asked me my name in a gruff but subtle South African accent. I stuttered my response, and he nodded for me to put my bag in the back before I stepped up into the front cab. We spent most of that short drive to RAF Halton in awkward silence.

I entered a camp bathed in bright sunshine and was taken to a hall where around forty other young men, with shaven heads and not a pound of body fat between them, were scattered around trying to look cool, or hard, but mostly looking nervous. The energy in the room was similar to my recent YTS experience, and I decided these lads were nothing I couldn't handle. We were ushered straight into a classroom for the induction, given no time to rest or settle in, split into groups, and the training began.

The following four days at RAF Halton were plain-sailing in comparison to what was to come when we moved on to the twenty-week Trainee Gunners Course at RAF Honington. But for now, we were issued our uniform and taught to march, polish our boots, use an iron, make a bed pack, and, as unbelievable as it sounds now, wipe our backsides correctly. We were allowed to visit the NAAFI every night, which was basically a sweet shop, and I rather enjoyed the steady marches and drill practice that lasted long into the mild late-spring evenings.

It was not at all what I had expected, and apart from the gut-wrenching episodical bouts of homesickness that involved lying on my bed listening to Beatles songs on my Walkman whilst swallowing down the lump in my throat and fighting back tears, it was actually not that bad. We were even allowed to phone home every night, and I phoned my parents and my ex-Marine grandad, who had been instrumental in my decision to join up, for regular moral support and advice.

The RAF Halton days flew by, and before we knew it, forty odd of us were loaded onto a coach and handed a paper packed-lunch bag, containing a corn-beef sandwich, a bag of crisps, a couple of biscuits wrapped in cellophane, an apple, and a carton of juice. I kept myself to myself and slept most of the two-hour journey east to Suffolk.

I hadn't really spoken to anyone since I'd arrived at the train station, and for the last four days had tried to look as mean as possible whilst projecting a stay-away-from-me kind of vibe, a vibe I had perfected growing up on the tough streets of Liverpool. I continued with this portrayal as we arrived at RAF Honington, and I stepped down from the cool coach and into the glorious East Anglian sunshine, to be greeted by a medium-height, thick-set, mean-looking man who had a dark navy-blue beret pulled tightly across his forehead, in a flat-cap style, the peak of which came to rest precariously on the thick brow that sat heavily above his small, menacing, pig-like eyes.

He lined us up in ranks of three outside an immaculate white building that was blinding in the bright midday sunshine and informed us all that we had ten minutes to get our "scoff" and get back out and lined up. I rather naively asked if I could smoke instead of eating as I wasn't hungry and didn't fancy my chances of getting in and out the mess in ten minutes. Without even glancing in my direction, he waved me away with a flick of his hand and assured me I could stay there and smoke outside the mess so long as I removed my headdress.

I immediately thanked him and whipped off my beret whilst simultaneously pulling out a crumpled twenty-pack of Regal King Size from the inside pocket of my DPM jacket, lighting one up, and deeply inhaling the thick, acrid, yet soothing, smoke. I quickly finished the cigarette and was about to get back into line when I had a brain wave – I'd have another one. After all, who knew when I would get the chance again. I pulled a second squashed cigarette out of the battered box, straightening it back into a respectable shape with my thumb and forefinger before lighting it, just as the other recruits ambled out of the mess and started to fall into three loose, disorganised ranks, all the while casually observed by our eagle-eyed sergeant.

When almost all the recruits had "fell in", he casually glanced at his watch before exploding toward me with alarming speed and murderous intent. He quickly and aggressively snatched the cigarette from my mouth, his fingers catching the lit end and spreading an eruption of fiery red embers all over the pair of us. I watched them bounce off his jacket and gracefully fall to the ground in slow motion, like spent fireworks, and in my peripheral vision, I caught the shocked looks on the other recruits' faces as he aggressively slammed his forehead against mine and screamed a tirade of four-letter abuse – mostly alluding to the fact that I was a Scouser and a bastard – directly into my face. He was so close that I could feel the warmth of his breath and the wetness of the warm flecks of spittle as they landed on my face. His eyes, bloodshot like those of a maniac, were bulging from his sockets, their gaze drilling deep into my brain as he continued to scream vile hatred and spit into my face.

I was in complete shock and didn't know what to do or how to react. My whole life, I had always tried to maintain an image. If someone came at me, I would be the one to strike first. I had boxed from the age of seven, so I would use my reflexes and hand speed to get in quickly with a flurry of shots and never back down, especially in front of my peers. But now, I just stood there, backed firmly into a recess, feet rooted to the spot, this man towering over me, spewing unadulterated hatred into my face. I had completely frozen. I felt exactly what I was: a little boy hundreds of miles away from home and missing his mum. My eyes began to well up and a lump formed in my partially closed throat, but I managed to quickly compose myself, the little pride that remained combining with a burning sense of deep shame to force me to snap back into the moment.

I was angry, and I thought, *Fuck it, I'm not going to let him break me on day one.* So, I stood there, pinned against that wall, shaking like a leaf, and lifted my head up, defiantly looking straight into his psychotic eyes, holding his stare. I could hear nothing now other than the heartbeat loudly racing in my ears, and my mouth was so dry my tongue was physically stuck to the roof. He suddenly and roughly grabbed the lapels of my jacket and physically threw me in the direction of the partially assembled lines, and I half stumbled, half jogged into a space that had opened up for me, my shaking legs so weak they were barely holding me up. I looked dead ahead and roughly placed the navy-blue beret back on top of my head.

I stood in line trembling and drenched in sweat whilst we waited for the last of the stragglers to exit the mess, watching as they were continually harangued by the demented sergeant screaming "*raus*" and "*schnell*" at them like a complete lunatic. Burning with embarrassment, I built up the courage to look into the faces of my new colleagues and found no humour, no mocking looks, just sheer terror, every one of those faces pale reflections of my own, *what the fuck am I doing here?* written in each of their eyes.

That was my introduction to my eventual saviour, Sergeant "Bastard", the man who would fight hard for me to remain on the course, despite, as I was later informed, the worst ever disciplinary record on basic training.

So, why have I started this book, which is essentially about my journey into and through Medicine, with a chapter about the infamous

Sergeant Mick Bastard? Because that split-second decision to stand and fight rather than run away was a "sliding door" moment for me. It was the first tentative step on the road to Damascus, the moment I went from streetwise hustler to soldier.

It's clear, on reflection, that the humiliating dressing down was simply a tactic employed by the good Sergeant Bastard, who had earned his nickname over the years for obvious reasons. He likely repeated this pantomime performance at the beginning of every training course, picking out the cockiest recruit to make an example of, as a way to stamp his authority, to lay an early marker, but it had been a knife-edge moment for me. I had been on the precipice, fully prepared to just walk away, like many other recruits must have done over the years, but I didn't. I mustered all my determination, all my stubbornness, what little was left of my pride, and I stood there and looked him in the eye. Despite shaking like a defecating dog, incapable of answering him back even if I had wanted to, I stood firm, and I never backed down. This was my first real test, and I had stumbled through it before using it to motivate myself. It was the spark that caught the kindling that eventually developed into a roaring fire.

This was the first of many challenges I was presented with on basic training, and indeed in the life that followed. But it was significant for being the moment I realised that, by my very nature, I am not a runner; I am a fighter. Those characteristics I had developed on the streets of Liverpool and honed throughout my relatively short military career turned out to be very useful assets in the world of Medicine. When everything is falling apart around you, when others are losing their heads and absolving themselves of all responsibility by fishing around in the wrist, performing an arterial blood gas for ten minutes, that's the time you have to stand up, steady your trembling legs, take a deep breath, roll up your sleeves, and step into the thick of the action.

If I had buckled on the morning of 25 May 1996, if I had thought *sod this for a game of soldiers* and thrown in my lot, then I would not be sitting here now writing this book. I don't know for sure where I would be, but it wouldn't be here. Up until that point in my life, I had been given every opportunity to succeed by my parents and my settled home environment, by my natural intelligence, and more than my fair share of sporting talent – not only excelling at boxing, but also successfully trialling for Great Britain at 800 m, and 4 x 100 m, in the early nineties. But up until that point, I had taken all of those opportunities and deliberately sabotaged my chances of success, choosing my friends and the streets over the inconvenience and hard graft of education and sports.

After that encounter with Sergeant Bastard, I gradually found my feet and started to mature. That's not to say there weren't many times I almost failed, almost didn't make it out alive. There was the time I fell out of a helicopter at a couple of hundred feet whilst abseiling. Then there was the time I was off skiving in the woods watching Hale Bopp illuminate the autumn sky whilst the fire position I was supposed to be manning was taken out by heavy machine-gun fire and completely levelled to the ground. Another time, I was held at gun point by a one-legged drunken Bosnian, whilst using a urinal. Or how about the time I stepped directly into a grenade blast to help out a mate who was about to get in deep shit, and left without a scratch? Or the time I fell into a peat bog whilst on night patrol and was saved by my GPMG, or the time I was almost shot outside a KFC in Belfast, or the time I was filling up my Land Rover and the ground immediately in front of the fuel tank was hit by a sniper… I could go on and on. I am often amazed I have somehow managed to get to the ripe old age of forty-six.

One thing I have learned over the years, though, and often the hard way, is that life is precarious and can end in the blink of an eye. Death can arrive at any moment and often arrives far too early. The attitude of an infantry soldier is often fatalistic and philosophical and, undoubtedly, gave me the confidence and bloody-mindedness to eventually decide that I was going to be a doctor, no matter what. A lack of education and qualifications wasn't going to stop me. That was just another obstacle I had to find a way to navigate around, or barge through, if necessary. I left the Regiment at the end of my minimum-term contract and bounced from bohemian artist to business owner, before deciding that Medicine was where I belonged, and the thought of failure never even crossed my mind. Well, not until my second first interview…

The Interview

Interview day arrived, and I was looking sharp, even if I do say so myself. I had trained for weeks to get into good physical shape, had bought myself a brand-new, expensive fitted suit, had a smart new haircut, and was cleanly shaven, for once. Not satisfied with just practising standard interview answers, I had been practising my charm for weeks. My self-depreciating smile was nailed down, and my humble confidence was on point. I was feeling good.

Rising early to ensure I had plenty of time, I managed to eat a good breakfast, before leisurely getting myself ready: shirt, bright-white and starched to within an inch of its life; jacket, pressed to perfection; trousers, creases sharp enough to slice bread; aftershave, expensive and liberally doused. I was smelling, looking, and feeling good. My wife had kindly agreed to drive me into the city centre so that I didn't have to worry about the parking situation, and we practised my humble and sincere responses to the continuous stream of questions she fired at me all the way there.

Pulling up outside the front doors of the administration headquarters for the University of Liverpool School of Medicine, Cedar House, I stepped out of the car into brilliant sunshine and straightened my trousers. Taking the suit jacket from its hanger in the back of the car and carefully sliding my arms into it, so as not to crease the front of my beautifully starched shirt, I was ready to go. I was going to absolutely smash this interview; nothing was getting in the way of winning my golden ticket.

Approaching the big, glass double doors, I paused briefly to give my reflection the once over. I straightened my tie for the thousandth time and gave my shoes a final buff against the back of my trouser leg. I was looking the part, every inch the young doctor, and I assured myself one final time that this was mine – I had it in the bag. At the grand old age of thirty, I had managed to traverse the most unlikely of paths from the mean streets of eighties Speke to the cool foyer of Cedar House. I was within grasp of the golden ticket, then all I would have to do was survive the tour and smash the elevator through the glass ceiling…

The first thing that struck me on entering that fabulous building was how quiet it was, which was unexpected because I knew there were medical interviews taking place all day. It was around this time I felt my first twinge of apprehension. Nevertheless, I followed the instructions on my interview letter, which directed me into a completely deserted waiting room with its abandoned reception desk.

Sitting on the corner of the reception desk was an old-fashioned brass bell. Okay, this was odd. My earlier confidence was ebbing away. Was this all a big hoax? Was I being stitched up? My mind was racing as I approached the desk and picked up the bell. I could hear muffled voices in the room behind. *Okay, calm down, you're overreacting. This is natural, it's just interview nerves screwing with your mind.* I rang the bell. Nothing. I waited what seemed like an eternity, but it was probably about half a minute, and rang the bell again, a little harder this time.

The door behind the desk opened, and a middle-aged woman popped her friendly face through the gap. "Can I help you, love?"

I informed her that I was here for my interview.

"I think you're mistaken, love. There are no interviews here today."

My stomach literally dropped through the soles of my highly polished shoes, and I instantly began to panic. I could feel my face flush and my cheeks start to burn with embarrassment. *Oh my God, is this really a set-up? Have I been pranked? I knew it had all been too good to be true; things like this didn't happen to kids from Speke.*

The floating head obviously picked up on my absolute horror and shouted to her colleague, who immediately walked out from the back office and fixed me with a look of motherly concern. "Can I help you, my love?"

I repeated that I was here for my medical school interview, and she reiterated that there were no interviews today, that they had finished yesterday. It was then that she dropped the bombshell.

"You're not Lee, are you?"

Oh no, what was she going to say, were the cameramen about to pile out of the back office led by an ecstatic Jeremy Beadle, clutching a massive envelope in one hand and a microphone in the other.

"Yes, I am."

"Your interview was yesterday, love."

I felt myself physically deflate within the perfectly starched white shirt, like a popped paper-mâché balloon. All that confidence, all that humble, self-depreciating practice… *Oh my God, I'm going to be sick.* I felt the colour drain from my face.

"Are you okay, love?"

I pulled the letter out of the inside pocket of my suit jacket and clumsily shoved it toward her. "Look. It's today."

She cautiously took the letter from my hand, and I could see genuine pity in her eyes as she read out loud: "Tuesday the seventh. That was yesterday."

"No, no. It's defo Wednesday. It's today, defo."

I took the letter back and read the word *Tuesday*, and the world collapsed around me. I was absolutely devastated. Standing there speechless, I tried to force out some words, any words, but none would come. How the hell had I got the days mixed up? I felt so embarrassed, and I started to flush again as beads of sweat gathered on my brow.

"Listen, love, don't worry. I promise you I will get you another interview. There's a second round for late entries at the beginning of September. I will get you in then, okay. Okay?"

I slowly nodded my head and thanked her profusely before walking out to face the music, the shame of admitting to my family and friends I had got the date wrong. But true to her word, the Secretary to the Dean of the School of Medicine, as I later found out was her role, got me that interview. Someone who had had no reason to believe in me or help me out, gave me a reprieve. She could easily have said that I had missed my chance. She could have stuck to the rules, but she never. She gave me a chance, and I am eternally grateful to her for that.

As you can probably imagine, the next few weeks were spent in a constant state of anxiety and uncertainty. Would she keep her promise? What had she said exactly? Did she say she would phone, or did she say she would send a letter? I was insecure and riddled with self-doubt, and by the time I finally got that letter and the second interview came around, there was no need to rehearse humility, or practise self-depreciation; all the cockiness and arrogance were gone. I followed a similar pattern. I dressed as smartly as I had previously, ate a smaller breakfast, and I was driven in my wife's car, but this time, I was quiet and nervous. There literally could not have been a greater contrast between the two interview build-ups.

Arriving at Cedar House early, I sat in the same cold waiting room, perched straight-backed and uncomfortable on a hard wooden bench. Tense and wringing my hands, I tried to focus by reading the names of previous deans, most long gone, engraved onto an old piece of hardwood that looked strangely out of place hung in this modern building of steel and glass. I had none of my normal confidence and was worrying that I was going to screw it all up and blow my second chance when my train of thought was suddenly broken by someone softly calling out my name. Looking up, I saw a tiny Mediterranean-looking woman with large, round glasses framed by a shock of dark, curly hair. She was not much older than myself and was beaming a broad friendly smile at me, head cocked slightly to one side like a curious little bird.

Smiling back, I said, "Hello," as I loosely shook her soft hand. She nimbly spun on her heels and quickly walked toward the open door that was now situated dead ahead of her, whilst I trailed behind, head slightly bowed, a condemned man on his final procession to the gallows. Briefly pausing at the door, I felt the wrenching sensation of nausea in my lower gut. I straightened my back and took a long, deep breath whilst simultaneously pumping out my chest. Looking dead ahead, I plastered a huge smile on my face as I confidently strolled into the interview room.

I told the panel of five people, sat behind the giant, dark wooden desk that dominated the room, exactly who I was and where I had come from, and more importantly, where I was going. I stood up at the end of the interview and looked steadily into each pair of eyes, as I firmly shook the accompanying hand, and I knew that I had done it.

I had absolutely no doubt whatsoever.

I was in.

From Small Acorns

And I was right. I had passed the interview and was accepted on the six-year course. The first year, year zero, was undertaken at a special centre for learning at Carmel College in St Helens, an old industrial town on the outskirts of Liverpool. The centre was technically a part of the college but was owned and run by the University of Liverpool. If I completed this year successfully, then I would progress on to the normal five-year degree in Medicine and Surgery, MBChB, at the School of Medicine.

There were twelve of us on the course, who had managed to stave off competition from the other thirty-five applicants interviewed for our places. Out of the twelve, nine were on the medical degree pathway and three on dentistry. We received excellent teaching in small groups, and in order to progress, we had to achieve the equivalent of an A grade at A Level in biology, biochemistry, and chemistry, and as a bonus, we had to do general studies. It was an amazing centre for learning, and I made it through to year one at Liverpool pretty easily as I had already passed the exams with an above 90% average on a community college access course the previous year. I had undertaken that course on the understanding that it would be sufficient to get me onto the five-year degree course, but during that year, the college course had been removed from the School of Medicine's approved list – hence, the requirement to join the six-year degree course and repeat my learning.

I spent that summer holiday mostly working as a gardener and window cleaner for my uncle's firm, the intense physical labour leaving me lean, healthy, tanned, and more than ready to get back to the cushy life of a student. However, what I didn't realise at the end of that summer was that the world I was about to enter would be new and strange, a world in which I would feel alien, alone, and an outsider for the next five years.

The first day of medical school was a pretty surreal experience for a thirty-year-old working-class Scouser. We had to attend registration in allocated time slots that related to the alphabetical order of our surname, and I arrived at the administration building slap-bang in the middle of my time slot, had a quick cigarette outside, popped a few pieces of Extra Ice chewing-gum into my mouth, and entered the foyer with my usual confident swagger, pushing open the heavy, old wooden door with a shove and instantly revealing my strange new world, inhabited by young people with smooth, hairless faces, most of them appearing to be not much older than my ten-year-old son.

I had never felt old until that moment, and I instantly felt the need to blend in, be anonymous, a movie extra milling about in the background whilst avoiding the camera's intense gaze. This became a feature of my time in medical school. I became obsessed with my age and would often say I was younger than I was when asked, which was absolutely ridiculous, but I felt my broad Scouse accent and my rather unusual background already made me stand out enough, and I really didn't want to bring any more heat down on myself. I actually got away with it most of the time… until my son got to around fourteen years of age and people started looking at me with more than a hint of suspicion as they realised I had been twenty-seven for the last four years and now had a fourteen-year-old son, the maths having become less believable by the year.

Taking my place at the back of the queue, I looked every inch the bearded, rough-arsed, worldly-wise ex-squaddie, but felt like the five-year-old kid, shyly approaching Alderwood Infants' imposing front gates way back in 1983. I had never felt so out of place, so claustrophobic. The urge to get the hell out of there was so overwhelming I could easily have run out of that building, pushing through the old wooden doors and back out into the bright light and the streets I knew so well, immersing myself in the safety of my city, my people.

But I resisted the urge to bolt, took a deep breath, stood up straight, pumped out my chest, and focused on the task ahead. I eventually got to the front of the queue and filled out my paperwork, collected my welcome pack… and I was in. I couldn't quite believe it. I was actually in. I had just handed Willy Wonka my golden ticket and was excitedly skipping through the gates to the chocolate factory.

As I walked out of the administration building, I bumped into my good mate from year zero, who was in the surname group immediately after mine. He invited me to a student event at the Walkabout in Liverpool city centre later that evening. I was slightly reluctant – after that first introduction to my new colleagues, my normally Teflon-coated confidence was slightly scuffed. However, despite my initial reticence, he managed to talk me round – it didn't usually take much persuasion when alcohol was involved – and promised that we would be meeting up with a "great bunch of lads".

I arrived at the Walkabout and was greeted on the stairs with a big bear hug and an introduction to his new mates from the rugby team as we walked upstairs to the balcony overlooking the stage. I engaged in some small talk but mainly stood on the periphery of the group of rugby boys, the odd garish-coloured shot of varying texture pushed in my direction as I silently observed their secret culture and bumbling, almost indecipherable language, full of guffaws and giggles with the odd perfectly pronounced swear word thrown in, to keep it real.

I listened, slightly amused by their blatantly exaggerated tales of sexual exploits and drinking games, which all seemed to involve large amounts of vomit. Standing on my own, like a Scouse David Attenborough, I watched my mate interacting with his new buddies and realised, with sadness, that I had lost him. He had completely reverted to his public-school, teenage, captain-of-the-rugby-team self, and was now well and truly "one of the boys". He had found his people and no longer needed the likes of me in his life, and it dawned on me that I was in for a long and lonely five years. I was a completely different animal, and this was not my world.

As I observed the Darwinian scenario developing in front of me, the music suddenly dropped off, and I was jarred back to the present by a voice announcing over the microphone that the moment we had all been waiting for had finally arrived: the president's inauguration. Following a brief pause, the speakers suddenly sprung back into life, belting out the classic instrumental, "The Stripper", as a young, obese male, wrapped in a feather boa and dressed in black, female underwear, stockings, suspenders, and six-inch stilettos, seductively sauntered on stage to wild raucous applause, whistles, and manic laughter.

This really wasn't my cup of tea, and I had seen enough for one night. I made my excuses to the year-zero buddy and left, later finding out that what I had witnessed was a Liverpool Medical Student Society (LMSS) tradition. Every new president had to strip fully naked in public, but it just so happened that this one had decided to take it to the next level. I decided the LMSS scene was not for me, only attending a further two social events over the next five years – the mid-course ball and the graduation party, although I left early on both occasions.

I continually felt out of place during my time at university, which was a strange feeling for someone who had always known how to fit in. I had been quite popular at school and in the forces, but I just couldn't be myself at university. I met some of the nicest human beings you could ever wish to meet during my time there, some really caring and genuinely lovely people who were friendly to me and always tried to include me in some way, but something always held me back, and in the end, they just stopped trying. I don't blame them really.

I suppose I felt too old to get involved in a lot of the organised fun aspects of university life, but I also felt a bit of a fraud, that I shouldn't really be there. I was constantly nervous and on edge, just waiting for them to realise they had actually, and rather embarrassingly, made a bloody huge mistake and unceremoniously kick me out, but not before ridiculing me in front of my suspecting peers.

Despite these feelings of inadequacy, I actually found the daily lectures of first year pretty straightforward. I also really enjoyed the introduction to problem-based learning (PBL). This would see a small group of us being given a clinical scenario by a facilitator and working together as a team to find solutions to the problem we had been given.

This seemed to really suit my style of learning, and I had no issues at all education-wise, comfortably passing the first year with flying colours.

*

The major life event of my first year was the passing of my grandad Keegan (I was lucky enough to still have all four grandparents at this point) from lung cancer, in the very same hospital in which I was a student. He had kept his diagnosis a secret at first, and being the tough Royal Marine that he was, he had just got on with it and never bothered anyone, even walking fourteen miles on Christmas Day to visit my nan at her EMI nursing home. There had been no room in the Christmas Day timetable for a bus up to Finch Lane, Huyton, so rather than putting anyone out, he simply walked, despite having advanced lung cancer and suffering from severe fatigue and shortness of breath.

He had reluctantly agreed to undergo chemotherapy without a murmur of complaint, but the cancer had metastasised, and he became very unwell over a short period of time. He was eventually admitted to hospital when he developed a large ascites (collection of fluid within the abdomen) and stopped passing water due to the pressure on his kidneys. He required an urgent ascitic drain to relieve the pressure.

I was informed of his admission, as I walked out of the old Florence Nightingale hospital wards, which now made up the clinical teaching part of the medical school, by a phone call from my dad, and I made the short journey, literally just across the road, to the hospital, looking every inch the junior doctor as I confidently strolled onto the ward with my rolled-up sleeves, NHS lanyard swinging with purpose. I noticed for the first time how run-down the ward was, paint flaking and peeling from the pink and cream walls, which seemed a strange colour combination for a geriatric medicine ward, now I came to think about it.

Putting that thought aside, I pushed open the powder-blue door into my grandad's side room and was immediately struck by the fluorescent yellow tinge to his skin, the massive ascites, and the red-brown crust on his lips and teeth, which all indicated he had been vomiting blood, was in acute liver failure, and in a pretty bad way really. He turned his head as I arrived, and I could see the pain and fatigue in his eyes for the microsecond before he put on his war face and gave me his best smile.

He was trying to look casual and was telling us all that he was absolutely fine and to "stop all the bloody fussing".

He asked me how I was getting on, and I instantly regretted that I had not been to see him as much as I should have. I told him all about my life as a student doctor, cracking off a few funny tales to try and lighten the mood, and he laughed along. I sat there with him for a while, thinking back to my teen years and how I had always tried to avoid going to my grandparents'. I had always had something better to do, somewhere better to be, and I regretted it then and suppose I still do.

He made me promise, no matter what happened, I would stick to Medicine and pass the course. I assured him in my cockiest manner that it was "a piece of piss" and not to worry about it. Smiling, he looked at me, and I could see genuine pride in his eyes. I already knew he was proud of me for joining the forces to get away from the bad situation I'd got myself into with drink, drugs, and gangs, and for coming to him to seek out his advice when I was at my lowest ebb, but I suspected he was most proud of me for breaking out of the class I'd been born into.

My grandad had been born into a world in which a person was defined by their class at birth, a world in which you stayed within that defining class. He joined the Royal Marines aged just sixteen in 1946, and despite long service, he never made it past corporal. Anyone who has been a soldier will understand how difficult it must have been to enter a unit that had just fought a world war together. Being thrown into this environment as a "sprog", no more than a baby, must have been extremely difficult, and I suppose that experience shaped him into the man he was to become. He was a proper soldier, and as such, he respected the rank system and would have likely deferred to his seniors and the officer class.

When he left the forces, he started working in Dunlop's tyre factory until it was closed down, and he then began working in the airport as a baggage handler. He looked after his family, he saved up and bought his council house, and he went to Yugoslavia every year with my nan as they got older.

He would never have imagined that one day his grandchild would smash through the established order of things and become "one of them", become a doctor. I had surpassed what someone from my class was supposed to achieve, and I think he respected that. I also think, deep down, he knew he had played a significant part in it all and was probably proud of that as well.

I was close to my grandad. We were similar people. Both small in height, but big in personality and attitude. Both fit and resilient and not easily deterred. I know it's not a very popular thing to be nowadays, but he was a proper man's man, and in the world I grew up in, we respect people who look after and provide for their family. We respect people with self-worth and honour, with morals and principles, and as such, I deeply respected my grandad.

And so, I watched this proud man slip away with the dignity I had come to expect. Never once did he complain, never once did he call out in pain, or express fear. He told his family that he loved them, closed his eyes, and died like a man. A Royal Marine, to the very end.

*

I progressed to second year without much difficulty. Every year ended with exams, both written and clinical, which needed to be passed in order to progress to the next year. Although I never felt fully part of the whole university experience, I certainly excelled on the educational side, passing exam after exam, and usually finishing toward the top of the year.

I was also developing well clinically, and despite being a nervous wreck taking my first set of bloods in the phlebotomy clinic during second year, I went from strength to strength. After a lifetime of working with my hands, I had good manual dexterity and, as such, was a natural at clinical procedures. My fellow students would always ask me to perform the difficult procedures, and as I progressed through the years, I would often be asked to help the foundation doctors with the trickiest of patients.

Although my course was going really well for me, I was still faced with many challenges, especially outside of my medical bubble. To allow me to continue to progress through my degree, my wife was the one tasked with supporting our little family, and following the credit crunch of 2008, her previously thriving business had begun to struggle, putting a lot of pressure on our family and requiring me to find work around my university hours and through the holidays.

On occasion, we really struggled financially. In fact, there were times we were so broke we had to choose between food and electricity. Despite this being extremely difficult and stressful for the both of us, it gave me even greater determination to succeed. And as I advanced through the years, it became increasingly easier to motivate myself through the struggle, as I could say, "I'm not going to let the last three years have all been in vain," and then four years, and so on.

It was hard to drop back down the ladder in my early thirties, to find myself at the bottom of the pile, especially after being a business owner and an employer since leaving the forces. I had been the boss, and now I was nothing, lower than nothing, and as such, a sitting duck for the egotistical narcissists and psychopaths who prey on the vulnerable and the weak. This class of human being seems to be present in much higher numbers in Medicine than most other walks of life, other than perhaps the military – which I can unfortunately attest to, having experienced my fair share of them during the Regiment days.

These people are essentially bullies, and due to being brought up in a staunchly socialist family, experiencing a childhood hanging around the violent working-class streets of northern England, and having been immersed in the oft brutal world of the infantry soldier, I am instilled with a strong sense of justice and struggle to back down from a bully. This made hospital placements quite difficult at times, as I would constantly have to bite my tongue or resist the urge to drag the perpetrators from the ward by their head, which would not have gone down too well in the more civilised world I now inhabited.

The hospital in which I underwent my training was a large inner-city teaching hospital with lots of unusual and severe pathology, meaning lots of potential for research and lots of wonga. Money and prestige attract specialist, highly regarded, and very senior consultants, and the only thing bigger than their reputations was their egos. As such, there were a fair few narcissists floating around our hospital, who loved nothing more than humiliating students. They thrived on putting you on the spot at the most uncomfortable of times, pulling you apart and pressing their immense superiority over you in front of the rest of the team, showing everyone just how much better they were than a mere medical student.

Don't get me wrong, there were also some absolutely amazing doctors who were a pleasure to work with and who would go out of their way to pass on their vast wealth of knowledge. It's fair to say, they are in the majority. However, as any medical student, or junior doctor, or indeed apple farmer, will have experienced first-hand, there are always a few rotten apples in every barrel.

I had handled the toughest and most aggressive sergeants and warrant officers in my time, and I considered myself pretty tough and streetwise, but these consultants used different tactics to those I had faced before. Their bullying was much more subtle and based on belittling the student or junior doctor in front of as many people as possible to make the subject feel as stupid as possible. Two such rotten apples were particularly well known in my hospital. They were terrifying for the young medical students, and to be honest, they were pretty daunting for me as well.

The first of the two was a professor in a surgical specialty and consultant on the ward on which I was on a six-week placement. I had been pre-warned to wear a white laboratory coat – despite them being long banned everywhere else by infection control – that was spotlessly clean and well ironed, with the sleeves rolled up to the elbows and neatly pressed. This was not an issue for me, as I always meticulously ironed my clothes and tried to look my best – a throwback to my military days. However, my one exemption to this rule was that I always had stubble or a short beard.

Apart from liking stubble and recognising that a beard hid a multitude of sins – well, my double chin – I actually had a valid reason for not being clean-shaven. I had suffered from terrible shaving rash, ever since my military days, and as such, I avoided shaving unless absolutely necessary. Little did I know, this particular prof was as anti-facial hair as he was dirty, crumpled lab coats.

I arrived for the first consultant ward round nice and early, as was my habit, my white coat gleaming and Daz-white with creases that could, ironically, have removed the offensive hair from my face. I joined the small team of foundation doctors and helped them to prepare the notes.

The whole team looked on edge, nervy, and the mood was serious, with none of the usual banter between the nurses and junior doctors. The notes were prepped, put in ward-round order, and the patient lists were printed off, the foundation doctors frantically scribbling down the most recent investigation findings and results in order to arm themselves against the upcoming onslaught of questions.

The minutes ticked past, and we waited like athletes before a big game – tense, focused, in quiet reflection. The doors swung open, and a disappointingly short and slight man with thinning yet impressively dark hair waltzed onto the ward, a rather fed-up-looking registrar trailing behind like a downtrodden dog.

They walked straight to the nurses' station without acknowledging a single team member, picked up a patient list, and headed straight into the first bay, the team quickly falling in behind like a brood of ducklings. The professor then proceeded to glide from room to room, snapping orders, completely ignoring the patient sat in front of him, as he projected a god-like air.

We eventually concluded the ward round, and I was relieved to have got through my first one without being asked a single question or receiving one the prof's legendary sarcastic remarks. He was walking away, and the team had visibly relaxed and started to go about the day's work, when suddenly, he stopped and slowly turned with Columbo-like drama. Looking directly at me for a few seconds, head slightly cocked to one side, he put his hand in his pocket and pulled out a disposable vibrant-orange razor, which he tossed in my direction. I leaned forward in a panic, almost stumbling, and caught it loosely with cupped hands. "Before the next ward round, make sure you get a shave."

And as quickly as he had arrived, he was gone. Thankfully, that was the last time I ever saw him, as he developed a severely debilitating, but fortunately recoverable, medical condition, which affected his mobility so much that he was unable to walk for the rest of my placement – every cloud, and all that.

The second rotten apple was a lot more sinister. He was the classic schoolyard bully, who used physical intimidation to bolster his own fragile ego. A medical specialty consultant, standing all of about five foot three inches in height and weighing around nine stone soaking wet, he would strut around the hospital corridors like the cock of the walk. Thankfully, I was only placed with him for one day, on which I was instructed to meet at his office for a teaching session with the rest of my PBL group. Unfortunately, only three of us turned up, and he seemed to take real offence to this – a slight to his egg-shell confidence.

I was the first to enter his office, and he showed me to the seat nearest to his desk, which I took whilst simultaneously pulling out the leather-bound notebook from my rucksack. Ever the diligent student, the notebook was never too far away from my hand. Suddenly, and without warning, he leaned across and roughly snatched it from my grasp before I could react. I sat there stunned as he started to leaf through the pages, pausing occasionally to read aloud notes that I had taken, ridiculing me in front of my colleagues and sneering at me. Eventually, he slammed it shut, and said, "What kind of crap is that?"

I felt the heat rising from my neck to my cheeks, and my heartbeat pounded in my ears. Feeling completely humiliated, it took every ounce of restraint I had to stay seated, keep my mouth shut and a disingenuous smile plastered on my face.

He slowly looked around the office, taking in the other two students in great detail, whilst deliberately avoiding my gaze. He then looked toward my waist and noted the Swiss Army belt-clip watch. Leaning across quickly again, he roughly pulled at it, almost tearing my belt loop clean off. He sneered sarcastically, "Who bought you this? Was it Mummy?"

Unfortunately, the watch actually was a recent Christmas present from my parents, and completely put on the spot, I couldn't think of anything else to say, other than, "Yes, it was actually."

I'd had enough of this game by now, though, and my voice was pure steel. He looked directly at me for the first time and must have noticed the fire in my eyes and my physical build. He suddenly looked very serious. "Do you play rugby for the university?" I informed him that I had never played a game of rugby in my life and explained that it was not a popular sport in the working-class area of Liverpool where I grew up. He looked me over again, and said, "You look like a sportsman." I informed him that I had played football but preferred boxing and had proudly represented Gemini Boxing Club in Speke and The Golden

Gloves in Toxteth, though my boxing career had come to a premature end when I joined the forces.

He began to look slightly concerned now, cagily asking me if I had been a medic in the forces. I informed him that I had actually been a specialist combat infantry soldier. He looked directly at me again, and I coolly returned his gaze.

"You could probably fight me, couldn't you?"

"I would fancy my chances, yes," I replied.

He continued to observe me for several seconds and then handed me back my notebook and started his teaching session as though nothing had happened. I occasionally bumped into him strutting around the hospital corridors like he owned the place, and not once did he ever acknowledge me. In fact, he wouldn't even look in my direction, keeping his gaze unnaturally directed forward.

*

Despite the odd bump in the road here and there, I managed to pass each clinical placement with flying colours, and as I approached my finals, everything seemed to be going swimmingly… until, bang, I was hit by the second major life event of the university years.

My uncle Paul, or "our P", who I was very close to and who was only forty-seven years old, was admitted to my hospital. He had been transferred to HDU with a severe sepsis of unknown origin, but likely intra-abdominal. I was sitting by his bed, with my nan Bell and mum, when the senior critical care registrar, who I knew from a previous placement, came in to break the bad news.

She nodded to me subtly and seriously, like a child playing the role of a grown up in a school production, before hesitantly informing us, in a slightly haphazard, bumbling manner, that it wasn't looking too good, and the medical team had decided to put in a DNAR (do not attempt to resuscitate) form, due to his significant frailty. Stunned, I studied my nan's face as the shock resonated around the room like a sound-wave. She looked confused, her skin gathered and crumpled around her cheek bones like sun-bleached paper, her deep-set eyes hollow and jet-black. *Well, that was a pretty shit demonstration of communication skills*, I thought.

My uncle gradually slipped away with all the people who loved him at his bedside. The scene was reminiscent of something out of *The Sopranos* – my aunties forming a tight semi-circle around him, fiddling with rosary beads, lips uttering silent prayers, whilst the male contingent of the family, fronted by my grandad Bell, fanned out behind – silent, strong, and dignified, heads respectfully bowed. My mum, the eldest daughter, seated at the centre, cradling my nan in her arms, wrapping her tightly in a futile attempt to stop her from shattering into a thousand jagged and broken pieces, all over the polished HDU floor.

I sat in the corner, numb, an observer rather than a participant, watching from the sidelines, as one half of my family's whole world literally fell apart in front of me. When the silence of the room was suddenly interrupted by a deep primal wailing, the verbalisation of my nan's heart breaking, I silently slipped from the room, completely unnoticed, and headed straight into the visitor's toilet, which was conveniently located immediately outside the bay.

Looking at my reflection in the giant wall-mounted mirror that took up a large section of the wall, I genuinely did not recognise the ghostly image staring gormlessly back at me. I watched this stranger as he pulled out his phone and dialled my wife. When she answered, I watched as he failed to speak, as he struggled to articulate the words he so desperately wanted to say. I tried to physically force the sound out, to describe the tragedy that had just befallen our family, but there was a massive lump in my throat, a blockage, and nothing could squeeze past it.

My wife asked me what was going on. Was I okay? I held the phone next to my ear for what seemed like a long time, before ending the call and breaking the bad news by text, instead. I composed myself, unlocked the door, and walked back to the HDU room – an important piece of my life, a good friend, gone forever.

Our P and Miss Indi

My uncle was one of the few people I knew who had had a more interesting life than me. On the surface, he had it all. He was tall, handsome, with a slim, athletic build, charismatic, and intelligent, and he possessed a rapier wit that could cut to the bone at will. He could be the most generous and loving person but could also be cruel and cold. He was a living contradiction, a man who adored his family and remained a child at heart, though his demons always lingered just below the surface, and his mood could turn on a sixpence, especially when he was on the vodka.

He was the second youngest of my mum's six siblings, my mum being the oldest, and as such, he was closer in age to me and my older brother. But unfortunately for him, he was part of the generation just before ours, the "scag" generation. He was an out-and-out rebel who never followed a single rule in his life and who would go out of his way to do the opposite of what he was told, even if it meant cutting off his nose to spite his face, which he often did.

His rebellious ways had started incredibly early on, and he was first caught "sagging" school at the age of just five, after his teacher called my nan to ask why he had been absent for most of the school term. It turned out he had been getting dropped off at school by one of his elder siblings and then would jump the fence and head over to Speke field to trap wildlife and set fires, the moment they turned their back. He got into smoking weed and taking LSD in his early teens and was eventually tempted by the brand-new opiate drug that had flooded the streets of

Speke, the very same drug that eventually ended the life of almost all his friends.

But my uncle was always "switched on" and realised pretty quickly the heroin was bad news. He decided he needed to get away from the city if he was going to clean up his act, so he bought a ticket for the promised land, and like generations of Irish (Scousers are almost all of Irish origin) immigrants before him, he set sail for America… well, he flew there, but that doesn't sound quite so romantic. At just eighteen years of age, that was the last we saw of him for a further eighteen years.

He travelled all over America, living in Indiana and Phoenix for spells, but his spiritual home was San Francisco, where he lived for twelve years in total. On his arrival from Speke, he found work as a busboy in restaurants, before working his way up to head chef and eventually restaurant owner. But being the rebel he was, he never followed the official process to become a legal citizen and happily revelled in the life of an illegal.

He never got clean of drugs either. He simply replaced heroin with work, before eventually turning to vodka, epitomising the old adage of "work hard but party harder". He drank to excess his whole life, destroying everything that was good, including all his personal relationships. Eventually, he pushed his luck too far and fell from a third-floor balcony whilst drunk and fractured his hip. After a brief period of rehabilitation, he was taken directly from a Californian charity hospital to a "lifers' jail" for three months, before being extradited to the UK.

He had been in Liverpool for a couple of years, continually plotting a way to get "back home", when he fell off a ladder whilst drunk and, at the age of thirty-eight, broke his spine. Now a paraplegic, he was wheelchair-bound for the rest of his life. He took it hard for the first year of rehabilitation in the Royal Liverpool University Hospital and the North West Regional Spinal Injuries Centre, Southport, drinking himself into oblivion and falling out with everyone who tried to help him, before he met a fantastic woman, who provided companionship for him until the end of his life, along with his beloved cat, Chollo – he never forgot California. At last, he settled into a new life of watching TV documentaries in his little Lark Lane flat, whilst chain smoking and drinking tea like it was going out of fashion.

He suffered further tragedy toward the end of his days, when the love of his life, the woman he had shared many happy years with, whilst living together all over America, was murdered during a carjacking. He had left her behind on extradition from the US and was informed of her violent end many months after her passing, by way of letter from her distraught parents. He took the news very badly and withdrew further into himself, whilst pushing us all away. Though surprisingly, he never returned to the bottle. He did, however, stop taking his blood-thinning injections, due to the annoying bruises on his stomach, and ended up suffering a massive stroke.

It was really difficult to watch this proud, handsome man, who literally could have been anything he put his mind to, wither and waste away. I found it hard to even look at him in the end, because he was so pained, so defeated, a spirit trapped inside a bottle. He had completely given up, and by the time we arrived around that HDU bed, he viewed his impending death as a blessed relief. I could see it in his faded blue eyes as he slipped away. He had always taken life on, squared up to it defiantly, stared it down, and told it to go fuck itself, but like all the brightest flames, he burned out far too quickly.

*

His death affected me deeply. I felt that I needed to honour him in some way, to make some good of such a tragic waste of talent. The opportunity presented itself not long after his passing, as I approached the end of fourth year and my upcoming “elective”.

Liverpool’s medical school is unusual in that we take our final examinations at the end of fourth year, not fifth year like most medical schools. If successful, we progress on to our final year, which is clinical- and portfolio-based. Sandwiched between those two years, occupying the summer break, we are encouraged to partake in an elective, which is essentially a four-to-six-week period of work experience. We can stay in the UK if we so wish, but we are encouraged to travel overseas, so we can experience different cultures and different ways of working.

Whilst most people chose to go to world-renowned centres of excellence that just happened to be situated on a world-renowned beach or conveniently located on the latest backpacker route, my wife and I decided to do something slightly different, as a result of attending a fundraising event for an English school in India. The school was located in Anandal, Tamil Nadu, which is one of the poorest regions of India and, as such, was probably one of the world's poorest regions at that time. The lucky residents of this area were about to get a month's free healthcare from one very inexperienced doctor for its fifty thousand "untouchable" residents. It was a fitting way to honour the memory of my free-spirited uncle, whilst making his death mean something – to these people, at least.

The fundraising event that started it all was a dinner hosted by a family friend who had first visited the region over ten years prior and had instantly fallen in love with the amazing people of Anandal. She had initially worked as a volunteer, reading to the local children in English, either in a crumbling mud construction that doubled as the chief's house and village school, or in the shade of a palm tree, dodging falling snakes and wandering scorpions. This experience gave rise to her dream of building an English-speaking school that would provide an education for the region's children whilst giving them the opportunity for a better life.

The death of her mother had been the impetus she needed, and for the next few years, she worked tirelessly, living and breathing the project to raise funds and build the school. The result is the fantastically modern English MH Memorial School, which provides a free education for almost five hundred local children at any one time, and that fantastic lady, Mrs M, also developed links with a call centre in Bangalore, providing employment opportunities for these previously "untouchable" children, legitimising them in the eyes of the state and gaining them recognition as real people, actual human beings.

Mrs M had been working hand in hand with the Rural Development Society (RDS) for several years, attempting to bring a permanent clinic to the region, and had previously used an outbuilding of the school to provide sporadic healthcare "on and off", which was entirely reliant on occasional international funding and charitable donations. She asked whether we would be interested in helping out, and the seeds of the clinic were sown. Instead of “helping out”, my wife and I decided to provide funds to open the clinic, which had been closed for eighteen months, for just one month initially, paying for all medications and employing a local nurse to supervise me and teach me Indian Healthcare 101, whilst my wife and son would volunteer to work in the school.

We were in. We part fundraised and part emptied what little we had left in our bank to provide the initial set-up costs, and before we knew it, it was early June, and we were sitting on an Etihad plane, heading for India. I was enjoying my traditional holiday tipple of gin and ginger with a lager chaser, whilst anxiously awaiting my final medical exam results. We were en route to Abu Dhabi for an onward transfer to Chennai, with our twelve-year-old son, Mrs M, and her twenty-year-old niece. We had booked the flight months before, not realising that it would result in me being stuck inside a metal tube, thirty thousand feet in the air, at the exact moment Liverpool University would be releasing the final exam results online.

I purchased internet credit and eventually managed to access the university system. Sitting statue-still, tense and rigid, in complete silence, I was scared to even breathe as I watched the page download at snail’s pace. The tension built by the second, becoming almost unbearable, and suddenly… the page froze and crashed. Okay, so that wasn’t going to work. Plan B – yahoo mail. I typed in my username and password and prepared to wait for an age but was shocked when my inbox instantly opened up, and I found myself looking at a long list of emails. Sitting pride of place, right at the top of that list, was an unopened email from Liverpool University School of Medicine.

I clicked on it and scrolled straight down to the bottom of the screen whilst the page was loading. Trying not to focus on the text, I partially looked away as my cursor hit the bottom of the page. I waited a few seconds, building up the courage to take a sneaky peek. Time slowed around me, my breathing heavy and loud in my ears. *Okay, let’s do this, this is it. This is everything I have worked for over the last six years. It’s all been leading up to this.* I swung my head back quickly and focused on the bottom of the email. *Congratulations*. I instantly stopped reading.

I had done it. All the years of sacrifice, all the hard work, all the struggle, all the nerves, all the sleepless nights, all the blood, sweat, and tears. I built up the courage to look at my phone screen again, noting the breakdown. Not only had I passed, I had passed in the top ten per cent of the year. I had passed with honours.

I took a minute and let it all sink in. Surprisingly, I didn't feel happy. I didn't feel relieved. I felt numb. I turned to my wife and told her the good news, and she exploded with a mixture of pride and relief. I suppose she must have been glad that it was all finally over and proud of how our joint sacrifices had paid off. I told my son and the rest of the party, and Mrs M informed the stewardess whilst ordering us all some champagne. The stewardess appeared to be as excited by the news as we were and instantly made an announcement over the PA system, to a polite round of applause from my fellow passengers, as she waived the price of the bubbly. I finally relaxed for the first time in months, if not years, and a weight that I wasn't even aware I had been carrying around with me literally fell away from my shoulders as I dropped back in my seat and closed my eyes, taking a deep breath in and exhaling slowly. I had done it. I was a doctor. A fucking doctor! Probably the most unlikely doctor ever, but still a doctor.

I thought back to my grandad Keegan's last moments on earth and the promise I had made him at his hospital bedside, and I thought about his wife, my nan, who had passed not too long after, and I thought about my other grandparents who lived opposite the airport in their little house in Speke. I thought of the only two teachers who had ever believed in me during my time in school, Mr May and Mr Gregory. I thought about my mum and dad and how hard they had fought for us as kids. I thought about the sacrifices my wife and son had made and the holidays we should have taken him on but couldn't afford.

I thought about sitting in my uncle's leather wheelchair in his flat on Lark Lane, drinking tea, smoking, and eating chocolate croissants whilst Chollo impatiently purred and forcibly rubbed against my legs, demanding his pouch of sardines or tuna. I thought about Sergeant Bastard and Corporal Williams – yet another person who believed in me when I needed it most. I thought back to my childhood in Speke, jumping off the enterprise roof and sailing sofas across the Big Daddy – a pond, well known to the residents of Speke, once located on the field now swallowed up by Liverpool John Lennon Airport. I smiled and took a sip of that sweet champagne and tried to swallow away the dryness in my throat, but it wouldn't budge. I felt happy, but I also felt sad. I felt proud of myself, a doctor from a family of dockers – not too bad for a kid from Speke.

*

We landed in Abu Dhabi late and had less than an hour to get across the airport and check in for our flight to Chennai. After a mad dash and James-Bond-style dive through closing train doors, we just about made it and fell into our seats on the cold and disturbingly misty plane. I instantly sunk into a deep sleep. A whole day of travelling, a fair amount of mother's ruin, lager, and champagne, with the added excitement of passing finals, had left me physically and emotionally exhausted, and I slept like the proverbial log.

The heavy landing rattled me from my slumber as we touched down in Chennai. We disembarked the plane at four in the morning into a cool and bizarrely deserted airport. We were quickly ushered through customs and headed toward the exit. A low rumbling noise escalated with every step we took toward the frosted-glass sliding doors. Stepping out into the cool, early morning light, we were greeted by a cacophony of squeals, clicks, shouts, screams, and pleading from the hundreds of impatient relatives, taxi chauffeurs, and tuk-tuk drivers who were assembled at least twenty deep and spread out across the whole length of the airport frontage, elbowing and jostling for position, whilst loudly and desperately touting for business as they fought their way to the front of the throng, making a literal grab for potential customers.

Our chauffeur was patiently waiting toward the far end of the line, and he smiled warmly when he saw us walking toward him, welcoming Mrs M back to India with a warm embrace. He insisted that we drop the bags exactly where we stood and jump into the minivan, whilst he loaded up. Exhausted and slightly intimidated by the cacophonous airport welcome, we were driven straight to our hotel on the main strip in Mahabalipuram, slaloming between insanely overloaded mopeds that contained mountains of tattered boxes and other valued possessions, whole families balanced precariously upon every exposed inch, and the sleeping sacred cows that were scattered across the motorways and dual carriageways like discarded litter.

We survived, somehow, and arrived at the strip, which was around half a mile of crumbling deserted and shuttered buildings with the occasional large pile of heaped rubbish, upon which the wild cows and dogs hustled for prime position at the feast, alongside the giant street rats and jet-black crows. We pulled up outside our hotel and walked across the dusty track, that served as a road, to purchase an Indian coffee from the vendor who was doing a steady trade, despite it being only around six o'clock in the morning, whilst the chauffer unloaded our bags.

We drank the coffee quickly, in thirsty gulps, tipped the driver with a stack of rupees and headed to the hotel room. My wife being the DIY genius that she is quickly knocked-up the mosquito tent for our son, and we all fell into bed, sleep instantly taking us into its comforting embrace.

I was awoken only a couple of hours later by a hum of noise working its way through the wooden shutters and into the stuffy, dated hotel room, with its loud ceiling fan and broken air-conditioning unit. I forced open the slatted wooden shutters, allowing warm fresh air to flood into the stuffy room, whilst revealing the most beautiful, vibrant, colourful, bustling street lined with stalls selling all the magic the mysterious East has to offer, from spices and local food produce to hand-crafted leather sandals and intricate marble sculptures. The dingy, scruffy, crumbling strip of earlier had metamorphosed from an ugly caterpillar into the most beautiful of butterflies.

I could write a book about my time in Mahabalipuram alone, a beautiful, allegedly French-influenced settlement – though there was certainly nothing French about it that I recognised – on the old sixties' hippy trail, famous throughout the south for its ancient temples, sculptors, and relaxed, laid-back atmosphere. It is the only place you will get an alcoholic drink in the dry state of Tamil Nadu – an under-the-counter Kingfisher accompanied every meal, usually more than five years past its sell-by date but tasting as good as any beer I have ever consumed – in the oppressive midday heat. We spent a wonderful week there whilst I worked in the local hospital to gain some Indian medical experience, and the others spent their days sightseeing. We all ate out together every night, experiencing the delicious South Indian cuisine, whilst staying strictly vegetarian for the first time in my life, to try and avoid the dreaded Typhi.

*

I worked in Suradeep Hospital, which was owned and run by a local GP, Dr Indira (Indi). She was the only doctor who actually worked at the hospital, being supported by a team of local nurses who performed clinical procedures, basic observations, and crowd control for the hundreds of patients who accessed the hospital on a daily basis. Indi was an immensely hard-working doctor, wife, and mother, who mixed long clinical hours with the traditional role of an Indian female, looking after her husband and her two almost fully grown sons.

She woke at the crack of dawn to prepare a traditional breakfast for her family, before opening the doors of the hospital at eight a.m. She would then see a constant stream of patients until midday, when it was time to close up and prepare lunch for her family, before returning at two p.m. to continue with the conveyor belt of amazingly varied patients, until six p.m., when she would duck out again to prepare the evening meal and then be back at work, until finally closing the hospital doors at nine p.m. Indi followed this routine for six days every week, whilst also providing a reduced service on a Sunday. A harder working doctor I have genuinely never met.

Suradeep Hospital was situated within an area of desolate, overcrowded shanty housing behind the bright lights and shiny façade of the strip. The area was home to the essential workers: manual labourers, shoemakers, sculptors, waiting staff, tuk-tuk drivers, and all the other grafters who made up the fabric of this complex society, ensuring the gears of Mahabalipuram remained well-oiled and continued to grind.

The hospital was a bit run-down compared to western standards, but it was spotlessly clean and housed surprisingly modern facilities, including its own biochemistry and haematology labs, which enabled the nursing staff to instantly process any venous samples they may have taken. It even boasted a radiography department that may have still used the old plain film and light box method of viewing images but had much grander ambitions, including purchasing a shiny new CT machine.

Indi lived above the hospital with her family, which consisted of her husband, who worked as a senior hospital administrator, and her youngest son, who still attended high school, whilst the guest of honour for the summer holidays, and her pride and joy, was the eldest son, who was following in his mother's footsteps and studying Medicine at Chennai medical school.

Working at Suradeep was an experience never to be forgotten. The large consulting room was at the near end of the hospital, closest to the front entrance and situated adjacent to the massive waiting area, in which close to a hundred patients jostled for the twenty metal chairs that were secured to the floor, packed together like sardines in their tin. The sickest of these patients lay, thin and frail, on the hard tiles, bones poking through thick, leather skin, tightly bound in saris. Undernourished, snotty-nosed babies clung to exhausted young mothers, faces pushed tightly against maternal bosom to stifle the empty bellied howls.

Others milled about the room, selling odds and sods to the waiting patients – never a missed opportunity – whilst skinny dogs idly wandered through this human carrion like circling vultures, picking up what little scraps they could, occasionally roughly swatted away by the claw-like hand of one of the pitiful floor specimens.

The consulting room itself was a large, high-ceilinged space with an interior design straight out of colonial India. A huge fan took up the vast majority of the ceiling, and the pale pink walls provided a stark contrast to the dark wooden bookshelves that rested lazily against them. It was separated into three distinct areas: the doctor's consultation area, essentially a desk and three chairs that took up most of the floor space; a curtained-off nook in one corner that housed an examination table and served as the clinical area; and almost hidden away in the furthest corner was a sink and some bins with high storage shelves that served as a kind of sluice.

The massive desk in the centre of the room was littered with medical paraphernalia and had two seats on the side furthest away from the door, that were reserved for Indi and myself, and one at the side of the desk, reserved for the patient. There were usually around ten other patients in the consultation room, who formed an orderly queue immediately behind the unfortunate victim sitting uncomfortably in the hot seat, straining to hear what the doctor was saying, some even leaning across the table to hear the conversation better, whilst others would chip in occasionally, give the doctor a confirmatory little nod, or even shoot a disapproving glare at the poor patient who was squirming like a fish on a hook.

The concept of patient confidentiality was completely alien. The occasional woman would be bent over the desk and injected roughly into her buttock, directly through the material of her sari, whilst more intimate examinations were performed behind the curtain in the nook, but still within full earshot of the next patients, who would gradually edge closer toward the curtain to ensure a more effective range for eavesdropping.

It sounds quite humorous but could be distressing and, on occasion, even sinister. On my last day with Indi, a desperate young girl, looking no older than sixteen, finally at her wit's end with the continual domestic abuse doled out by her violent drunk of a husband, was dragged into the consultation room by her enraged family, much to the initial annoyance of those waiting their turn patiently in the queue. She was crying hysterically and continually retching and vomiting small amounts of fluid, likely the bleach she had just drunk in an attempt to end her miserable existence.

The room quickly erupted into shouting and screaming, and she looked terrified as she was harangued and harassed, pushed and pulled in all directions by the angry queue, a few even giving her a slap around the head or a hard toe-kick to the shins for good measure. I stood up and made my way through the throng to try and protect the girl, but Indi had reacted first and quickly took control of the situation, shouting stern instructions in Tamil at the nurses, who quickly and roughly dragged the girl into the nook, pulling the curtain tightly closed behind them. As quickly as it started, it had finished.

The room instantly settled down and carried on as normal, seemingly oblivious to the loud sobbing and retching coming from behind the spotlessly white, flimsy curtain. It was a truly bizarre experience. I had seen a lot of shit in my life, but that really shocked me. I was shaking with adrenaline and felt upset over the girl's distress, the miserable life she must have endured so far, and I couldn't help wondering what the hell I had let myself in for.

This was my first glimpse into the darker side of Indian society, but it would not be my last.

Anandal

After a week of acclimatising to the South Indian way of life, it was sadly time to leave the relative comfort of Mahabalipuram and Miss Indi's impressive Suradeep Hospital and head for deepest, darkest India. We were corralled into two air-conditioned minivans which had been preloaded with gallons of fresh water, cigarettes, and food supplies. This was the point it started to feel less like a holiday and more like an expedition.

We drove six hours south and inland, leaving behind the traffic smog, rancid pollution, and general stench of the ramshackle shanty towns that sprawled out from the massive city of Chennai and surrounded Mahabalipuram in a vice-like grip of extreme poverty, deprivation, and filth. The dual carriageways soon gave way to pitted muddy tracks, flanked by a dense wall of lush green vegetation, the odd gap like a missing tooth, occupied by an old wood and palm-leaf shack.

We stopped a couple of times to purchase an Indian coffee from one of the ancient leather-skinned locals who seemed to litter the side of the road, or for a much-needed comfort or cigarette break. The air, thick and polluted as we left the city, had initially become wet and heavy with the promise of rain as we travelled south, but became drier and lighter the deeper inland we headed, and the vivid green blur was now replaced by an overwhelmingly bright rusty-orange colour that emanated from the soil, only occasionally broken by clustered strands of thin, yellow grass and spiky moth-eaten shrubs.

As we closed in on the Anandal region, everything opened out and became much more expansive, a Jurassic barren wasteland framed by turquoise-blue vistas. The endless landscape was only occasionally interrupted by a haphazard pile of smooth, black boulders which formed perfectly balanced pebble mountains that erupted through the bright sandy soil to reach high into the perfect blue sky. The standard ramshackle mud-and-palm-leaf hut constructions of the region peeked from the shadows of the giant pebbles, with the obligatory bare-boned cow loosely tethered to a peg outside, prehistoric-looking chickens pecking at unseen insects through the thin, dry grass that sprouted between the cow's spindle legs. The whole place had a timeless quality about it, and I half expected Fred Flintstone to come "yabba dabba dooing" past us in his foot-powered car, a sabre-toothed tiger in hot pursuit.

*

We finally arrived at a brilliant-white compound, blinding in the reflected afternoon sunshine, making it visible to us for some distance before we reached it, a white oasis in an otherwise vast expanse of nothingness. It seemed completely out of place, set on a large piece of flat land between two hills. As we neared the massive iron gates, a large, freshly painted sign proudly informed us that we had arrived at the *MH Memorial School*, our destination and our home for the next few weeks.

We drove through the gates and into the dusty school compound to find the children arranged in the perfect military formation of an "open square" (U-shape), facing a central raised stage, green-and-beige school uniforms clean and neatly pressed, faces scrubbed clean, and hair neatly brushed into side-partings or perfectly plaited into pigtails. They excitedly shifted from one bare foot to the other whilst waiting to welcome these strange foreigners, desperately trying to keep eyes forward and faces straight to avoid the wrath of the teachers, but failing miserably.

Standing in the centre of the stage was an important-looking, unusually tall, and stick-thin Indian man who was cleanly shaven, apart from a thick moustache that was neatly trimmed to the lip. His hair was thinning but carefully combed into a slick side-parting, and he was dressed in a spotlessly clean and perfectly pressed polyester khaki safari suit with polished, brown leather sandals on his feet.

He was flanked to one side by a rather dishevelled, bare-footed, obese woman, who like him was tall for the region. She was decked out in a sun-faded purple sari stretched almost to breaking point around her bulging midriff. Her hair was roughly gathered into a short ponytail, sat atop a broad face with bulging eyes and heavy jowls, her oversized mouth set in a rather unpleasant scowl.

To his other side was a tall and very thick-set young girl, dressed immaculately in her spotlessly clean and crisply pressed school uniform. Her hair was perfectly plaited like the other schoolchildren who stood facing her in military formation, but she stood out from the rest of them like a sore thumb. She was in no way overweight but was much taller than all the other schoolchildren, both boys and girls, and probably weighed as much as at least two of them. Surprisingly, she was wearing shoes, brand-new, black leather sandals over perfectly white, knee-high socks. To the periphery of the stage was a group of smartly dressed, stern-looking, young adults, who had their eyes fixed rapier-like on the children in the ranks, mentally logging any infringements for later retribution.

We exited the vans and were greeted by a formal welcoming party, which seemed to appear out of thin air, dressed uniformly in white shirts with a school sash draped from shoulder to waist. I presumed they were teachers, and the leader bowed in a graceful and exaggerated manner to Mrs M, before embracing her warmly, and enthusiastically shaking our hands, one after the other – starting with the doctor, of course. After all, this was India, where social status was still a big deal. We were then led up onto the stage and introduced to the chief of the six villages that made up Anandal, Manhoran, whose primary residence was situated in his home village but who spent most of his time running the region's business from the school whilst living in a small brick-built construction that he shared with his wife, Madam, and his daughter, both currently flanking him on the stage.

Manhoran welcomed us to the school with a warm and enthusiastic handshake and thanked us for visiting his region, with humility and genuine gratitude, an instantly likeable character. Madam eyed us suspiciously throughout, those huge eyes never leaving our own, whilst the daughter, appearing much older than her tender years, had the overwhelming confidence of one who has been born into a position of power and well and truly knows it. There's an old Liverpool saying that someone could "buy and sell you", and I'd say it summed up this twosome perfectly.

A heart-warming speech was delivered by the head student, thanking us for supporting the school and providing funds to open the clinic. Then we spent the following hour being shown around the complex by Manhoran and the welcoming party, all the while trailed by a stream of giggling children. I was shown to the clinic and provided with a couple of able-bodied assistants to help my wife and I set up the room, whilst the rest of our party went off to play games with the kids, before they were all loaded onto American-style yellow school buses and taken for a "ride-along" on the school drop-off – an essential service in this part of India, which remains a dangerous place for a child to grow up, with many not making it to adulthood. Most missing children are suspected to have drowned in the huge uncovered rural wells that dot the countryside, but with a body rarely to be found, the cause of their demise can often only be speculated upon.

The clinic was made up of two adjoining rooms, the largest of which we used as a consultation area, a desk and two chairs dominating the centre of the space, and the furthest corner sectioned off with sliding medical screens, an examination table skilfully concealed behind in an identical arrangement to that of Suradeep – well, if it's not broken… The second room was pretty impressive and set up in the fashion of a mini hospital ward. It contained three beds with a drip stand positioned next to each. The wall furthest away from the door was lined with grey metal shelving units, a lockable cupboard, and a sink, instantly providing us with an all-in-one ward, medication storeroom, and sluice.

After a couple of hours' hard graft, and a bit of *Changing Rooms* magic from the wife, we had it looking pretty impressive, even if we did say so ourselves. Exhausted and drenched in sweat from hard physical labour undertaken in the oppressive dry heat of southern India, we darted across the empty yard in a half jog, looking forward to a nice refreshing shower and an early night in our "luxury accommodation", which was located on the opposite side of the school playground from the clinic, above the administration offices and next to the chief's small family house, which itself was sandwiched between our apartment/admin block and a couple of rickety, brick toilet stalls with ill-fitting wooden doors, situated next to a long row of communal sinks that the children used to wash their hands before each meal.

I used the ancient law of proclamation to stake my claim to the shower by loudly shouting, "First in the shower," at my wife, as I picked up the pace and took the steps up to the room two at a time, in exaggerated leaps, the light quickly fading all around me. Eager to check out our accommodation, I excitedly burst into the room, throwing a beam of light down the stairs toward my trailing wife, the door swinging open to reveal a large, open-plan space, containing six beds scattered in a completely haphazard fashion, interrupted only by a couple of old pine tables and a large stack of five-gallon plastic water containers that occupied one whole corner of our room. Three of the beds had already been claimed by Mrs M, her niece and our son, and I mentally noted that there was no sign of running water, or even a toilet.

The beds, in the loosest sense of the word, were two gym benches pushed together with a thin mattress rolled across the top. My face, never one to mask emotions well, gave away my complete surprise as I took in our rather modest surroundings and naively asked, "Where's the shower?" An amused Mrs M informed me that our shower facilities were actually a tap and plastic bucket, which could be found in one of the toilet cubicles that flanked the school playground, behind a row of tall palms.

My wife burst into the room behind me, slightly out of breath, just as I was being advised to take a torch, "keep an eye out" for scorpions and wandering snakes, "run under the trees" to avoid dropping spiders, and not to worry about the pack of free-roaming security dogs. Mrs M assured us they wouldn't attack, as long as we stood our ground. I half hoped she was joking, but deep down, I knew she wasn't. I now understood why Mrs M had been so vague when questioned about the living conditions and facilities at the school. She had simply said it would be a surprise. Well, it was a surprise alright!

The light had completely faded by the time we had been given the tour of our digs, so we decided it was probably safer to venture to the toilets as a whole group. Picking up the two torches that had been left for us in the room, we cautiously stalked toward the rickety cubicles, linking arms as we traversed a now pitch-black compound. We quickly sped up to a jog on reaching the treeline and swung the torch beams wildly at the ground in front of us to ward off any cobras and avoid stepping on a scorpion. I was at the end of the mini human chain, right arm anchoring me to my closest companion, knotted towel tightly gripped in a white-knuckled left fist to prevent a potentially disastrous disrobing, shoulders hunched toward my ears, head bobbing and weaving like a drunken boxer as we cautiously passed under the low-hanging palm leaves.

I let out a rather effeminate squeal as a leaf brushed my ear and picked up the pace to an almost full sprint for the last couple of metres, unintentionally breaking the chain and alerting the pack of security dogs who instantly started barking in unison, not too far away from us, but out of sight due to the impenetrable cloak of darkness. We let the two youngest group members use the cubicles first, whilst we stood guard outside, silhouetted by the weak electric torchlight that radiated from the large gaps at the top and bottom of the cubicle doors.

It was eventually my turn. I pulled the door tightly shut behind me and slowly shone the torch around the pitch-black wooden box, carefully allowing the beam to linger over each nook and cranny of the three-foot-by-three-foot stall, imagining some ferocious beast hidden just beyond the penetrating reach of the fingers of light. Flipping across the latch-style lock, I began to fill the white plastic bucket that was already handily beneath the tap. I stripped off the towel before pouring a handful of freezing-cold water over my head with cupped hands, instantly inhaling with shock and letting out a loud involuntary gasp whilst I quickly and roughly lathered myself in shower gel, already dreading the rinsing-off process.

We made it back to our accommodation, slightly traumatised, but still all in one piece, and I climbed up onto the open terrace, formed by the flat roof of our apartment, for a quick cigarette. Sitting on the low wall that topped off the building, legs dangling perilously over the edge, I watched the drifting cigarette smoke throw a translucent veil across the stars shimmering like diamonds in the crystal-clear sky. The barks, snarls, and howls of the dogs were more distant now, and I felt every inch the modern Columbus as I took a last deep lungful of smoke and flicked the cigarette as far out as I possibly could into the inky blackness, watching the orange light sail gracefully toward the ground and erupt in a shower of sparks as it landed, bounced once, and abruptly stopped. I swung my legs back over the wall to the safety of the roof and walked back downstairs to the sanctum of my bed, which in all honesty was an insult to the word.

The next day was uneventful enough. We decided that I would travel into the nearest city, Tiruvannamalai, with Manhoran, Mrs M, and a couple of bodyguards to purchase some medical stock for the clinic, whilst those remaining behind would officially start working in the school. We squeezed into the chief's battered old, white Toyota Corolla with its bizarre caramel-coloured leather interior and drove for a good hour until we arrived in the city centre. Quickly purchasing what we needed from one of the city's huge medical warehouses, we stopped only for a quick coffee – all eager to get back to the rest of the group and set up the clinic for tomorrow's big launch.

We awoke early the next day, nervous with anticipation but ready for the opening. I headed up to my new smoking spot on the roof terrace above our room and excitedly watched the queue of people forming outside the locked gates of the school. There was initially about ten of them, but I could see many more blurred figures far off in the distance, partially obscured by the haze of the early morning sun and the dust storm kicked up by their feet whilst navigating the ancient tracks that led down to this natural plain. By the time I was ready to open up, there must have been at least fifty people waiting in that queue.

I had never seen a more rag-tag bunch. They were of varying heights and ages, but all were painfully thin, dusty, generally dishevelled, and eagerly awaiting the opening of our doors. I walked over to the clinic with Manhoran, and he introduced me to my new nurse, Anastasia, who, just like the chief, spoke decent English. They sat me down and gave me a two-minute crash course in Tamil. Well, "crash course" would be slightly overegging the pudding. What actually happened is they told me a few rudimentary words, such as head, belly, pain, hot, cold, and cough, which I diligently jotted down in the little handmade notebook I had purchased from Mahabalipuram market. I left it open and within easy eyeshot upon the consultation desk.

The first day followed the exact pattern as a typical Suradeep clinic – patients lined up, one after the other, inside the consultation room, again with not even the pretence at confidentiality, the queue snaking through the open door, out of the school gates, and occasionally, all the way around the corner and along the white compound wall.

My first patient took a seat in the chair opposite me, about a foot away from the next in line. She was probably middle-aged – although it was difficult to tell – with sad eyes set deep in a small head that was perched delicately on top of a long, thin neck. The skeletal frame below was wrapped tightly in mummy-fashion with a faded, torn, and dusty old sari. Taking the seat directly in front of the desk, she fired a barrage of indecipherable words and sounds directly at me, like hot lead. Her head was tilted to one side, eyes squinting, face wearing a look of pained almost physical sorrow that bordered on pleading. The weight of the world sat heavy on those narrow shoulders. I suddenly realised she had stopped talking and was now just sat there, staring at me, in total silence.

Realising I didn't have a bloody clue what she had just said, she leaned forward slightly and stretched out her arms, cupping her hands in front of me, head rhythmically swaying in a side to side nodding-dog motion that seems specific to the people of South India. I desperately searched the list of local words which I had scrawled in my notebook, still open on the desk directly in front of me, and I recognised nothing she had just said. *Did I hear a* talai *or was it a* vali*?* Giving up, I looked over toward Anastasia, who was standing to the side of the desk. Smiling, she pointed to the open jars of multivitamins and painkillers that had been strategically placed next to a large pile of neatly cut squares of yellowing newspaper. I took a rough handful of paracetamol, ibuprofen, and multi-vits, and wrapping them in separate squares, I offered them to the patient.

Quickly snatching them from my hand, she stuffed them into the front fold of her sari, smiling shyly to reveal a full set of oversized, bright-white buck-teeth. The years seemed to fall away from her, and I realised she was much younger than I had initially thought. She touched her cupped hands to her forehead and bowed slightly toward me, whilst performing the nodding-dog motion again. Gingerly rising from the chair, hand pressed into the small of her back, smile now gone from her face, the years piled back on as she was roughly nudged out of the way and replaced in the hot seat by patient number two.

Before she could escape, however, she was pulled to the side of the desk by the thick-set and muscular Anastasia, who cupped her face in both hands, expertly pulling down the eyelids with her thumbs, whilst simultaneously pushing her fingers deep and hard into the cheek muscles, forcing open the mouth to allow inspection of the tongue and gums. The shocked patient was then bent over the desk and injected roughly through her sari, deep into the upper buttock, the bright-red shot of Vitamin B almost instantly disappearing into the muscle via the large-bore needle. With barely time to even register a protest, she let out a loud shriek, much to the amusement of the rest of the queue, and was sent on her merry way, sobbing loudly and muttering indecipherable curses to the laughing faces in the line as she half ran, half stumbled toward the open door, rubbing her buttock lightly and tenderly, back pain forgotten for the time being. The whole process had taken just seconds, and whilst infection control would have had kittens about the "trans-sari" injection technique, I was mightily impressed by the efficiency.

That was pretty much how it went for the rest of the day and, in fact, for the weeks that followed. Every patient was given a handful of tablets by myself, whilst every female with conjunctival pallor (pale skin inside the eyelids) was given a Vitamin B shot, through the sari, of course, by my heavy-handed and slightly sadistic nurse. Any raised temperatures or clinical signs of infection were given an intramuscular shot of gentamycin, again straight into the buttock, and were brought back the next day for a further shot, and so on.

Sicker and frailer patients would be carried into the clinic by concerned relatives, often following an uncomfortable night's journey, pushed along on a battered old bicycle through the dark hours, to exploit the cooler temperatures and arrive at our gates for first light. They were cannulated by me then placed on one of the beds in our makeshift ward and given a couple of five-hundred-millilitre glass bottles of saline and a single bottle of IV antibiotics for their troubles, and then sent on their way again. Everyone had to be out by closing – physically kicked out, if necessary, by Anastasia who basically ran the whole show whilst graciously allowing me the pretence of being in charge.

*

I manned the clinic Monday to Friday, from eight in the morning till five in the evening, with Anastasia and, occasionally, my wife. On our days off, we would all head into Tiruvannamalai, sightseeing and following the old hippy trail around the temples of Shiva, or rummaging in the famous haberdasheries whilst sampling the local culinary delicacies.

Our time at the school provided us with some pretty strange and memorable experiences, most of them involving Madam in one way or another. She was a larger-than-life character, appearing devoid of any sense of shame, an out-and-out comedy villain who would regularly help herself to any food we may have had stashed away in our room, not even attempting to cover up the theft after she had been caught red-handed. I could include many stories in this book about the infamous Madam, from the time she calmly beat a cobra to death with a branch and her bare hands when the poor creature tried to slither its way through the school gates, to the time she paraded around the playground in a size 10 Primark T-shirt, which she had stolen from Mrs M's young niece, somehow managing to stretch it across her considerable girth. But the image that stands out most for me is of her force-feeding my poor wife handfuls of boiled rice in what will forever be known within our family as "the Typhi episode".

Our food was delivered to the school, by motorcycle courier, three times per day, after being freshly prepared for us by Manoharan's mother in her little house, situated in the family village just a short drive away. It was a strictly vegetarian diet and was particularly bland, apparently to suit our western tastebuds. Only the bottled water we had brought with us from Mahabalipuram was used to prepare the food. Overall, the whole process appeared very hygienic, as attested by the fact that she had provided food for every previous group of European visitors to the school without a single issue occurring – until the fateful day on which the alleged Typhi incident occurred.

The chief had tasked a new delivery driver to drop off our breakfast of mild curry, chapati, idli (savoury rice cake), and dosa (rice pancake). As usual, Madam had been up at the crack of dawn and helped herself to the prize pickings from the selection of pots that had been laid out in our small canteen, located next door to the clinic, and was walking out of the dining area as we walked in, empty banana leaf in hand, curry liberally smeared across her beaming face.

We ate breakfast as normal, forcing as much down as we could handle in order not to appear rude, but at the end of the day, there is only so much curry and rice you can tolerate for breakfast, especially a couple of weeks in. I got my first clue that something was amiss as I walked across the schoolyard to the small outside toilet cubicles, the route taking me directly past the front porch of Mahoran's house. As I passed by, I could hear loud wailing noises and looked across to the front stoop of the little house. There, rolling around wrapped in a thin, white nightdress that was drenched in sweat and alarmingly translucent, was Madam, alternately vomiting and stuffing handfuls of boiled rice into her oversized mouth. She looked directly at me before shooing me away with her non-rice-eating hand, and I gladly made my way back to the clinic and my endless line of patients.

That day just happened to be our wedding anniversary, and my wife and I spent the latter part of the evening celebrating by watching the sunset from our roof terrace whilst swigging on two out-of-date Kingfishers that Mrs M had somehow managed to score for us in the driest part of the dry state. My wife hadn't felt a hundred per cent all day but seemed okay to me as we observed the ancient scenery that surrounded the school from our vantage point up on the roof, in the rapidly fading dusk light.

Refreshed after our long-awaited beers, we were making our way back down to the room to rejoin the others, when my wife suddenly started to feel pretty rough. We decided to take a rapid detour across the deserted yard toward the toilet cubicles. Escorting each other had become our group's custom, for protection against the pack of wild security dogs that roamed the grounds and all those snakes who now had a major axe to grind after Madam's brutal murder of one of their own. Whilst I stood outside and waited, I could hear my poor wife vomiting pretty intensely. We walked back over to the room, and when I saw her in the full light, I was surprised by how awfully pale and clammy she looked.

The vomiting and severe diarrhoea continued, and we spent most of the night stumbling between the apartment and the toilets, the associated dangers of the journey becoming less worrisome and, eventually, the last thing on our minds. By the morning, she could no longer muster the strength to even make the short journey across the yard and was semi-permanently attached to a white washing bucket that we had stolen from one of the cubicles. I decided the time was right to start some IV fluids, due to her decreasing oral intake combined with the increasing outside temperature, before heading off to the clinic to make a start on the growing queue of patients forming outside the gates.

Around mid-morning, a messenger from the school came over to inform me that my wife was not looking "too good". However, as I was stuck with a sick patient, I sent Anastasia across with a couple of bottles of fluid to check her over whilst I finished up at the clinic. I later found out that the old trouble and strife had also been subjected to the standard dose of intramuscular gentamycin, but not through a sari.

I eventually returned to the room and found a miraculously resurgent Madam trying to force handfuls of boiled rice into my wife's mouth, whilst my wife used the last of her strength to fight off this assault. I chased Madam out angrily and put up another bottle of fluids. My wife was very pale now, and her blood pressure was dropping, despite fast fluids, and as a baby doctor, I felt I was rapidly getting out of my depth. I thought it was probably about time I sought some professional help, so I asked Manhoran to take us to the Catholic hospital, in Tiruvannamalai.

We were loaded into the back of the old Toyota, my son in the front seat, and my wife sandwiched between me and Mrs M in the back, head hovering precariously over the edge of the white bucket that she had brought with her, continually moaning and dry retching, nothing of any substance remaining for her digestive system to eject, despite Madam's best force-feeding efforts earlier.

We arrived at the Catholic hospital, following what must have been an hour straight from hell for my poor wife, and Manhoran and Mrs M got straight down to haggling at the finance desk, eventually agreeing on a private "luxury" hospital room, with ensuite toilet facilities and all necessary medications provided upfront. We settled into the "luxury" suite, whilst Mrs M kindly took my son back to the school with the chief.

Now I fully understand that luxury is a subjective concept, but that hospital room was pushing it, even by Tamil standards. It was a small, narrow room, the faded white paint flaking from its walls, a colonial shutter-style glassless window at one end that did nothing to either filter out the traffic noise from the busy road or provide a defensive barrier against the swarm of fat-bellied mosquitoes lazily hovering around the hypnotic pulsating light emanating from the ancient portable TV sat precariously on an undersized swing bracket high up on the window's opposite wall. The ceiling fan, although a long time out of service, provided a comfortable home for the local spiders and was lovingly adorned with generations of cobwebs. The bed was narrow and hard but dressed with pristine, crisp, white cotton sheets, and the hard wooden visitor's chair, which was to be my perch for the next thirty-six hours, partially obstructed the entrance to the ensuite. Now "ensuite" was also stretching the definition of the word to the very limit. It was essentially a peach-tiled box with a filthy hole in the floor, a foot groove placed conveniently either side, and an old brass tap positioned about six inches from the floor, just enough room beneath for an old, scratched and faded, red plastic bowl and water scoop that I presumed was intended for personal hygiene. The ensuite was shared between my wife's room and the neighbouring room, in a Jack-and-Jill fashion, and of course, the locks were not working – come on, would you really have expected anything else? But thankfully, we had no neighbour in the adjoining room – one small mercy, at least.

We spent the night providing a living feast for the mosquitoes, whilst my wife's blood pressure continued to steadily drop, despite fluid resuscitation. The Catholic hospital's rehydration policy was designed for your average seven stone Tamil resident, and the odd bottle of five hundred millimetres, just wasn't cutting the mustard for a five foot eight, severely dehydrated westerner.

Around three a.m., she started to feel really unwell, and her blood pressure plummeted even further, as low as fifty systolic at one point, with a racing heartbeat and very cool peripheries, which, for the non-medics amongst you, is bad news. I raced to find a nurse to request some more of their preciously guarded fluids, only to be told that our money had run out. Mrs M had wisely told us not to take any cash with us, as it would likely be stolen during the night, but not to worry as everything would be paid for upfront. Apparently, the money Mrs M had paid was for a basic medication package only, and we had now exceeded this package. As such, they would not be giving any further treatment.

Mrs M's plan was looking less sensible by the minute. I explained that I was a doctor… well, almost, and that my wife was in a very precarious situation and needed fluids urgently. But it was falling on deaf ears. I asked to see the on-call doctor who just agreed with the nurse's financial assessment. I pleaded that we would obviously have the money in the morning when Mrs M returned, but again, there was no bargaining. They were literally going to let her die. I was absolutely flabbergasted, and as a last resort, I offered my watch as collateral (thank God I had ignored the advice to send it back to the school with my son), and after a brief examination and a slight impressed nod of the head, I was guided to the finance office, which thankfully, remained open and fully staffed for twenty-four hours a day. I was given a written chit for unlimited medications, which I took to the pharmacy, where I purchased my own eight bottles of fluid, which were then literally emptied straight into her veins. As the night progressed, she slowly picked up.

Now, those Catholic doctors may have been protective of their little glass bottles of fluids, but they certainly had no issue with the liberal use of antibiotics, possibly because they charged us well over the odds – hence the rapid burning through of our funds. On discharge, a couple of days later, when analysing the bill, we realised they had been administering four different kinds of antibiotics, which doesn't sound like a massive issue, but the lasting effects were significant for my wife

– including an acute kidney injury that required daily IV fluids on our return to Mahabalipuram.

As if that wasn't enough, India also gave my wife a couple of other parting gifts. The first was a prolonged case of c-diff, which lasted for several months after we returned to the UK, and the second was ototoxicity, which is irreversible damage to the nerves of the ear, resulting in "reverse deafness", which has left her with the choice of wearing a hearing aid, or annoying everyone senseless by constantly saying "what" for the rest of her life – she usually opts for the latter option.

*

We passed the rest of our time in Anandal without too much drama. Obviously, Madam continued with her antics, but we were more than used to them by now and mostly found them funny.

Our time to leave came around eventually, though. All too soon, we found ourselves standing on the stage for the leaving ceremony with heavy hearts. More than a few tears were shed from our party, as well as the teachers and school kids.

Despite the hardships, I had really enjoyed my time at the MH Memorial School and was dreading leaving. I had fallen in love with the region and its people, their strength and resilience striking a chord with me and reminding me of the people of my own city. They had been dealt the worst possible hand in life, but they never moped about or complained about how difficult it was for them. They just got on with it and worked as hard as they could to improve their own situation, and they did it with a jovial attitude and big beaming smiles.

After the leaving ceremony, we were packed into the air-conditioned minivans and made our way back toward the refreshing breeze of the coast, stopping off at the colonial French settlement of Pondicherry, made famous by the book, and film of the same name, *Life of Pi*. We spent a day on the beach drinking alcohol and swimming in the Bay of Bengal, much to the annoyance of the beach police who repeatedly chased us out of the sea with loud whistles and bamboo canes. Apparently, there was an unusually high presence of sharks in the area that day, so maybe we should have listened, but the Dutch courage from the alcohol coupled with the oppressive heat meant we were more than happy to participate in this game of cat-and-mouse for most of the afternoon.

We headed from the beach to the home of a friend of Mrs M's, who kindly let us stay for the night, and we got a proper shower for the first time in weeks before heading down to the waterfront for candyfloss and carnival games in the shadow of the giant Ghandi statue. Sitting on the breakwater with my wife and son, enjoying the cool sea breeze whilst listening to the rhythmic lapping of the waves against the shore, the occasional ringing of a bell accompanied by excited cheers from the fairground games behind, I almost felt normal. It was like being back in my world, a Bengal Blackpool… until our eyes adjusted to the low light levels, and we realised that the gleaming shimmering movement below us was not the sea working its way through the narrow corridors of space between the large chunks of stone making up the breakwater wall. It was actually a steady stream of thousands of dark-coated rats scavenging amongst the flotsam that had been washed into the spaces, just metres below our feet.

I'm not going to lie, that realisation kind of killed the mood slightly, and we decided to wander into the town for something to eat. We found a Pizza Hut – Indian-style, of course – which had passable branding but tasted like no Pizza Hut pizza I had ever tasted before.

We had a thoroughly enjoyable couple of days in Pondicherry before returning to Mahabalipuram for a week's rest and relaxation. I spent the mornings accompanying my wife to Dr Indi's Suradeep Hospital for ongoing IV fluid rehydration to help repair her broken kidneys, then our afternoons were spent relaxing around the pool, sinking Kingfishers and sunbathing. We were mere shadows of our former selves. I had personally lost over two stone by sticking to a strictly vegetarian diet for the first time in my life, and my poor wife, who had had no weight to lose, left India with half the kidney function and a third of the hearing capacity of the woman who had arrived.

We flew from Chennai to Abu Dhabi, and after more than five meat-free weeks, I headed straight for McDonalds and absolutely devoured a double quarter-pounder and a Big Mac. But the drama was not quite over as we almost missed our flight, and it required some serious pleading for them to agree to hold the aeroplane. Thankfully, half the passengers were as late as we were, but that's a story for another time.

Touching down on the obligatory grey and miserable Manchester Airport runway, we took a forty-minute taxi ride, and finally arrived back home in Liverpool. Taking turns to shower, we fell into bed exhausted and slept for almost twenty-four hours.

*

Without wanting to sound like the pretentious art student of my post-soldiering years, Tamil Nadu had left its imprint on our very souls. As such, we couldn't just walk away and leave the good friends we had made over there in the lurch. I had felt a deep bond with the people of Anandal and a burning desire to continue my uncle's legacy in any way I could, so we promised to continue funding the clinic we had named after him as a family, and we continued to do this for a further four years. We scraped by, we scratched around, we fundraised, and we borrowed, and we sent that money every single month, right up until Manhoran sadly passed away from TB, after years of recurrent exacerbations had left him increasingly frail and skeletal.

After Manhoran's passing, one of his underlings took over, and it became obvious that he was misappropriating the funds we were sending over to the clinic, so after much soul-searching, we decided to stop sending our monthly contribution. We had set up and established the clinic, and we had provided four years of free healthcare to a region that contained at least fifty thousand residents, a region that had previously had very limited access to medicine or medical treatment.

The RDS had been obtaining other avenues of funding from international aid charities for the last couple of years, and our money was not as essential as it once had been, and the clinic went from strength to strength, and remains in my uncle's name – The Paul Bell Memorial Clinic – to this day. It satisfies me to know that there remains a little corner of India where he is remembered and where he continues to make a difference to the lives of some of the most desperate people on the face of this planet. I think he would have been buzzing with that. It would definitely have appealed to his adventurous spirit.

But that would all be in the future. The elective was done. Now, there was just the small matter of fifth year to get through.

Graduation

As mentioned in the previous chapter, my wife and I had committed to keeping the clinic running, and as a result, a lot of my time during the early part of fifth year was spent attempting to raise funds, whilst most of the rest of it was spent in hospital working on the wards, or running the football club that my wife and I had started with a rag-tag bunch of kids from Speke five years previous and had developed into a pretty professional outfit with four established teams, boasting well over fifty youth members, ranging from early to late teens.

On starting fifth year, I had made the decision I was going to be the best foundation doctor my hospital had ever seen. I am ultimately a perfectionist, highly ambitious and extremely competitive, although I often keep it well hidden to capitalise on being the perennial underdog. For example, as a soldier, I had never fired a weapon before joining the Regiment, had never even held one, and was not a natural shot. In fact, I was pretty shocking to start off with and couldn't so much as hit the proverbial barn door. However, by the end of basic training, I was one of the top marksmen on the course because of my obsessiveness on and around the range. I lived and breathed target-shooting, learning to effectively calculate trajectory of projectiles and the rationale behind adjustments for wind and distance – all on the quiet, obviously. I was far too cool to be seen doing this out in the open.

I was the same in the years that followed at art school, where I was the only student who would slave away all day in the life studios or spend days on end locked in the dark rooms located in the eerie basement of the old John Moores building on Hope Street, the very same building in which John Lennon and Paul McCartney had studied together. I would experiment, over and over again, with length of exposure and development times, until I got my photographs exactly how I wanted them.

And I was the same again when I became a gardener. I was meticulous when it came to shaping lawns into geometrical shapes and would continually strive to provide the best possible gardening service. I wanted to be better than everyone else, and I was. As a result, my customer base exploded, and I could have continued on very successfully, if Medicine hadn't come calling.

Not surprisingly, I took this same attitude into university, and it paid off. I was awarded honours and finished within the top ten per cent of my year, and to be perfectly honest, I have carried that attitude right through my medical career to my current dizzy heights of medical consultant. However, it would be fair to say that, during fifth year, I was displaying a particularly intense level of obsession.

I had no doubt at all in my mind that I was going to be the best foundation doctor, a real-life, thirty-odd-year-old Doogie Howser M.D., and to achieve this, I had a plan. A plan which involved attending hospital every single day. Whilst a lot of my year had taken their eye off the ball after successfully passing finals, I had not. Instead, I persistently shadowed the foundation doctors and learned my trade "on the job". By the end of fifth year, I was well prepared, and to be honest, I would have confidently pitted my skills against any of the junior doctors I was shadowing. I could get venous or arterial bloods from anyone, could cannulate a stone, and there was not a man alive whose penis I could not place a catheter in. I had learned all my medical mnemonics, and although I was undoubtedly nervous about starting, I was also extremely confident in my own ability. And I must have been going about it in the right way, because I had become popular and well-respected amongst my seniors, the nursing staff, and patients alike.

I had given myself the best possible preparation to take on the challenge of Black Wednesday – the Wednesday in early August when junior doctors start their first job, the day we are finally let loose on the wards, the day we feared above all else. However, before I took on this challenge, I had the little matter of a graduation ceremony to get through.

*

The day itself is a bit of a blur now. I remember queuing up outside the Catholic cathedral – Paddy's Wigwam, as we know it locally – on Hope Street, with my wife, son, and parents, for what seemed like an age, on an overcast and unusually cold early summer's afternoon. It was a striking scene, with hundreds of black caps and gowns lining up on the concourse and spilling out onto the wide stairway in front of the church. It was a solid mass of black, contrasting sharply against the brilliant-white shirts, beneath the dark cotton-wool-dotted grey skies above, and the reflected light from the pale limestone paving slabs that wrapped around the grey concrete structure of the striking cathedral. A perfect monographic image, only occasionally interrupted by the odd splash of vibrant pink silk flashing from the lining on the inside of the gowns.

I had to leave my family so I could be seated early, in a special section of the cathedral reserved for the honour students, enabling us to be awarded our degree first. As a result, I was seated away from most of my friends and amongst a mixture of students who I didn't really know, a group composed of the honour students from the year above who had taken a gap year, the best of the four-year programme students, and what could only be described as the biggest nerds of my year, myself included. We were disproportionately represented by mature students, of which I was probably one of the most mature in age if not mentality – as attested by the fact that, even now, I am referring to people as "nerds".

I remember feeling a sense of pride that I was graduating in my city and in my cathedral, a sense of accomplishment at what I had achieved – something most people had probably thought nigh on impossible just six years previous. Other than my wife and myself, I really don't think anyone truly believed I would succeed when I announced to the world and his mate that I was going to be a doctor. A lot of friends who I haven't seen since school or the forces still probably wouldn't believe it possible. I sometimes don't myself, even after all these years.

There was also an element of relief that it was finally all over, and I would soon be getting paid a salary. But I would say the overwhelming emotion that stands out for me, on the actual day, was boredom. We had gone up to receive our degrees first, and it was over so quickly. We then had to wait for the rest of the year to be awarded, and the ceremony dragged on, and on. I was also desperate for the loo, after having had a couple of pints of lager for Dutch courage, making me even more eager for it to end. It's a shame really but typical of my time in university. I was always looking toward tomorrow, eager to get it over and done with, even during my own graduation.

When it was finally finished, we headed to the marquees in Abercromby Square for the drinks reception. The atmosphere was relaxed, a collective sense of relief that we had done it, and it was all over. Five years is a long time to be in university, and I think even the most hardcore party animals must have had enough of it all by then. Most were just milling around, not really knowing what to do with themselves. It felt a bit like the airport in Bosnia, after we had finished our tour and were waiting to fly back home, but a lot more civilised – there were certainly no flutes of champagne in Banja Luka!

The whole graduation ceremony was pleasant enough, and it was nice for our families to get involved and feel a part of it, but it wasn't really my scene. I briefly chatted to a few friends from the course and awkwardly introduced them to my parents and wife whilst we drank champagne for a couple of hours and watched the course awards being handed out – some funny and some as serious as a heart attack.

It all appeared to be naturally winding down, and we were getting ready to make a move, as my wife had arranged for us to meet up with the rest of our clan for a meal in the city centre – kindly emptying what little she had left in her bank account to pay for it. We were just putting on our coats and saying our final goodbyes, when a painfully thin young girl, sporting a floral headscarf, was assisted onto the stage by what looked like two of her friends. Shaking her stick-like upper limb free from the security of one of her friend's linked arms, she stumbled slightly before gripping the microphone with one of her skeletal hands and shakily announcing over the PA system that she would like to say a few words, if that was okay.

I initially felt slightly annoyed, as I was ready to leave, had almost escaped. But noticing how nervous she was and how small she looked up on that big stage, I felt a twinge of guilt and exaggerated my turn to make it obvious that I was now giving her my full attention, whilst she steadied herself, and plucked up the courage to start her speech.

She looked very young, but I suppose was in her early twenties, the same as the other graduates of normal age. The paper she held in her hand, which must have contained her written speech, was now shaking vigorously as she extracted her second arm from the safety of friend number two's steadying embrace and, unsupported, bore the weight of the sheet in her frail hand.

Opening the speech, she informed those of us who didn't know that it was also her graduation today, but she was sure many of us may not recognise her as she'd missed so much university over the past two years and had changed so much in her appearance, and she was right – I didn't have a clue who she was. She then went on to tell us how privileged a position we had achieved at such a young age and how it was so important to retain our humanity throughout the upcoming madness and to remember to always treat our patients with respect, like a person and not a patient. Always speak to them directly and not about them. Essentially, treat them how we would like to be treated ourselves.

She informed us that she had been in hospital a lot over the last couple of years and had actually studied for her finals from a hospital bed, and had received a mixed bag of care, to say the least. Without once looking down at the paper in her now rock-steady hand, she went on to explain how it had been a struggle at times and how she had felt like giving up on many occasions, but she had stuck with it and had overcome adversity and serious illness to pass her exams and become a doctor. Achieving her lifelong dream and making her family proud by becoming the first doctor amongst them was tinged with sadness, as she had recently come to the realisation that she would never go on to practice. Her condition had deteriorated, and she now had just months left to live.

At this point, she paused for a couple of seconds to gather her composure. The marquee was in complete silence as we hung on her every word. She swallowed down the lump in her throat and bravely continued with a tremoring voice, telling us to be the best doctors we could, and reiterating how important it was to treat patients with the dignity and respect they deserve. She then paused again, for longer this time, thanked us and broke down as she was helped from the stage by her two helpers to rapturous applause from the emotional crowd.

I was absolutely stunned. I am not an emotional person but don't mind admitting I was moved to tears by her powerful speech, as was every other human being there. I couldn't believe that this young girl, who had been so energised and passionate as she relayed her message, who radiated so much beauty and so much humility, had just months left to live. It was an absolute travesty. Life can be so cruel sometimes, and so unfair.

Up until that speech, the day had really just been about a sense of relief for me, thanking God it was finally all over, drawing a line under it and moving on to the next phase in my life. There was obviously pride at what I had achieved and at how unlikely my journey had been, a sense of "I told you so", but if I'm honest, I was just happy I would finally be earning some cash. We had struggled so much financially over the last couple of years that I was ecstatic I could finally contribute and provide for my family, finally look after my wife and repay her for all the hard work she had put in over the past seven years, for enabling me to stand up on stage that day, to follow my dreams, at the expense of her own. She dreamed of becoming an architect and she would have been amazing at it, but she had stepped aside, sacrificed her dream for mine.

I had not once that day stopped to think about how privileged I was to be healthy and alive. I had thought about how I was going to be the best doctor I could be – I was obsessive about it – but I hadn't thought what that really meant. Was the best doctor the one who instantly sited a cannula in a sick patient and could answer all the questions on the ward round? Or was it the one who held a patient's hand when they broke bad news, the one who showed real empathy and humility, the one who hugged the old lady with dementia to allow her to feel the warmth of human contact, the one who stayed behind after work to sit and chat with the lonely old man who hadn't had a visitor in months?

My priorities had been wrong. I was too focused on technical ability and knowledge, and this young lady had opened my eyes. As tragic a situation as this was for her, her family, and her friends, what a gift she had imparted upon us, as the next generation of doctors. She had given us the kind of wisdom that would normally take years to accumulate, and to those of us doctors who had listened to her message that day, and took the true meaning of her words on board, she changed us forever and undoubtedly for the better.

Although the girl's name now escapes me and her face has become blurred with the passing of time, I will never forget the message of her speech that day, and for as long as I work in Medicine, I will try and live by the lesson that she taught me. The world lost an amazing young mind and a truly compassionate human being, but even if I was the only doctor who took her message to heart that day, she has indirectly affected so many lives and improved the care received by thousands of patients.

I left the reception, and I met the rest of my family in a Brazilian restaurant in Liverpool. I ate and I got drunk. I got extremely drunk, and I appreciated just being. For once, I was not distracted by thoughts of tomorrow. I sat and I was.

Not Such a Black Wednesday, After All

My university career was over and done with, my little protective bubble about to burst. I was to be cast out into the real world, to start at the bottom, yet again, and slowly work my way back up that slippery slope. My first foothold would be Black Wednesday, and I waited with a mixture of nervous excitement and trepidation to discover where I would be starting out on my medical journey.

Finally, the day arrived. I opened up my inbox, and there it was. I clicked on the email, watching it download excruciatingly slowly. *Come on, hurry up. Is it surgery? Is it medicine?* At long last, the page opened up to reveal my jobs list:

1. *Neuropsychiatry: Brain Injuries*
2. *Elderly Medicine (DME)*
3. *Orthopaedic Surgery*

Neuropsychiatry: Brain Injuries! What? Did I have the correct list? I checked the name and my ID number, rechecking them at least ten times. It was definitely me. When I had completed my choices, I hadn't even noticed neuropsychiatry was an option. How the hell had I been given it as my first job? I was not at all happy. I had finished in the top ten per cent of the year but hadn't been offered any of my first-choice jobs. It felt like a slap in the face. I needed to speak to someone, urgently. I had been psyching myself up for the challenges of the ward, and now I wouldn't even be working on a ward. Instead, I would be a glorified medical student on psych. Black Wednesday had been stolen from me.

As an ex-soldier, and an infantry one at that, I thrive on challenges and love nothing more than being right in the thick of it, digging in and fighting shoulder to shoulder in the trenches. I love the camaraderie that ensues, the feeling of being in the shit and successfully making it out the other side, the collective sense of achievement and satisfaction in knowing we were all pushed to the edge. We may have buckled, but we were never broken. We got through it, and we did it together as a team. That was what Black Wednesday represented for me. It was a rite of passage for all doctors, and I was being denied my rite.

I contacted the deanery and asked if my jobs could be changed, perhaps even swap the order and keep the same jobs, so I started on the ward first. But it was to no avail. I had given it my best shot, but the die was cast, and I was to start on neuropsychiatry, or more specifically: brain injuries.

When I eventually calmed down – and it took a good while – I realised that it wasn't going to be all bad. I had been placed in an old community hospital, which was a fifteen-minute walk from my house. There would be no on-calls and no weekends, and I even had every Tuesday morning allocated for teaching, and every Wednesday afternoon set aside as study time. It was basically like being a student again, with wages, and I would be eased into the world of Medicine in the gentlest way possible. Okay, it was a bit too gentle for my liking, but I had to stop complaining and just get on with it. There were certainly plenty of worse ways I could be earning a living – I knew this for a fact because I had done most of them. A few days later, I was sent my rota, which advised I would be working primarily in the brain injuries rehabilitation centre, but I would have placements with the hospital psychiatric liaison team, the crisis team, and the community mental health team.

*

Black Wednesday finally arrived. I was to attend my induction at nine a.m. in the community hospital. It was a glorious day, and I drove my brand-new 125 c.c. scooter the short journey from my house to my new place of work. Whilst my contemporaries were nervously gearing up to start life on the wards, I was sat in a large, high-ceilinged Victorian living room, bright sunshine flooding in through the giant bay windows, as I ate bacon butties followed by Danish pastries, washed down with plenty of strong coffee.

We were introduced to the computer systems and given a couple of short lectures on the principles of psychiatry and the upcoming placement, finishing at twelve on the dot. Following the lectures, I wandered up the corridor to the brain injuries rehabilitation centre to meet my new consultant, who was waiting at the reception desk to greet me. He was tall, at least six foot five inches, and painfully thin, with a pale Celtic complexion and a soft Irish lilt that put me in mind of TV's Mathew Kelly. He was dressed very smartly in a pressed suit, plain shirt, and matching tie, and was well-groomed, but he didn't radiate confidence, seeming uncomfortable in his own skin whilst holding himself at awkward and unusually stooped angles. He was relatively young for a consultant, and I got the impression he was naturally shy, despite having chosen a career that involved talking to people pretty much all day, every day. As a result of this shyness, he was incapable of maintaining eye contact, and our initial conversation was stilted and slightly uncomfortable.

As time went by, and I got to know him more, I got the distinct impression he enjoyed the neurology part of his job much more than the psychiatry aspect. It made me wonder if he had been unsuccessful in his training application and had just fallen into psychiatry. I was not convinced he enjoyed his work or living away from home. He had an air of loneliness or even sadness about him, and he flew back to Ireland every Friday, seeming to tread water through the working week, just doing enough to get him to that Friday flight, counting down the days like a prisoner – ironically, in a similar position to most of his patients.

I realise that I probably haven't painted the most flattering picture of him, thus far, but he was actually very good at his job, despite all of the above. He was a highly intelligent man who turned out to be really down to earth, and I genuinely liked him as a person. He didn't seem to fit in, and I suppose I identified with him on that score.

Anyway, back to my first day. He quickly showed me around the ward and introduced me to the staff. We then sat in his office for twenty minutes whilst he asked me about my expectations from this job and life in general. I hadn't really thought about these things, and I replied that I wasn't sure, as I had no idea what I wanted to specialise in yet and was keeping an open mind until I had completed all of my foundation jobs. He seemed more than satisfied with this answer and told me to take the rest of the day off and meet him back on the ward Monday morning, sending me on my way with an awkward half pat, half tap on the back.

It was just after lunch on Black Wednesday, and I had managed to survive my first day… well, half day, in the new job. I excitedly jumped back onto my new shiny black scooter and drove as fast as I could to my parents' house for a nice spot of lunch.

The rest of the week continued in this vein, with an induction lecture and introduction to the trust teaching programme on Thursday, breakfast and lunch included, obviously. Then "break away" and self-defence training on Friday, which was delivered by two male community mental health nurses and was right up my street. I absolutely loved it and finished off the hard day rolling on the mats with a couple of refreshing pints of lager in my old local, which was located a short and convenient five-minute walk from the community hospital. All of a sudden, this psych lark didn't seem so bad after all.

*

The brain injuries unit turned out to be an interesting place to work. It was an eight-bedded unit and most of the patients were young and healthy. The unit was full of unique characters – real "scallies" as we call them in Liverpool – with the most fantastic back stories. I consider myself pretty streetwise, being an ex-squaddie who was brought up on the mean streets of Liverpool, serving an apprenticeship in some of the toughest boxing gyms in the country, and graduating into an early life of street gangs and violence, but I must admit that some of the antics these boys got up to shocked even an "arl arse" like myself.

We had some stories to tell between us. One patient had suffered such severe knife injuries during a bungled robbery that the cardiothoracic team had decided to open up his chest in A&E to perform manual cardiac massage – something that is only ever done as a very last resort. He died on multiple occasions, but due to the resuscitation team's absolute heroics, he eventually survived to tell the tale, all be it with an oxygen-starved and permanently damaged brain. Another patient was injured in a major car crash, following a high-speed police chase, whilst yet another had been beaten to death in Liverpool city centre and resuscitated twice by the medical team, the last time ultimately proving successful. One patient had fallen out of an open second-floor window whilst snorting cocaine from the ledge, and an ex-squaddie had a piece of shrapnel lodged in his brain from an IED explosion in the Middle East, and simply couldn't adjust to civilian life. We even had a failed suicide attempt following a major news story that made the front page of most English red-tops, which I obviously can't go into for reasons of patient confidentiality.

It was an interesting introduction to the world of Medicine. My role was essentially to replace the GP who had provided a twice-weekly drop-in service, usually ignored by the patients as most had no physical health needs, and as a result, I found myself with a lot of spare time on my hands. I tended to fill this time by sitting in the communal area and playing music or drawing and painting with the patients. As you can imagine, with such a unique group of characters all thrown together in one place, we had the occasional clashes of personality that could often turn violent.

We even had an escapee one Friday, who was rather bizarrely apprehended by the police in my local pub, just as I was walking in to meet up with some friends.

He was a diagnosed schizophrenic who had developed a brain injury following multiple drug overdoses, and although he didn't strictly fit the criteria, he had somehow managed to get placed in our unit on several occasions. He was currently on a Section 3 of the Mental Health Act, which means he had been detained for treatment, and he had been moved to us a few days earlier from an acute mental health hospital. We were under clear instructions that he was not to leave the locked unit, but it was Friday afternoon, and he liked to party. As such, he was desperate for a "pint and a line" as he had been telling anyone who would listen to him, including me.

Getting no joy from anyone, he decided to make his great escape in the most blatant and daring fashion of all: by busting straight through the front door. It will not come as a shock to you that this was no criminal mastermind we were dealing with here, and even if he hadn't told half the staff that he was going to make a break for it, the simple presence of a six and a half foot, rakishly thin, unkempt and bearded, fidgeting, wild-eyed, cold-turkeying schizophrenic idly hanging around a locked security door may have aroused at least a little bit of suspicion. Not surprisingly, he was quickly escorted away from the front entrance and back into the locked unit. However, this did not deter our daredevil, who simply moved on to Plan B. He asked if he could go out for a cigarette, and whilst being escorted to the smoking area by a female nurse, he made a sudden dash for the sixteen-foot wire fence that surrounded the garden, his long legs quickly eating up the distance as he made his break for freedom. About halfway there, he hit a divot and his lead ankle buckled, sending him stumbling for a couple of yards before he completely lost his balance and face-planted into the overgrown grass that bordered the neatly cut lawn.

Rooted to the spot, we watched with morbid fascination as he picked himself up and continued to desperately stumble toward the impassable green mesh, none of us holding out much hope for his escape attempt as he slammed heavily into the fence. It appeared the impact might have knocked the wind out of his sails, but he somehow managed to swing one of those long, gangly arms upward, and he found a finger grip. Before we knew it, he had gone up that fence, like a rat up a drainpipe, expertly swinging his long legs over to the other side, before finally losing his grip and falling. Fingertips desperately grasping for the small rectangular gaps in the metal wire, he fell the last twelve foot or so, hitting the ground with a heavy thud. He lay still for a couple of seconds on his back, before jumping up with a big smile on his face and throwing up a double two-fingered V-sign in our direction. He then turned and ambled away, dragging his leg with a slight limp, the back of his dark jumper covered in dry soil, twigs, and grass.

It was an unexpected and impressive escape, and the staff, most of whom had stood statue-still throughout the whole episode, suddenly sprung into life, making a beeline for the nursing station to organise a posse, phone the police, and compile a rather embarrassing incident report.

We spent the rest of the afternoon searching the local park and liaising with police, but it was no good – he was nowhere to be found. I phoned my consultant to inform him of the events. He didn't appear to be overly concerned and told me to take an early "knock off" and let the police deal with it, adding that I should enjoy the weekend. I decided to take him up on his advice and arranged to meet up with a couple of friends at a local pub, just a few short minutes' scooter ride away from work.

It was a beautiful late summer's afternoon, and I drove my scooter with short sleeves, enjoying the cool, refreshing breeze rushing in through my open visor as I eased open the throttle. I pulled up outside the front entrance of the pub and pushed my scooter up onto its stand, noting the two police cars that seemed to have been abandoned in the terraced street running alongside the pub, blue lights silently flashing.

Gently twisting my new helmet side to side to loosen it, I pulled it up and off my head, throwing my gloves inside, before swinging the shiny black lid rhythmically back and forth as I walked toward the double front doors of the Fulwood Arms public house. At the exact same time, the doors were flung violently back in my direction, almost knocking me off my feet. Instinctively, I jumped backward and just about avoided a tussling group of policemen struggling to contain a large, gangly, bearded drunk, who turned his head in my direction and, looking directly at me with a daft intoxicated grin on his face, shouted, "Alright, doc!" as he was roughly pulled away toward one of the waiting cars.

*

That was about as exciting as it got on the brain injuries unit, but I had quite a few hairy experiences whilst placed with the community team, one involving an incident caused by the sheer stupidity and "pigheadedness" of an arrogant psychiatric registrar.

The patient we had been asked to see in A&E was a middle-aged gentleman with a long psychiatric history, who had found himself in crisis and turned up at the emergency room with a fifteen-inch, silver LCD television for company. When we arrived to assess him, he was cowering in the corner of the curtained cubicle, hiding behind the unplugged TV. He looked terrified as he peered around his protective shield at us, like an animal backed into a corner.

Completely ignoring the patient's distress and the obvious danger posed to us, the registrar walked straight toward him, stopping only a couple of feet away, where he towered over the crouching man. He put out his hand and asked for the TV, making that little up-and-down, backward-and-forward, four fingers together movement that teachers and others in authority tend to make when demanding something be handed over. You know, the one that is usually paired with a stern look of disapproval from the finger-wagger.

It was blatantly obvious, even to a foundation doctor with a couple of months' experience in mental health, that this man felt threatened, was ready to come out fighting for his life, and it wasn't going to end well for any of us. Ignoring the blatant signals radiating from the patient, the registrar continued forward and attempted to pull the TV from his grip. In response, the patient turned the air blue with threats, and pulled the TV back aggressively.

We took a quick step backward. Feeling a rising level of anxiety and concern for my own safety, I asked the registrar if he really thought it was wise to keep goading the patient, who was clearly frightened. Turning his head slowly, the registrar looked at me as though examining a piece of dog turd he had just noticed on the sole of his shoe. He completely ignored my question. With a look of smug determination, he stepped forward again, straight into the corner of the silver LCD TV that had been swung with murderous intent, fortunately only glancing the reg's forehead. I had to stifle a laugh, because if anyone deserved to be hit with a TV, it was that arrogant bastard.

However, I soon stopped laughing as the patient sprung out of the blocks like a cat and ran toward us both, swinging the TV wildly, focused on us with the special type of crazy eyes solely reserved for the bayonet-wielding soldier and the severely pissed-off schizophrenic. I used my best boxing footwork to sidestep a couple of swings and rolled behind the registrar just in time, before the crazed patient retreated to the corner of the room and launched the TV across the cubicle, hitting the registrar square in the chest. The patient returned to his crouching position, all fight suddenly spent, cowering and whimpering like a beaten dog between the curtain and the bed.

We backed slowly out of the cubicle, never taking our eyes from him, the TV lying smashed between us, both ready to turn and run, if necessary, the smug look long gone from the registrar's face. "Still think it was a good idea to pull the telly from his hand?" I asked sarcastically as we left the bay. He didn't even look at me, simply turned and walked in the opposite direction, probably wanting to put as much space as possible between him and me, before he acted on the temptation to swing a TV at me. *Another early finish then*, I thought, as I headed toward the A&E exit.

That was about the worst experience I had with the liaison team, but I had several dodgy experiences whilst placed in the community, including one occasion when I was trapped in a living room by a twenty-five-year-old, six-foot-six-inch, twenty-stone schizophrenic who had only recently been released to Care in the Community, following a long period of incarceration for a near fatal hammer attack on his own father. In fact, "near fatal" is an understatement – "miraculous" was the word used by the medical team to describe his father's survival.

Again, I was paired with a registrar, and we had broken the golden rule of never allowing a patient to get between yourself and the door as we entered the room and took a seat on the sofa that was situated in the barred bay window of the old Victorian room. I instantly knew we had made a mistake, but I had instinctively followed the lead of the registrar as he was the senior doctor.

The moment the patient was escorted into the room by a female carer, who was at least sixty years of age and around eight stone soaking wet, I had the overwhelming urge to get out of there. He immediately occupied the armchair that was blocking the only exit and eyed us suspiciously as he was poured a cup of tea by the carer.

My registrar asked him how he had been getting on, and he instantly replied he was being spied on by government agents who had microchips implanted in their heads, and the only way to stop them was to smash their heads open with a hammer – the very weapon that he had attacked his father with – and remove the chips.

As we progressed through the assessment, it became clear he was listening to voices speaking from behind him as he would abruptly stop talking, cock his head to one side with a look of concentration on his face, before giving a little confirmatory nod, then immediately turn toward us to begin a fresh line of questioning. He was becoming more suspicious of us by the minute, and at one point, mid-sentence, he suddenly turned and informed me that he had a hammer in the drawer of his TV cabinet that he used to protect himself from intruders.

It was genuinely one the most intimidating experiences of my life, which is a big claim for a man who has faced enemy fire on multiple occasions. He obviously thought we were spies, requiring the chips removed from our heads, and it took all my charm and "gift of the gab" to get past him and out that door. We couldn't get out of there fast enough or on the phone quick enough to get him re-admitted to a secure unit, as he was clearly psychotic.

That was without doubt the most frightening experience of my placement, but the most bizarre occurred as I was leaving a community mental health hospital in South Liverpool on an overcast and miserable day in late September. I was standing outside the front doors of the old hospital that was located behind the car park of a well-known supermarket chain. Ironically, it was the hospital in which I had been born, over thirty years before, when it had been a "proper" hospital. I was in the process of wrapping a thick, woollen scarf around the exposed skin in the rather inconvenient gap between the top of my leather bomber jacket and the base of the helmet, when I heard muffled shouts. My spider senses tingling, I turned toward the sound, and my heart instantly sank as I saw a man known locally as "the Zulu" rapidly approaching me, in a rather threatening manner.

The Zulu was an African gentleman who, urban legend claimed, had once been a respectable businessman. Standing at well over six foot in height, he wandered the streets of Toxteth in a permanent state of semi-nakedness, sporting a body that looked as though it had been chiselled from the finest anthracite. He was usually mild enough in manner but had somehow managed to progress from successful businessman to a batshit crazy, self-styled Zulu – hence the nickname.

He was currently heading toward me with great haste whilst dressed in a "traditional" African outfit made from the finest matted polyester, with a white leather Stetson upon his head, and white sunglasses with shutter-style glassless lenses and funky flashing LED lights embedded in the rim. A pair of lacy fairy wings spread across his huge shoulders and upper back were fixed in place by a thin piece of white elastic that was looped over his immense anterior deltoids and disappeared into his armpits. To finish off the look, he was rocking a pair of knee-high, white fur boots. But most worryingly of all, he was walking straight down the middle of the thin tarmac pathway that was my escape route, shouting, "I never fucking said that."

"Are you okay, mate," I replied, as I threw my leg over the scooter, opened the throttle, and pressed the ignition switch. The engine clicked a few times and went silent. *You've got to be fucking joking!* My engine had never failed before. Butterflies suddenly fluttered in my stomach.

"I never fucking said that," he repeated, speeding up now.

"Listen, mate, I never said anything," I replied, as I turned the key again and rolled the throttle hard with my right hand until it could move no further whilst simultaneously hitting the ignition switch with my left thumb, silently praying to a god that I didn't believe in, as the engine slowly caught and chugged once, twice, and then sprung into life. This alerted him to the fact I was trying to make a break for it, prompting him to pick up the pace, closing the distance alarmingly fast.

The scooter suddenly lurched forward, and I drove straight toward him at speed, hoping against hope that he would move out the way. He didn't. I swerved at the last minute as he swung a ferocious kick toward me, barely glancing my left thigh but causing the scooter to wobble precariously and lean alarmingly to the right. I pulled the brake sharply and touched my foot to the ground, allowing my knee to collapse and my weight to shift toward the ominous-looking gravelly tarmac before forcefully extending my right leg and throwing my weight sharply to the left. The bike wobbled viciously and righted as I pulled the throttle back and leaned forward to steady myself. The whole manoeuvre took a couple of seconds, but glancing in my wing mirror, I saw he was almost upon me, at full sprint, closing the gap fast.

I wrenched the throttle back fully and pulled away, heading toward the end of the driveway and out onto the main road. I prayed there would be no traffic coming as I slowed the last couple of metres before the gate posts and quickly glanced behind. He was still coming. I looked to my right and noted a bus approaching. I had to make a choice, and fast. I decided to take a chance on the bus and sped off as quickly as I could into the bus lane, an angry blast of the horn following behind me for the first ten metres or so before I escaped to safety.

But my time on neuropsychiatry eventually came to an end. As interesting as I had found it, and as much as I had enjoyed my time, I was more than ready to get back on the wards and get my teeth stuck into some real medicine. I was ready for Black Wednesday, Part Two.

Black December

After my cushy neuropsychiatry job, I was more than ready to get my teeth into a bit of medicine and finally experience a real Black Wednesday. The actual day in early August is not what it once was, as hospital trusts tend to be a lot nicer these days and will prepare for the madness by overstaffing the wards and the on-call rota to ensure there is enough physical and emotional support available, if and when required. There are special protocols in place. Everyone is aware of the situation, and most are pretty sympathetic, as they know from experience how terrifying it can be for all involved, especially the nursing staff and poor patients.

Despite the jokes and horror stories, it's actually a relatively safe period to be in hospital these days, as the modern F1 is so well supported and so closely monitored. That is unless your second job happens to be your first actual hospital job, as it was in my case. If you spend your first day on the job sitting in a lecture theatre, drinking coffee, eating Danish pastries, and laughing at your poor terrified contemporaries via social media posts, then it's a pretty safe bet that karma is going to bite you on the arse further down the road, and that's exactly what happened to me when I was quite literally thrown to the lions at the start of my second placement. There was no extra support on the wards or the on-call rota, no understanding from the consultants, as four months into the job is deemed long enough to have learned the ropes, and sympathy is certainly not a word within the known vocabulary of the average nurse by early December. If you start in hospital on that dark Wednesday in December, then believe me, there really is no bedding-in period – you either hit the ground running, or you crash and burn.

There are certain landmarks in your F1 year that nobody can fully prepare you for, situations that have to be lived through to be believed. In many ways it is similar to a soldier's learning experience, though starkly different in other ways. There's nothing quite as sobering as your first death, or as shocking as your first cardiac arrest, or as exhausting as your first round of chest compressions. However, the one thing every new doctor fears, above all else, is the first experience of a patient "going off" when you are the only doctor – and as such, the most senior doctor – on the ward. That terrifying period of deterioration that must be endured before you can legitimately pull the arrest cord or put out a 2222 call and get someone who actually knows what they are doing on the scene.

And like every other fresh-faced baby doctor – not quite so fresh-faced in my case – I spent the first few days of work in a state of perpetual fear, maybe even abject terror, that one of my patients was about to go off right in front of me. And low and behold, a couple of weeks into the job, and exactly as I had feared, it happened.

My first hospital job was in the Department of Medicine for the Elderly (DME), which to the blissfully unaware, is what was once known as the geriatric wards. DME was set aside from the rest of the hospital with just one corridor in and out. A montage of pictures made up the walls of the corridor leading to the department, reminding you that you were in Liverpool, the city that had once put the "Great" in Great Britain. The collage of images spanned the city's recent past, illustrating the glory days of the patients who were currently contained within the sanctum of the DME. Images from a bygone era of long-demolished, bustling tenement blocks adorned with Union Jack bunting, tables of faceless, black-and-white, hollow-eyed ghosts in the foreground, excitedly waving plastic flags as they celebrated the coronation of a young Queen Elizabeth. A monochrome docklands scene centred around a group of proud flat-capped dockers, hard men staring defiantly down the lens of the camera. The mini-skirted Cilla

Black look-a-likes swarming outside the swinging Cavern club, in stark contrast to the gritty, leather-clad, spike-haired punks of Eric's.

This montage was probably missed by ninety per cent of the junior doctors who hurried through those corridors with great trepidation on their first Black Wednesday. But as I entered the fray, on my very own Black Wednesday, I studied them intensely, making my way slowly along the corridor toward what would be my place of work for the next four months, feeling strangely emotional and proud in equal measures.

Upon arriving at the ward and swiping through the magnetically locked door, two sensations instantly hit me like a baseball bat in the face. The first was the horror of the yellow glow emanating from the artificially lit magnolia walls, a pulsating and palpable light that seemed to envelop my uninitiated psyche, making me recoil with squinted eyes, the seed of a headache instantly planted. Whilst uncomfortable, this sensation at least became bearable after a couple of minutes of acclimatisation. However, the second sensation changed from minute to minute, hour to hour, day to day, never doing me the courtesy of letting me get accustomed to it. Anyone who has worked on a DME ward will be familiar with the assault of the ever-changing smell. It is unique, to say the least, especially during norovirus season, which this currently was. It infiltrates your every pore, every fibre of your clothing, and just when you think you have become immune to it, a new pungent delight is freshly served up from the bowels of a constipated elderly patient or from the murk released by the unwinding of a matted leg dressing. It sounds overly dramatic and possibly even a bit precious, but it really is an experience that has to be lived through to be believed.

My first impression of the ward, after the visual and olfactory onslaught, was that it was rather tatty-looking, and by tatty, I don't mean dirty or unclean. Rather, it looked worn and tired, almost as though the depressingly magnolia walls had seen more than enough misery, suffering, and death and had given up on even being walls anymore. This perfectly mirrored the expressions on most of the ward's nursing staff, as they buzzed in and out of the bays and side rooms like worker bees flitting from flower to flower, never really stopping, but never quite achieving whatever job it was they had set out to achieve in the first place.

It was in this environment that my medical career was truly born. After the gentlest of introductions, this was the real deal. I staggered onto the ward like a fawn onto the plains of the Serengeti, my steps unsteady, legs trembling, to be imminently faced with two choices: run with the herd or be torn apart by the hyenas in blue.

I spent the first few days on the ward keeping my head down and trying to find my feet, learn the computer systems, not piss anyone off, and make sure I was never the most senior doctor on the ward. However, being the diligent junior doctor that I was, and being on a mission to always be prepared for ward rounds, I had established my own daily routine in which I would arrive half an hour early to prepare the notes, print off the handover list, and swot up on all of my patients. I ensured I arrived well before the consultant set about her daily routine of pulling my preparations apart and making me feel totally useless.

Our ward was one of three within the DME/stroke department, and it contained thirty-six patients, divided equally between three teams, which were made up of a consultant, an SHO, an F1, and a registrar providing middle-grade cover for two teams. This sounds like excellent staffing levels, but once acute on-calls, nights, weekends, and annual leave were factored in, it usually left a consultant or registrar and a junior.

Mornings were taken up by three consultant ward rounds per week, a registrar round, and on the remaining morning, the SHO or F1 was left to their own devices as the lunatics officially took over the asylum. Afternoons were occupied by jobs generated from the ward rounds, death certificates and crematorium forms (there were a lot of these during the winter months), clerking new admissions onto the ward, teaching students, and any other craziness that can suddenly develop on a hospital ward.

I was in team one, the A team, and into my third week. As usual, I had arrived early, greeting the nurses with a little bit of a swagger. I was starting to get into the rhythm of this doctor thing now. Like the first shoots breaking through the soil and reaching out for the sunlight, I was growing, and wasn't it mighty oaks that grow from small, green shoots? And then, bang, right in the middle of my unsuspecting complacency, it happened.

I was at the doctors' desk happily printing out my personalised patient list when a nurse uttered the words I had feared the most. "Doctor, can you have a look at this patient? He doesn't look well at all." Fifteen little words, fifteen words that, individually, might appear completely harmless, but when placed together in that particular order were enough to make my heart plummet. Slowly, my eyes rolled up, caught in the magnetic pull of the large clock above my computer screen. Desperately not wanting to know, but observing, nonetheless, that it was 08.35. Eight. Thirty-five. At least fifteen minutes before any of my colleagues would arrive on the ward. *Why the bloody hell wasn't I sitting in Costa, having a nice bacon barm right now?*

I stood up, simultaneously sending the wheeled computer chair shooting backward toward the wall with my buttocks, as I slowly made my way to the gallows, trailing the nurse like a puppy. We headed past the A team's bay and side rooms (my patients), and into B team's area (not my patients). *Great, I didn't even know the patient!* However, it didn't take the brains of an archbishop to figure out who was the cause of the nurse's angst. He was in the far corner of the bay, writhing in agony on the bed and clutching his chest, face grey, thick Eddie-the-Eagle-style glasses knocked to a jaunty angle, giving the whole scene a comedy twist that I was definitely in no frame of mind to appreciate. *Okay, so it was his heart.* I had figured that much out. But was he a known cardiac patient?

"I've done an ECG, doc," said the nurse, as she thrust the cool, smooth, crisp 12-lead trace into my hand. Now, another fear of mine, at this point in my fledgling career, which I had not yet admitted to, was the 12-lead ECG trace. We had all been told the horror stories of junior doctors interpreting an ECG as normal sinus rhythm and sending a patient home to die of a cardiac arrest, when in fact there had been an obvious ST-elevation. I looked at her face as I clamped the paper between my fingers, and my own sheer terror was mirrored in her dark eyes. It suddenly dawned on me that not only was this man's life in the hands of the ward's most junior doctor, but also the ward's most junior nurse. *What a bloody team!*

Okay, so I wasn't going to be getting any help. This was it – I had to do something. I turned to her, and summoning up my most authoritative voice, I almost steadily asked for the patient's notes and obs chart. A look of instant relief spread over the nurse's face as she realised she was temporarily relieved of any responsibility, and she happily scurried off to get the notes. I was alone. In my peripheral vision, I could just about make out the shape of the patient still clutching at his chest, and like every victim in every horror film, I began to turn slowly toward my resigned fate. Just then, I remembered the ECG. I studied it intensely for a few seconds, trying to delay the inevitable, but it may as well have been written in ancient Aramaic. Then, out of nowhere, MONA B popped into my head. I felt an almost instant relief. Beautiful MONA B… and then SOCRATES – I was on fire!

MONA B is a pretty rudimental medical student mnemonic that is used to memorise the management of a myocardial infarction and stands for: Morphine, Oxygen, Nitrates, Aspirin, and Beta blocker. SOCRATES is another classic medical student mnemonic to identify differentials of pain, which stands for: Site, Onset, Character, Radiation, Associated symptoms, Time/duration, Exacerbating/relieving factors, and Severity.

So, back to the patient. I turned to him. He was still grey and still rolling about on the bed, frantically clutching at his chest, which was no surprise really as I hadn't actually done anything yet to help him. A mental fog began to roll in like a heavy mist from the Mersey on a crisp autumn morning. I fought it back and started to ask some relevant questions, relating to the site of the pain, its onset, character… going through SOCRATES, simultaneously running through MONA B, just as the ward's most junior nurse arrived back with a heavy set of hospital notes. "Sit him up, please, nurse, and put some high-flow oxygen on him," I said as calmly as I could.

"Fuck that, doc! I'm not sitting up, not with this pain," was the patient's instant retort, as the nurse connected him up to the oxygen without sitting him up. *Okay this isn't going to pan out like an episode of* Casualty. I felt my confidence ebbing away, once again. "Has he had morphine, nurse?"

"Yes," she replied.

Okay, that's two down.

"Aspirin. Give him 300 mg, please." He hadn't had aspirin, yet. *Well done*, I congratulated myself, just as Eddie the Eagle yelled at me to hurry up and do something about this effing pain. The nurse looked at me with genuine sympathy. I desperately looked at the big white clock on the bay wall, realising it was still about ten minutes before the other doctors usually arrived on the ward. My heart sank.

With a mixture of pity, hope, and desperation, the nurse said, "He's MEWSing a five, MET call?" A MEWS score is the Modified Early Warning Score that uses clinical measurements such as blood pressure, heart rate, oxygen levels, etc., as a way to assess the severity of illness which ranges from 0–14, and five was the threshold to put out an emergency bleep – a distress call to the Mounties (the MET: Medical Emergency Team) who would currently be prepping for handover and looking forward to a warm comfortable bed after a long, hard night shift.

Like a field marshal surveying his defeated army on the battlefield, I mumbled yes, almost inaudibly. With tangible relief, she hurried off to put out the MET call, leaving me totally deflated, useless, a complete failure. I lifted my heavy head slowly and noticed the GTN spray (a spray that opens up the blood vessels in the body, including those in the heart, and as a result relieves chest pain) on his bedside table. "Have you taken your GTN?"

The patient slowly shook his head, grimacing behind the oxygen mask. I handed it to him, and he lifted the mask, and sprayed the GTN beneath his tongue, just as a medical registrar arrived on the ward in a blaze of frenetic energy, a general at the head of her troops. The MET was here. With a mixture of relief and horror, I realised that it was my ward registrar. She snatched the ECG from my hand, muttering what I presume were curse words in her native Gallic tongue, barely glancing at it as she tossed it toward the bedside table. I watched it float gracefully through the air and softly land, skidding almost the whole width of the bedside table before it stopped, perfectly balanced on the edge.

"Have you done trops?" she snapped at me. Trops refers to the troponin level test, which is a blood test that can be used to detect a heart attack by assessing the level of damage caused to the heart muscle itself because of a lack of oxygen. If the heart muscle is starved of oxygen, it initially panics and releases troponin in the early phase and then eventually dies and breaks down releasing more troponin as the heart attack progresses.

I turned to the patient and watched his symptoms literally melt away in front of my very eyes as the GTN spray kicked in. It suddenly struck me that I had put out the MET call way too hastily. "No," I replied sheepishly, my voice barely concealing my burning shame.

The registrar looked at me, and I watched the anger in her eyes dissipate slightly as she registered how embarrassed I was about the whole situation. She asked for a quick handover, which I tried to make as cardiac-sounding as possible.

"So, it was angina then?" she asked.

"Yes," I replied, barely audible, again.

Turning to the rest of the team, she said, "It's okay," dismissing them with a shooing motion of her hand. Relieved, they turned in unison and headed to handover, one step closer to their beds. Grabbing the notes and flipping to the latest page, she quickly scribbled up the events of the MET call, as one by one, the ward doctors arrived for their shift, casually glancing into the bay before going about their daily business. I stood behind the registrar, head bowed like a naughty schoolboy, whilst she completed the notes, before closing them shut with a loud snap and passing them back to me without a word. She then turned on her heels and walked away. I stood motionless for a second, the heavy notes cradled in the crook of my right arm, wanting the earth to open up and swallow me whole.

I walked back to the doctors' office and dropped, deflated, into the tattered leather seat next to team two's F1, who just happened to be my old mate from year zero, the new leader of the rugby boys. "So, Mr H had another angina attack then, did he?" he asked me, feebly trying to contain a snigger.

"Fuck off," I replied, as I printed off another copy of the patient list. Just then, my consultant popped her head through the office door, giving me a stern look before eyeing her wristwatch and asking, "Are you ready?"

I stood up and handed over a copy of the patient list. *Why the hell did I choose to do this?* I thought for the thousandth time, as I fell in behind my impatient consultant. Humiliated, smarting, and angry with myself, but determined to improve, I swore I would never repeat the same mistake again. And to be fair, I never did.

Death

A lot of junior doctors will experience death for the first time early on the job. Most doctors are barely in their twenties on qualifying and, as such, will likely have relatively young parents and living grandparents, and thoughts of death probably don't occupy too much of their time. After all, we all feel relatively invincible, even immortal, when we are young, don't we? I remember walking into some dodgy situations as a nineteen-year-old soldier, and I can honestly say the thought I may not walk back out again never crossed my mind, not even once.

That mentality changes pretty quickly when we start working and become surrounded by death, immersed in it, even. There can be periods in which you lose three or four patients in a week, patients who you may have developed a good rapport with, in some circumstances, even a friendship. At first, this can be really difficult to take, even more so if one of these special patients arrests in your presence and you become a part of the team attempting to resuscitate them. This post-arrest period can be most surreal for the new doctor – the sudden lull following the storm, as the other doctors steadily drift away and the nurses silently busy themselves with the body, detaching drips and removing cannulas, whilst the patient, who was a living breathing person only minutes before, lies still in the centre of all this chaos, usually in the most undignified of positions. A once proud and private person, now topless, chest concave, airway half in, half out, tongue protruding and head rolled to the side, lifeless eyes fixed in your direction.

Images like these can be difficult to shake off, and at first, I would take ten minutes to myself and grab a coffee, if I could spare the time. If I couldn't, I would quickly phone my wife or my dad for a random chat. I would never talk about what had just happened, but it made me feel a bit more normal to hear about how my wife's morning was going or discuss last night's match with my dad for five minutes. It would bring me back down to earth and push out the image of those lifeless eyes peering into my very soul. Over time, the impact lessened, and it got easier. Eventually, I would walk from one arrest to another and then straight home to bed without giving a second thought to what I had just witnessed, to the personal tragedy that had just unfolded before me, to someone's world ending.

I had seen dead bodies before I entered the medical world, both in my job as a soldier and in my personal life. I had lost several family members and close friends, and coming from a predominantly Roman Catholic city, many families, including my own, would take bodies home and lay them out in the front parlour for a period of mourning. These cadavers were beautifully presented in their plush silk-lined coffin, dressed in their Sunday best with blemish-free waxy complexion and a faint whiff of formaldehyde adding to the surrealness of the whole scenario. It was as though the person who I had once known had been swapped out for a Madam-Tussaud-style lookalike, making the situation bizarre enough that it was easy to detach myself from. However, witnessing somebody die in hospital, in what is essentially your place of work, is a different ball game altogether. Being present and observing the last breaths, the exact moment of passing, can be an emotional or, in some cases, even a spiritual experience.

The first dead body I encountered in Medicine was as a third-year student. Being the stereotypical mature student nerd, I had randomly turned up on a ward – in my own time, of course – and asked the nursing staff if they had any interesting patients for a diligent hard-working medical student like myself to take a history from. I was directed toward a bed which had the curtains drawn around it. I shouted a cheery hello as I pulled the curtain slightly apart and nimbly slipped through the gap, only to be confronted by an elderly patient lying stone-cold dead in his bed. He looked as though he had been dead for a good while, having that telltale grey, waxy tinge to his skin and was flanked on either side of the hospital bed by what looked like his elderly grieving wife and middle-aged daughter. I froze, instantly rooted to the spot, mortified. I apologised profusely for intruding on their private moment of grief, before gathering my wits and quickly returning to the nursing station to confront the group of giggling nurses, telling them, in no uncertain terms, what I thought of their sick joke, before leaving the ward.

Most doctors' first experience of death comes when verifying a patient. Each patient needs to be physically checked by a doctor (or increasingly, these days, by a trained nurse) to confirm, or verify, the patient has passed away, before they can be taken to the mortuary. We have to check for absence of heart and breath sounds, and the absence of a central pulse, before checking the light reflexes of the pupils, and finally testing for lack of reaction to a painful stimulus, usually a stiff sternal rub.

I found the act of verification a very profound and peaceful experience in my early days. I would always talk out loud to each patient, explaining what I was doing to them, obtaining permission for each step of the process. I would often feel a presence in the room, a heaviness in the air, the weak magnetic attraction of another being close behind me. I always put this down to an overactive imagination, or maybe even a bit of residual Catholic angst, but I still never dared turn around to look behind me, eyes fixed dead ahead as I subconsciously made the sign of the cross and silently mouthed *rest in peace* before rushing out of the room as quickly as my little legs would carry me.

Death is often horrendous, and tragic, and sad, and unfair, and cruel, and unjust, but it can also be beautiful and serene at times. I have sat and held the hand of an elderly patient during her final moments of life, a patient who had suffered for so long and had endured so much pain, and who longed for the end. I watched her slowly slip away, watched all that pain and stress, all that weight she had been carrying, instantly disappear as she passed, replaced with relief, peace, a sense of calm. It was a very spiritual experience, maybe even bordering on religious.

I am often asked whether I believe in God, and if I have seen anything that has convinced me of an afterlife. I was born and christened

Catholic, but I would now consider myself an atheist. As such, I don't believe in the religious concept of heaven and hell, but I have seen some pretty strange things in my time, in both the military and Medicine, that I struggle to fully explain. I have seen feet running up hospital stairways then disappearing into thin air. I have heard children crying on empty maternity wards, and I have seen floating cigarette embers accompanied by a strong smell of smoke on a dark and long-abandoned urology ward.

As strange as these experiences were, it's often not what you see, but what you can feel or sense that is most convincing. I was once attending to an elderly female patient in the final minutes of life. I had been called to the ward by my SHO because the patient had no DNAR in place but was clearly dying, despite my SHO's sterling efforts. I entered the room to assess the patient and could see that she was close to death. Her eyes were closed, and she looked very hypoxic (blue around the mouth) despite being on high-flow oxygen. Her breaths were shallow, ineffective, and becoming less frequent.

I turned off the oxygen at the wall and carefully removed the mask, cradling her face in my hand and pulling her forward slightly so that I could slide the green elastic of the mask over the back of her head. As I bent her neck slightly toward my chest, she suddenly opened her eyes wide and swung her head to one side, gaze fixed on a position in the corner of the room immediately behind me, and softly and lovingly uttered a man's name. I instantly froze, and the hairs on the back of my neck pricked up as I felt a towering presence standing close behind me, the air thick and pulsing with electricity. I became acutely aware of my own breathing, my heart pounding in my ears, and I dared not turn around. The patient's face initially registered surprise before she beamed with joy for a split-second and took her final breath, eyes fixed on the same spot, glazing over and closing, smile remaining on her face.

I stood stock-still with the patient's head resting against my arm for a moment or so, whilst the energy in the room slowly dissipated. I laid her head back gently and exited the room without once looking behind me. I told the SHO that she had passed away and ordered him to verify the patient. I went down to the staff room, had a coffee, and tried to calm down, and I have never told anyone about that experience until now.

As frightening as that situation was, it didn't feel menacing in any way, and whatever or whoever that presence was, it clearly brought a lot of joy to a dying old lady… whilst scaring the wits out of me. I suppose it was comforting for the patient, and in a strange way, it was for me as well.

But I have also experienced scenarios that certainly did not bring any measure of pleasure or reassurance to the poor unsuspecting victim. I was working as a cardiology SHO, based on the coronary care unit (CCU), daydreaming whilst half-heartedly reviewing the long list of blood results on the computer located at the nursing station. Lounging way too far back into the soft, leather ergonomic chair to be deemed professional with my smart phone resting precariously on my thigh, I was suddenly shaken into the present moment by the shrill and piercing howl of the arrest alarm. Springing cat-like from my seat whilst sending the iPhone freefalling toward the vinyl floor, I instantly felt the familiar knot of apprehension deep in the pit of my stomach and the rush of nervous excitement as I quickly scanned the department to ascertain whose light was flashing.

Each of the nine rooms had an orange light outside that would have looked more at home on the top of an AA rescue vehicle than in a state-of-the-art CCU. The light would flash when the arrest cord was pulled and indicate in which room the arrest was taking place. It was a bit unorthodox, but you certainly couldn't miss the alarm.

I realised that it was the primary (PPCI) in room three, who had suffered a heart attack, or myocardial infarction (MI) in my language, whilst in the community and been brought straight to the catheterisation (cath) lab for coronary artery stenting. He had arrived on CCU only the night before, following the insertion of several stents into his left main stem, which is essentially the blood vessel that supplies the left side of the heart, and the worst possible place to be affected by a clot.

Despite being on CCU for a relatively short period of time, the patient in room three had certainly not endeared himself to the resident staff, having earned quite a reputation so far. He was, to put it politely, a very difficult patient and, to put it not so politely, was one of the most obnoxious and generally unpleasant patients I'd so far encountered in my short medical journey, an opinion that seemed to be shared by every doctor, nurse, healthcare assistant (HCA), and domestic who had had the misfortune of crossing his path.

I ran into his room and quickly felt for a pulse. There wasn't one, despite noticing that the monitors showed electrical activity. The advanced nurse practitioner (ANP) and I started CPR at a rate of thirty compressions to two breaths whilst a third nurse connected the wires dangling from the sticky defib pads, that had wisely been left in situ on his chest wall, to the defibrillator. I took the chest – arms straight and right hand tightly gripping over my left clenched fist as I pushed firmly and rhythmically deep into the centre of the chest, feeling minimal resistance, no cracking of ribs or sternum. I focused zen-like energy on the job at hand, so much so that I was startled when the arrest team suddenly burst onto the scene.

I was still relatively junior at this point and, as such, instantly took a back seat once the consultant anaesthetist, cardiology registrar, and cardiac surgeon entered the fray. I let the nursing staff take over the chest compressions whilst I stood back to take on the role of official scribe and documenter of the arrest. After about fifteen minutes, he responded well, managing to maintain a cardiac output, and he was regaining consciousness.

He began writhing on the bed and moaning loudly in a strange otherworldly voice for a few seconds, before screaming, "Fire, fire," and, "I'm burning, I'm burning." We looked around the room at each other, all slightly freaked out, as the patient, drenched in sweat, eyes bulging out of a severely flushed face, became more agitated and continued to scream that he was burning up.

I turned to my mate, who had joined the excitement from ITU next door, and whispered, "That's because you're in hell, mate," a little bit too loudly, just as the anaesthetist gave him a stat of sedative. Instantly relaxing, he sank back into the bed and settled, at peace. His personality completely changed after that. He was withdrawn and quiet for the rest of his admission, polite even, and he certainly didn't give the staff any more trouble.

Now, I don't believe for one minute he had actually been to hell, and if he had been, then what a complete stereotype hell really is, but it was a strange situation, all the same, and whatever it was that our obnoxious friend had seen that day, it certainly did not provide him the level of reassurance and comfort that the presence in the dying lady's room had brought her.

As much as the above experiences have made me question my atheistic beliefs on occasion, I still don't really buy into organised religion. However, this doesn't mean I don't believe in anything at all. People undoubtedly contain a physical energy, almost like electricity, and watching a person as they pass away, right at the very last moment, you can see this energy disappear. Whatever makes us human leaves the body, that vibrant, loving, physical being disappears, that spark of life departs, leaving behind nothing more than a lump of meat. This normally occurs over the proceeding minutes that follow the final breath. Normally, it slowly seeps out, but it can also be instantaneous, as drastic as switching off a light. It's at times like this that I question my atheism the most. Is this evidence of the fabled human soul, or is it simply the transfer of one source of energy into another?

Ultimately, death is a part of life for the junior doctor, and it's something that does get easier over time, a lot easier. But should it? Is it a good thing that death becomes so trivial? I suppose it's a defence mechanism, and if we were to mourn each death, we would probably lose our minds or end up in a state of permanent depression. Recurrent exposure to death, to tragedy, puts doctors at risk of losing compassion, or even their humanity. But do we have a choice? And does this easy co-existence with death mean we have lost our humanity, or is it just a temporary mechanism, necessary to survive. I wonder if the terminally ill girl who spoke at my graduation would think it was a sign that I had stopped seeing my patients as human beings? These are questions I will explore in further detail later on in the book, but all this talk of death leads me nicely into my first cardiac arrest.

First Arrest

Back in DME, I was well over a month into my first real medical job and had already hit several of the doctor milestones. I was settling in pretty well and was starting to find my feet on the wards. I was diligent, hard-working, and after a slightly shaky start, I was becoming more competent by the day. In fact, I was beginning to forge a bit of a reputation amongst the nursing staff as the foundation doctor of choice, especially if there was an unwell patient to be dealt with.

I enjoyed the day job on the ward, but I really thrived when on call. For the non-medics, "on call" is when we provide out-of-hours medical cover to the wards, encompassing evenings, nights, and weekends. We are basically given a list of jobs and a bleep (pager) at handover and spend the rest of the shift ticking jobs off the list in order of priority whilst continuously answering bleeps, reviewing sick patients, and roaming the wards unsupervised, like a real doctor.

This was proper medicine, and I absolutely loved it. I was already very confident in my clinical abilities, and had been since medical school, but I was developing my skills in early diagnosis and intervention, and not only was I good at it, I was in my element. I never complained about my workload. I was organised, kept my head down, and I simply got on with it. I never felt so alive as when I was dealing with a sick patient. After all this time, I had finally found my purpose in life.

In many ways, it was, and still is, similar to being a soldier walking into a dodgy situation. That bleep suddenly goes off, and you get the knot in your stomach, the nervous energy, the sharpened razor-like focus as you enter the room, breathing intensified, heart rate picking up, every noise amplified, the slightest twitch of movement instantly registering, and you become aware of the faintest of smells. Muscles flood and tighten, engorged with blood, the acute awareness of their potential, the raw power, as the feeling of euphoria washes over you like a tide, causing an intensification of the butterflies and a giddiness that can quickly turn to blind panic if not harnessed and controlled, but becomes highly addictive if you are up for the challenge.

This feeling, the altered state of focus, the heightened awareness, the sheer aliveness, is a drug, and a potent one at that. I was well and truly addicted. In the early days of frontline medicine, I lived for this high, and in some ways, I still do. I need it. I chase it, in the same way that skydivers chase the thrill of hurtling toward terra firma in free fall, or surfers face up to the destructive power of a giant wave on nothing but a flimsy piece of board.

You never fully appreciate being alive until you face potential death. In the case of true acute medical doctors, they never feel so alive as when they are standing up to death, facing it down, and taking it head on, fighting death for the life of their patient, pitting their wits against the Reaper. Not all doctors enjoy this feeling, though. Most actually hate it and, as a result, choose to avoid acute medicine.

I once read a book about the last twelve months of the Second World War and the hesitancy of the allied soldiers to engage in combat during this period, knowing the war was all but over, and they would be going home soon. A general observed in the book that there are two types of soldier in this situation: one who faces the enemy guns and runs directly toward them, continually firing back, a blur of perpetual motion, and the other who takes cover, digs in, hides behind a tree, doing anything to avoid getting shot. Ironically, it's the first type who tends to survive and who makes the best soldier. The exact same principle applies to acute medical doctors.

There are the doctors who walk into an arrest and spring into action, fighting back, never backing down, not stopping until they reach the objective. Then there are the others who mill about in the background, volunteer for chest compressions, spend ten minutes trying to get a blood gas from the wrist, or linger around machinery, looking serious, essentially taking cover and treading water until the cavalry arrive. The first type of doctors are true acute medical doctors and will survive and thrive in the field, whilst the second group are not cut out for the challenge and will gravitate toward a safer, less challenging job. This probably applies to surgeons as well, although that is not my world – they are the fighter pilots, the "fly boys", and we are the infantry soldiers.

Anyway, I digress. At this fledgling point in my career, I was yet to learn all of the above and had somehow still not been involved in a true cardiac arrest situation. My colleagues joked that I was a good luck charm, as nobody ever seemed to arrest around me, but I have different ideas about that. I think the trick is to avoid your patient arriving at that situation in the first place, by applying early and aggressive intervention. However, this isn't always possible, and I was about to find that out first-hand.

I had well and truly recovered from the shock of that first patient "going off" and had re-established my habit of getting onto the ward nice and early to prepare for the ward round. The thought of being the only doctor around no longer terrified me, and I actually enjoyed the peace and serenity of early mornings, taking my time to set up the trolley and prep the notes. However, on this particular day, one of my colleagues, my chatty rugby-loving friend from year zero, had already arrived and was ruining the serenity of my doctors' office. Not only was he encroaching on my time, but he had the audacity to engage me in trivial conversation.

I am generally a very outgoing person, but I also really like my own space, and I have my own routines that I do not like to be disrupted or changed in any way. Even now, I enjoy the routine of lunching on my own, having a bit of me time. There is nothing better than finding a quiet corner table, well out of the way, and catching up with Netflix or BBC iPlayer on my phone for half an hour or so. As I am normally very sociable, people will often come and sit by me – probably thinking I must be lonely, sitting all alone over in the corner – with the good intention of brightening up my lunch break. Outwardly, I will happily pass the time with them, but deep down, it annoys me. As did this intrusion into my morning routine of coffee and music on my phone whilst leisurely perusing the notes. I went along with his conversation and tried not to let the annoyance show on my very expressive face.

I had just sat down at the middle computer of three – he was already sat at my favourite computer – and was in the lengthy process of starting it up, when the arrest alarm suddenly went off. Instantly flooded with nervous excitement, we simultaneously stood up and headed in the direction of the heart-wrenching sound. *Was this to be the day? My first proper arrest?*

We quickly arrived at my colleague's bay of patients to find a stressed-out and struggling nurse side-saddle on the edge of a hospital bed, firmly pinning down the shoulders of a seizing female patient in a desperate attempt to stop her shaking her way out of the bed.

I looked into the face of the patient, which was framed by a halo of vomit that had worked its way deep into the strands of grey and silver matted hair, forming an almost perfect semi-circle around her head. She seemed to recognise my colleague and me, which settled her for a second. She was looking directly at me, holding my gaze, her eyes burning into mine. Despite being elderly, she had an innocent, almost childlike expression on her face and was clearly scared. She attempted to speak but no sound came out as she mouthed a silent and indecipherable plea, before starting to shake violently again, eyes rolling up into her head, the voiding of her bladder visible by the dark stain forming in the region of her groin area and slowly spreading out across the pale yellow hospital blanket.

Luckily, my colleague was the first type of soldier and a real acute doctor in the making – although he rather disappointingly ended up in the world of general practice. We both immediately sprang into action, quickly gaining venous access and assessing her using the A to E approach, which to the layman is basically an assessment that starts from the mouth and works its way downwards. Is the airway patent? Is she making any respiratory effort? Does she have a pulse at the neck? And so on.

We quickly discovered she was no longer breathing and had no detectable pulse, so I started chest compressions immediately whilst my colleague obtained an airway and started "bag and masking her", simultaneously checking with the nurse that she had put out an emergency call. She hadn't, so we asked her to go and do that right away and get us the arrest trolley, containing the defibrillator, on her way back.

I continued the compressions whilst time slowed around me, looking directly down at my hands as I pumped the chest, concentrating on the tight, white skin stretched taught over my knuckles, I blocked out all distractions and focused on maintaining a regular depth and rate whilst visualising the ALS algorithm in my mind's eye. I tried to avoid looking directly at the patient, wanting to remain detached and focus on the job at hand, but I could feel her eyes burning into me. I turned to look at her face, and time instantly stopped dead, the world frozen and silent. Her huge, bulging, lifeless eyes filled my consciousness. Like a deer in the headlights, I couldn't look away, and for a few seconds, I stopped the chest compressions.

I watched as her eyes slowly glazed over in front of me, and she was gone, departed from this world. I wasn't prepared to give up that easily, though. I pulled myself together, sound instantly returning, loudly filling my ears as my hands pushed through the soft skin and struck the hard sternum again, pushing firmly and deeply toward the spine. I was back in the moment. I was focused. I heard my voice shouting for somebody to take over the compressions as the crash trolly arrived, and I quickly switched on the defibrillator before attaching the sticky chest pads.

I had lost all concept of time, completely focused on the job. A thought suddenly popped into my head: *adrenaline*. I asked for a pulse and rhythm check. My friend shouted, "No pulse," and the defibrillator told me that no shock was advised. I was pulling the grey plastic cap off the 1 ml syringe of prepared adrenaline just as the arrest team came bursting into the room, led by a rather cool-looking critical care registrar (CCR), who immediately took over the proceedings and started dishing out jobs. I was left on the defibrillator, and my colleague was instantly demoted from airway to chest compressions.

It must have been around nine o'clock now, as my consultant popped her head into the bay and looked directly at me. Not even acknowledging the unfolding drama, she asked rather tersely whether I was planning on attending the multi-disciplinary meeting (MDT) – a meeting that took place weekly with our medical team, the physiotherapist, occupational therapist, and nursing staff to discuss progress and discharge plans of our twelve patients. I looked directly at the CCR, who replied, just as tersely, "No, he's on the defib," without even looking up at the consultant.

As she spun on her heels and briskly left the bay, the CCR looked up at me with a half-smile and a slight nod of the head, which I returned whilst getting back on with the job at hand, making a note of the time now as I awarded myself the role of note-keeper. I looked back at the patient, who now looked clearly dead. Her unseeing eyes stared blankly at the ceiling, and her thick, swollen, purple and pink tongue protruded from the side of the endotracheal tube, lolling like a Labrador puppy with every heavy downward thrust to the centre of her chest. She appeared to have physically collapsed in on herself, like a partly deflated helium balloon, and I had serious doubts about the benefit and appropriateness of continuing CPR. However, we ploughed on for another twenty minutes or so whilst she fluctuated from pulseless electrical activity (PEA) – a rhythm associated with a poor prognosis and not responsive to an electric shock – to any number of variable shockable rhythms, and we bounced from adrenaline and vigorous chest compressions to direct electrical current focused through the pads stuck to her chest wall, which I took very seriously as the chief button-presser and bed-clearer.

It was a physically and mentally draining process, and by the time we started to look around the bed at each other questioningly, we were shattered and undoubtedly on the edge of rebellion. That was when I heard the CCR utter the word I never expected to hear: "ROSC." He was telling us the patient had a return of spontaneous circulation. Her heart was now beating for itself and providing blood pressure consistent with life. Remarkably and unexpectedly, we had done it. We had saved this woman's life.

The CCR left the bay to arrange for a bed on ITU, leaving the operating department practitioner (ODP) to manage the airway. But on his way out, he stopped to thank me and my colleague for our hard work, informing us that we had done a great job, before relieving us of our duties with a firm handshake. With a barely contained sarcastic smile, he turned back to me and said, “Enjoy the MDT.” And just like that, it was all over.

I walked out of the bay as though I were twenty feet tall. I was flooded with adrenaline and had a feeling not too dissimilar to that of leaving a nightclub in the early hours of the morning, soaked in sweat, ears ringing as you’re emptied out into the cold and deathly silent surrounding streets. The serenity and tranquillity of the normal world a stark contrast to the experience you have just lived through. I was on a high. My heart was racing, my legs were trembling, and I was all hyped-up with nowhere to go… other than the boring old MDT, of course.

I floated down the corridor and into the meeting room, politely apologising for my lateness and taking a seat at the back. As soon as I sat down on the uncomfortably hard plastic chair, the enormity of the situation suddenly hit me. My head was swimming, and I couldn’t concentrate or focus on what anyone was saying. I was tormented by constant images of a head softly lolling in time with my chest compressions, bloodshot eyes bulging out of the sockets, the nightmare image repeating over and over again in slow rhythmical motions, like the slow, dark spread of urine seeping through the hospital blanket.

I left the MDT with no clue of the plan for any of my patients. Grabbing my trolley of notes from the doctors’ office, I wheeled them over to the bank of ward computers and bumped into one of the nurses who had been involved in the arrest.

“How is she? Did she get down to ITU?” I asked.

The nurse told me that, shortly after I had left for the MDT, the patient had arrested again and had unfortunately passed away. I was absolutely devastated. I couldn’t believe it. The shock must have shown on my face because the nurse informed me, rather casually, “It happens,” with a shrug of the shoulders, and walked away, leaving me standing rooted to the spot.

I had been involved in my first arrest and, in fairness, had handled it impeccably – in stark contrast to my first experience with an unwell patient. I had learned from my mistakes and had shown that I had the potential to become a proper doctor. I had also got my first real taste of that high. I was hooked, but I was also conflicted. At home that night, I couldn’t concentrate and kept zoning out as the images from earlier in the day continued to haunt me. I couldn't shake them off, and I found I was questioning myself, wondering if I could have done anything differently. It continued to affect me for several days, and I had a couple of sleepless nights, but the images became less frequent, and I eventually closed them out.

I have had arrests that have got to me since, usually because I can relate them to a family member. But I have never had one affect me on the scale that the first one did. I don't believe I consciously decided to close off a part of myself as a protective measure following that arrest, but I can honestly say I have not allowed myself to be so affected by anything in Medicine, since that day.

Positive Feedback

As mentioned previously the foundation years are full of milestones and firsts for a doctor, especially F1, from the first arrest to the first dead body to the first drunk vomiting all over you or swinging a wild punch in your general direction in A&E. It's the first time many of us will work over eighty hours in a week, long weekends or nights, and it's the first time many will miss seasonal holidays with their family and friends. It's the first break from many of the family traditions of our youth and childhood, and it's the first time we will work until dropping into an emotionally and physically broken pile of creased clothes and pale sun-starved skin at the end of yet another run of nights.

I had been an infantry soldier and a business owner and, as such, was used to manual labour, to physically hard work, and long, unsociable hours, but it grinds even the hardiest of us down in the end. Foundation medicine is a different type of work. It's both physical and mental; it's emotional and frustrating; it's intimidating and, at times, even terrifying. And it's a constant bombardment of shit, day after day after day. It starts off exciting and new, a rollercoaster of the dizziest highs followed by the most plunging dark and depressive lows, and by the end of F1, you are ready to do twenty years in jail for murdering the next nurse who bleeps you at four in the morning to prescribe a bag of fluids.

Whilst I loved the acute side of on call and thrived in this environment, deciding early on that I was definitely a budding acute medic, it's all the other day-to-day stuff that gets to you in the end – the constant grind of ward work and the associated shitty jobs, the endless blood rounds, the rewriting of drug chart after drug chart, the inappropriate handovers from colleagues, the nonsensical jobs from irate nurses, and the bizarre demands from insane power-crazed consultants. It's such a relief to just survive to the end of the year and know you are no longer going to be bottom of that pile, that some other poor fucker is in for the year of hell you just survived. There is a well-known saying in the military that shit rolls downhill, and it's such a relief when you are no longer neck-deep in faeces at the foot of that humungous hill.

I don't want to depress anyone who may read this book prior to starting F1, but I can assure you that you are in for a hard year, let's be under no illusion here. It will test you physically, mentally, and emotionally. There will be tears and tiaras, tantrums and strops, but it will be the making of you. It will make you a stronger, tougher, and more resilient person. It will mould you into a doctor, whether you like it or not, and believe me, it does get a lot easier… well, until you hit your registrar years, but that's a whole other story.

*

I was on my third and final rotation of F1: orthopaedic surgery, a difficult, demanding, and intense job with insanely long hours that officially started as an eight a.m. ward round, but inevitably resulted in a seven thirty start to prep the notes, followed by an hour of being alternately completely ignored, spoken down to, and ridiculed by some of the biggest arseholes in the medical profession – the consultant orthopaedic surgeon being the inevitable culmination in the career of the rugby boys.

In fact, the only thing I found worse than the macho ortho consultant, was his ultra-macho, one-of-the-boys female registrar, who believed the secret to breaking into the ultimate boys' club in Medicine was to out "lad" the lads, which they attempted to do by terrorising the foundation doctors. However, I had dealt with much bigger and tougher opponents over the years and would quickly put them in their place, which, ironically, tended to win me favour with the consultants. I had absolutely no desire to pursue a career in surgery, which meant I didn't have to play their little game.

As annoying as this part of the day was, and as unsupported as we often felt by our seniors – who completely washed their hands of any ward-related work, once their whirlwind round had finished – it was all over by nine when the real job would begin: the orthogeriatric ward round. This was as polar opposite to the first one of the day as could possibly be imagined. It was split between two elderly medicine consultants, who covered alternate days and were both frailty specialists. They took the job of keeping our patients alive a lot more seriously than the ortho jocks ever did. The second round tended to take up our whole morning and was much more intense than the first, involving endless trolling through blood results and old clinic letters. It would usually end with a light-hearted grilling around lunchtime, though it could occasionally reconvene after eating and take up a decent portion of the afternoon as well.

After both rounds were completed, we would finally get started on the job lists we had generated, whilst being continually harangued and harassed by any one of the medical outlier or specialist ward rounds that would be spread across the afternoon. The amount of our time these occupied would vary wildly depending on who the on-call or specialist consultant happened to be. Some would simply ask us for a list of outliers and then leave us to get on with our jobs, whilst others, usually the renal consultants, would drag us around to see their patients again, and would grill us endlessly on the most irrelevant of details, whilst generating an insane list of jobs for each individual patient that would be grudgingly – as we couldn't really hand these jobs over to the evening on call without looking like complete arseholes – added to our other two lists.

If we happened to be on call until eight p.m., then the first couple of hours would be spent juggling our own job list from the day with the endless shite jobs that would be perpetually handed over by the less competent amongst our colleagues. If lucky enough to be on a normal day, we would sit in the little office between the A and B sides of the ward and smash through the list of jobs until around six or seven p.m. most nights, and then it was back home before all the fun began again the next day, and the day after, and the day after, and so on. Added into this hectic schedule, we had to balance nights and weekends, audits, revision for our exams, our portfolios for appraisal and completion of each rotation, and let's not forget any locum shifts we could pick up to earn a bit of extra cash – £2,000 pounds per month doesn't stretch too far when you have just accumulated almost £100,000 of debt getting through university.

This relentless slog seemed to go on forever, and it felt as though I was never at home or present for my family. Even when I was there, I wasn't there. My mind was persistently preoccupied with tomorrow's work plans, or my head was wedged in front of a laptop screen or buried in one revision book or another. It was difficult for my family, and it put enormous pressure on my relationship, adding to the overall stress, especially since my wife's business had gone under following the credit crunch of 2008. As a result, we had become increasingly financially destitute, going from the heady heights of a posh semi-detached house in an affluent suburb of Liverpool city centre, moving steadily down the property ladder and culminating in a one-and-a-half-bedroom bungalow, in which you could not swing a cat – rather unfortunate, seeing as we had two decent-sized dogs and a rapidly growing teenage son who found the cramped living conditions very difficult.

It was against this backdrop that I entered one of my final ever surgical nights as an F1. The last of a run of four, where I had not slept well at all, probably accumulating around nine hours' sleep in total over the past three days. I was tired, dead tired, a level of tired I had not felt since basic training, but I had been thirteen years younger on basic training, which makes a hell of a difference. My days of digging a trench for three days continuously, with no sleep, were probably behind me at this point.

I arrived into handover immediately after a rather heated argument with my wife, and I was in no mood for a list of shit jobs. I was living on my very last nerve, which was stretched almost to breaking point, and of course – I received a horrendous handover. Most of the jobs should have either been completed by the day team or could easily have been left until the next day. I quickly filtered through the shit. I was an expert in shit-filtering by this point in my career, ungraciously accepting the important jobs, whilst telling a couple of poor, unsuspecting young doctors where they could stick the unnecessary jobs, before heading off in one of my famous diva-like strops straight to the surgical ward, muttering and cursing to my equally pissed-off and dog-tired registrar the entire way there.

I sat in the doctors' office, staring at my haggard reflection in a blank computer screen. I felt low, as low as I had ever felt in my life. Nothing seemed to be going right for me or my wife. We were in debt up to our eyeballs and our combined wages were simply not cutting it. I was under extreme pressure, the type of pressure that manifests itself as a physically uncomfortable sensation within your skull and makes your cheeks feel permanently warm and flushed. I was jittery and anxious, which was probably down to the endless mugs of strong coffee that were the only reason I was currently functioning on any level, and I wondered for the four hundred and twenty-nine thousandth time that week, what the hell had I been thinking, starting from scratch again at my age, putting my family through all the hardship of the university years and now working myself to death, flogging myself every spare weekend that I could, just to try and stay afloat. I was struggling personally, and we were struggling as a family, and I had no idea what I was going to do about it, or how I was going to get myself out of it.

I begrudgingly pressed the rectangular power button that was slowly and invitingly pulsing orange at the bottom right-hand corner of the computer monitor and watched the screen flicker into life, instantly erasing my tired image. With a heavy sigh and a dropping of the shoulders, I melted into the chair as I simultaneously entered my log-in details and waited for ICE to fire up so I could quickly check the list of bloods and image results that had been handed over to me.

I was feeling pretty sorry for myself by the time I logged off the communal computer and headed to the ward, a condemned man carrying the weight of the world on his shoulders. I arrived at the nurses' station and acknowledged the sister with a sullen nod of the head.

"Are you Dr Keegan?" one of the nurses asked me.

"Yes," I replied, a little too tersely.

She informed me that a relative had dropped a thank-you card off for me earlier that evening and had asked for a message to be passed on to me. The relative had asked them to tell me that I was the best doctor she had encountered, and she thought it made a refreshing change to have a "normal Scouse lad" working as a doctor in our hospital.

The nurse offered me the card, and I instantly knew I couldn't open it on the ward. I knew that if I read it now, when I felt so low and so vulnerable, I would not be able to hold it together. I took the card from her and thanked her, before quickly walking to the toilets, where I opened it as cautiously as if it might contain a bomb. It was the most beautiful thing I had ever read in my life, and I cried. I cried for the first time in a long time. I hadn't cried at my grandad's funeral, or at my uncle's. I never cried. I was a tough guy. But this completely floored me. All the hard work, all the struggle and sacrifice, all the stress and long hours away from my family, all the debt and chasing our tails, it all became worthwhile as I stood alone and inconsolable in that small, cramped, poorly lit toilet cubicle.

I eventually pulled myself together, straightened my back, pumped out my chest, and put on my game face, strolling back onto the ward, feeling six feet tall, which is actually quite tall for a short arse like me. I had a spring in my step now, and I no longer felt nearly as low, the weight having dropped from my shoulders. The exhaustion didn't seem quite as exhausting, and I wouldn't say that I felt on top of the world, but I was certainly a different man from the one who had started the shift that night. I can no longer remember what was written in that card, and to be honest, I probably couldn't have told you what it said by the end of that night shift, as I had so much going on in my head at the time, but the sentiment will always stay with me. It was exactly what I needed at the exact moment I needed it. I had hit rock bottom, and I really was down and out, but that thoughtful message had given me the shot in the arm I needed, and it was timed to perfection.

I had clerked the patient in question onto the ward the previous night. He had liver cancer and severe ascites, a similar presentation to my grandad, and despite the tiredness, the problems that I was facing at home, and the overall shit period of life I was going through, I had pushed it all to one side and tried my best to treat the person in front of me as a human being, not just a hospital number. I chatted to him about his family, and he told me all about his daughter who had accompanied him onto the ward and who was currently waiting in the family room for him. She was evidently the apple of his eye and the lady who had kindly written the thank-you card to me. We passed the time with trivial chat as I inserted a drain into his hugely distended, drum-tight stomach to relieve his painful symptoms. I had then left his room, moved on to the next patient, and never gave him a second's thought again that night. I had been straight on to the next pressing issue, to the next drama, but in the short time I had spent with him, I had made a difference to that man, and to his family. It's so easy to forget, when you are caught up in it all, that that's what we are actually there to do – to make a difference, and to care.

The act of writing a thank-you card probably seems rather insignificant to most people reading this book, but when you are at your lowest ebb, when you feel like a failure, totally worthless, a simple act of kindness, such as buying someone a coffee or a pint, paying them a compliment or a kindness, or writing a card or letter can make such a difference. I suppose I had started to let doubt creep in, my confidence flatlining. I was depressed, and I was miserable, really miserable. I had needed an arm around my shoulder and someone to tell me it was all going to be okay, I was a good doctor, and I was doing a good job, and this card provided the validation I so badly needed.

If I could offer one piece of advice to non-medics, it would be, if you appreciate someone, let them know it, because you never know what another person is living through and how much they may need that kind word or that hug, or just a compliment to make it all seem worthwhile.

If I could offer one piece of advice to medics, then it would be to always remember, however hard your life is at that moment, however tired or stressed you may be, it's a person in that bed, not a patient. It's a person like your mum or your dad, or your grandparents, or your brother or sister or son or daughter. It's not a number; it's a human being, just like you, who may be just as tired, just as stressed, and who is likely in pain and alone and frightened about what the future holds for them or their family. They might need a kind word, some reassurance, a bit of warmth and humanity at a very difficult time, possibly the most shit time of their life. It works both ways – if you want respect then you have to give it, and earn it. Like everything else in life, it doesn't come for free.

And so that was the end of year one.

Cardiothoracics

It was finally done. I had successfully navigated my way through F1 and made it out the other side. I was ecstatic. It had been a hard year. Despite some fraying around the edges, I was still in one piece, and I still had a roof above my head, a family, and food on my table… just about.

Prior to finishing the first year, I had had the task of selecting my pathway for F2, which is traditionally A&E, GP, and one other specialty. After my slightly unfair allocation in F1, I had been promised my first choice of the rest. The prospect of A&E excited me, but GP held no interest for me, and I was struggling to pick a specialty that I had any interest in from the list of specialist surgeries, gastro, and psychiatry that were arranged in a variety of permutations – fifty-two of them to be precise.

That was when an opportunity arose that set me on the pathway to where I am today, one that required some of the best wheeling and dealing I have managed to pull off in a lifetime of striking favourable deals and successfully grasping at long shots. I had heard on the proverbial grapevine that my hospital trust had accidentally overfilled the F1 posts and, as a result, had three more doctors than F2 places. I had also heard, on that very same grapevine, that it was giving the admin staff the mother of all headaches trying to find a solution to this problem… which is where I take the stage in a rather Machiavellian manner.

After performing a bit of out-of-hours research, I had discovered that the local cardiothoracic tertiary centre offered an SHO programme, which was at the level of F2, and which was usually closed to local trust doctors, being offered exclusively to overseas and out-of-trust doctors looking to move into the area. The programme consisted of three four-month rotations of cardiothoracic surgery, critical care/ITU, and cardiology, which sounded like a dream to me, and the fact that the on-calls were half of what I would be doing in hospital/A&E – meaning I could work locums and earn extra cash at weekends – majorly sweetened the deal.

So, armed with this information, I headed to the admin office and offered the rather unsuspecting head of programme at least part of a solution to her problem. I would leave my trust and transfer over to the specialist centre and enrol on the SHO programme. She liked the idea but said that I still had to put three jobs down from a list of seventy-five available from all local trusts, and I would be guaranteed at least one of my choices. I agreed and took the piece of paper offered, instantly filling in:

1. Cardiothoracic surgery, Cardiology, ITU at cardiothoracic centre

2. Cardiology, Cardiothoracic surgery, ITU at cardiothoracic centre

3. ITU, Cardiology, Cardiothoracic surgery at cardiothoracic centre

She took the paper from me and paused for a second as she looked down at my list. With a half-laugh, half-sigh of resignation, she said, "Okay, you win. Cardiothoracics it is, then."

And the rest is history. I left my trust and entered the glorious world of cardiothoracics.

I walked into the centre for the induction on day one, bacon sandwich in one hand and large cup of freshly ground coffee in the other, and I was instantly in love with the place. It was the most satisfying and best environment I have ever worked in and, without doubt, my happiest time in Medicine. I honestly loved every minute of it – well, almost every minute: there were obviously some major egos to deal with – but I thrived there. I developed into a highly skilled, highly motivated, and, without blowing my own trumpet, pretty knowledgeable doctor. It was also where I developed the habit of prescribing Magic Mag (magnesium) to my patients, which would eventually lead to me being nicknamed Dr Magnesium (Mg^{2+}), although $MgSO_4$ would be more accurate as that's how it's prescribed, but let's not split hairs.

My first rotation was ITU/crit care, and I was hooked from day one. I went above and beyond, volunteering for every clinical procedure I could, and within four months, I had sited well over a hundred central lines, was proficient in transthoracic and transoesophageal echo, bronchoscopy, direct current cardioversion, and intubation. I could handle an airway like a boss, and not only was I an anaesthetist in the making, but I was an absolute natural at it. I was the proverbial blue-eyed boy of the anaesthetic department, and I had the complete confidence of my senior colleagues, being trusted to site subclavian central lines and even asked, on a couple of occasions, to "throw a femoral line in" mid-arrest, which probably doesn't sound like a big deal to most readers, but these were honours usually reserved for registrar-level trainees and certainly not lowly F2s like me. I was developing into a valuable member of the team, and I was operating way beyond my level of seniority.

I had found my home, and I loved every single second of it, almost jumping out of bed of a morning to get to work. My relatively cushy rota meant I could also locum weekends across the whole north-west, gaining invaluable experience of working with teams of different personalities and variable skill sets. One of the valuable lessons I learned on my weekend travels was to always establish what boundaries are in place within each hospital and to know when not to cross them. I learned this the hard way following a stern reprimanding – otherwise known as a complete bollocking – by an on-call acute medical consultant, after I had placed a right internal jugular central line into an intravenous drug user, whilst working on the acute medical unit (AMU), on one relatively slow Saturday locum shift in a Manchester hospital.

I was so confident at this point in my career that I threw it straight in with minimal fuss in less than five minutes after the on-call registrar had been unable to site a peripheral cannula despite multiple attempts. This was deemed a highly skilled and dangerous clinical procedure, and I was told, in no uncertain terms, that F2s don't take it upon themselves to throw random central lines into patients with no senior support or agreement from the responsible consultant, especially on a weekend. It was a slap-down designed to put me back in my place, and to be fair, it worked, as I was pretty embarrassed by the whole incident. However, it was delivered by a consultant who subsequently went on to offer me multiple long-term SHO, registrar, and consultant posts, which leads me to believe that he was secretly impressed, deep down.

More importantly though, by working weekend locum shifts, I was finally able to help ease the financial strain on our family. My wife had also landed herself a plum job as a national food development manager for a large company, so we now had a decent combined wage coming in, enough for us to leave the cramped hell of the tiny bungalow and put in an offer on a beautiful, grand Victorian terraced house that was currently separated into four separate student flats, and needed plenty of TLC to bring it back to its former glory. The house had the added bonus of being conveniently located just a few minutes' drive away from my new place of work.

Back to the job, and as mentioned, all was rosy in the cardiothoracic garden. I completed my rotation in critical care and seamlessly transferred into cardiology, absolutely loving it. I threw myself into it with the same level of vigour and enthusiasm I had thrown into anaesthetics. A veritable Scouse Max Fischer (one for the *Rushmore* fans), I volunteered for everything, including the post of British Medical Association (BMA) union representative for my trust, just as the junior doctors' dispute caught fire. I made three good friends at the centre, from Italy, Sudan, and Sheffield, and we socialised a lot around work. But I got on really well with the whole SHO team and felt I actually fitted in for the first time since enrolling on the medical degree. My son was now in his mid-teens, and my wife and I had a level of freedom we had not experienced before. We were happy, happier than we had ever been in our life together, and I had everything I had ever wanted. These were my salad days (for the Spandau Ballet fans), and I never even realised it.

I formally applied for anaesthetics in the December of that year, whilst on cardiology, and eventually moved on to cardiothoracic surgery, but not before a chance encounter would change the course of my career and have a monumental effect on the rest of my life. It is probably the very reason my daughter is in existence today.

I met a young doctor who was on a gap year and had travelled for six months around Australia and New Zealand before running out of cash and returning to the UK to top up his savings and eventually head back off on his merry way. He had landed a four-month SHO job in cardiology and was pulling in £50 an hour. I couldn't believe it: £50 an hour, all day, every day. Prior to meeting him, I had only thought of locuming as a way to earn a bit of extra cash on the odd weekend, but he regaled me with tales of doctors who had worked their way up to consultant level whilst earning a fantastic locum wage. I initially dismissed his stories as fantasy, but a seed was sown deep in my psyche, an idea germinating, a possibility I had not even been aware existed previously.

I moved on to cardiothoracic surgery just as the junior doctors' dispute was turning ugly. I wasn't quite as keen on surgery as I had been on my first two rotations. Surgeons can be a strange bunch, as alluded to earlier in the book, and I had my fair share of run-ins and clashes of personality with the consultants, but nevertheless, I still enjoyed the rotation overall.

One of my good friends, the Sheffield one, who we will call Mark from now on, was on the same rotation, and we managed to wangle ourselves a deal with the surgeons, whereby we could scrub in at the start of a procedure and alternately open up the chest or harvest the leg vein as required for the bypass grafts, and then scrub out. We could then be bleeped once the procedure was drawing to a conclusion and would scrub back in to wire and close the chest, thus saving around five hours of standing around and twiddling our thumbs whilst also allowing us to hit the hospital gym for at least two hours every day. Not only was I happy, I was in the best physical shape I had been in since leaving the forces. I was even playing eleven-aside football again, for the first time in well over a decade, as well as attending circuit training three evenings a week with Mark.

The year in cardiothoracics was not without challenges, incident, and tragedy, but on the whole, it was very enjoyable. I felt it healed me as a person, a husband, and a father. I was truly happy for the first time in a long time, and I felt fit and young, strong and healthy. I had just hit my prime, and although still very junior as a doctor, I was at the top of my game. I was confident and good at my job, and I knew it.

However, life has a habit of throwing curveballs, and unbeknownst to me, there were certainly a few of those heading my way. But it's our ability to handle these challenges that makes us the person we are, and for every knock I have taken in my life, I have always got back up, sometimes battered and bruised, sometimes changed forever and permanently scarred, but I've always put one foot in front of the other, taken tentative steps forward, no matter how shaky or unsteady, always forward. As a young boy soldier, I was told by a battle-scarred old corporal, "It's when you stop moving forward that you die," and I have tried to live by this ever since. And as of writing this book, I'm still here.

The first of said curveballs was just about to be launched ferociously in my general direction…

Politics, Strikes, and Ricky Tomo

I have always been around politics in one form or another.

In fact, one of my earliest childhood memories involves sitting in the small, overcrowded living room of the house my grandad Keegan had proudly purchased from Liverpool City Council, conveniently located just across the road from what is now John Lennon Airport – less than 100 metres away from my other grandparents' house – where he worked as a baggage handler at the time. I was sunk deep into the corner of the large, pinkish-coloured settee, happy in the familiar embrace of the worn material whilst intently studying the sharp needle points of Artex – responsible for the removal of countless layers of skin from my elbows and knees over the years – that covered every square inch of wall and ceiling, apart from the chimney breast. In contrast, the chimney breast was neatly constructed from natural stone that made up a large fire surround, which doubled as a display area for an assortment of treasured ornaments and brass trinkets, precariously balanced on overhanging edges and mounted dark wooden shelves, and a shelter for the rather underwhelming electric fire that stood in its centre.

I was happily listening to my dad and grandad heatedly debating a variety of topics, from politics to football, even down to the distance between the traffic lights at the top of Western Avenue and my grandad's house on Damwood Road. This was a standard Sunday in a working-class Liverpool family household, traditional for me as a roast dinner, a scene that would be replayed time and time again throughout my childhood. Politics was in their blood, you see. They had previously been union men and shop stewards when they worked in Dunlop's tyre factory, as had my great-uncle Ted.

All three had protested the closing of the factory, eagerly joining the picket line when management had announced they were set to devastate the local community, and economy, by moving overseas to exploit emerging cheaper labour markets. My dad had even joined the flying pickets in Birmingham and had been put on the infamous blacklist that is currently being exposed by TV celebrity and fellow union man Ricky Tomlinson, who is most famous for his role in the British TV comedy, *The Royle Family*. He's another person whose future job prospects were left in tatters following inclusion on that infamous list.

As a result of this early indoctrination into political debate and socialism, a sense of justice and fairness runs through my blood, an innate part of my DNA. The apple does not fall far from the tree, and like my dad, and indeed my grandfather, I am a keen debater – or "an argumentative bastard" as we are fondly called in Liverpool – as is my son after me. I truly love a good debate, and it's for this reason that I jumped at the first chance to take up the role of BMA representative for my trust whilst I was working on cardiothoracics.

I had been intensely following the media coverage and general furore surrounding the Conservative government's proposed new junior doctors' contract for months, and I was angry. I was ready for a fight, a fight we turned out to be hopelessly underprepared for, and one we never really had a chance of winning. We were just inexperienced kids attempting to take on the masters of the political dark arts, and predictably, they tore us to pieces, outplayed us, out-thought us, and outflanked us at every turn.

We were painted as spoiled little rich kids who had no real understanding of the world, who spent our spare time sipping champagne on beautiful, exotic, white sandy beaches, or taking helicopter rides over New York City, preaching to the masses about how unfair this new contract would be on our bank accounts whilst greedily funding this lavish millionaire lifestyle with our princely wage of £2,300 per month, before tax.

But it had never been about money for us. It was about ensuring patient safety by maintaining safe working hours and safe staffing levels. Unfortunately, all of our fears were proven well-founded in the pre-Brexit years, as staffing levels plummeted across virtually all specialties in all trusts across the country, and we struggled to cover training places. This unprecedented situation led to large rota gaps, unsafe working hours, and practices that undoubtedly had a negative impact on patient care, and it led to an over-reliance on out-of-trust and overseas locums and substantive doctors, who had little or no support settling in to a new way of working. This situation has been exacerbated tenfold in recent years, following the devastating effects of Brexit and COVID measures on the NHS, but the rot well and truly started with the hated junior doctors' contract.

Ultimately, the forced contract ended up costing the NHS more money in staffing costs and made many of our hospitals unsafe places to work in, or to be sick in. I have seen this at first-hand, over and over again, on my travels across the country, working in many of the hospitals most affected by the enforced contract, witnessing the unappealing career prospects it resulted in, and the combined effects of Brexit and COVID. It is so frustrating, because it's exactly what we predicted would happen with both the contract and Brexit.

Anyway, back to cardiothoracics, when I was still wide-eyed, passionate, naïve, and ready for a good scrap. My first act of war was to paint protest signs whilst organising the logistics of picket lines for the inevitable strike action that was coming our way. I attended the meetings and was vocal. We had to strike, we had to go all out, all together, or they would pick us off like Thatcher did when she divided and conquered the miners. There was no point going in half-hearted and providing emergency cover, not whilst we had public opinion on our side.

My position was that we had to go hard and fast, go for a full all-out strike, a mass walkout. This move was deemed highly controversial and was roundly attacked by the majority of the right-wing media, who claimed it would lead to widespread deaths. However, at the time, it was overwhelmingly supported by the general public, as shown by poll after poll. My argument was that senior doctors (consultants were not included in this contract dispute) would be more than capable of covering the wards and providing safe management of patients, and even if this action led to a blocking of hospital beds and delayed discharge of patients, which obviously came with some risk, stopping this contract would save countless lives in the long run.

Whilst us unionists pondered, and essentially sat on our hands, the government set its attack dogs on us, and as the old saying goes, their lie was halfway around the world before our truth had even put on its running shoes. We eventually, and belatedly, decided to strike, in the very half-hearted way that the government had hoped we would. We continued to provide emergency cover for acute areas and out-of-hours services, whilst circling the wagons and setting up our picket lines.

I remember the first few days were bright but bitterly cold, and we had lots of support from the community, which included them bringing us hot drinks and food. These were great days of solidarity and unity, and we all bonded over fighting for a just cause, for patients' lives. We had public support, and we had the moral high ground. All we had to do now was call out the government and press our advantage.

And surprisingly, we did. We went on TV, and we stuck to the script: it was not about money; it was about patient safety, and the safety of us as doctors. It was a hard time, but it was a great time to be a doctor. It was the first time in living memory we had taken strike action, and we all felt we were part of something much bigger than just ourselves – we were part of a cause.

We set up our pickets on the front gate and took allotted shifts, although most of us stayed for the whole day to keep up the numbers. We displayed our witty placards, banners, and flags, that mostly targeted our mortal enemy, Jeremy Hunt, and I pulled out my ace in the pack. I had managed to get hold of the email address of Ricky Tomlinson's wife and asked if she would get Ricky to attend the picket line. She replied almost immediately and explained he had not been in the best of health, but that he would try and get down if he could.

The following day was another bright day with clear blue skies and not a breath of wind, but it was perishingly cold, the type of cold that creeps up from your feet and works its icy fingers deep through the fibres of your muscles and into your bones. We had been set-up for about an hour or so and were all huddled around our big catering flasks of tea and coffee, kindly provided by my wife, like extras huddled around one of those flaming oil drums in an American film, when this little old fella came walking across the road toward us. He was wrapped up in a big cream mackintosh jacket with a flat cap perched on his head, and he was partially bent over against the cold. I thought it was an elderly local coming over to show his appreciation and support for our cause, until he got within a few metres and beamed that big trademark smile of his at us. I recognised him instantly, and excitedly introduced him to the other doctors.

It was Ricky Tomlinson, and he was on top form, keeping us entertained for hours and even calling a couple of journalist friends who came down with film crews to interview us all on the picket line, with Ricky, ever the star, pulling off hilarious one-liners and spinning story after story about his times on the picket lines as a young man. It was a thoroughly enjoyable day. Unfortunately, though, it proved to be the dizzy high before the crushing low. We found out later that night that our leaders had been in secret talks with the government and had started negotiating a deal.

The “deal” turned out to be the new contract verbatim as originally proposed by Jeremy Hunt. We limped on for a while and held a couple more strikes but were continually undermined by our own leadership, and eventually, we completely folded and struck the worst possible deal for ourselves and for our patients. Like the miners before us, we turned on our leaders, and one after another fell. We had been divided, and we were conquered. We had let the public down and we had let ourselves down. I was devastated by the turn of events and resigned from my position as union representative, cancelling my subscription to the BMA shortly after.

I refused to sign the contract, and I still, to this day, have not signed and never will. I am probably one of only a handful of doctors of my grade in the whole of the UK who hasn’t signed it. Like the handful of Japanese fanatics who continued to fight a personal war in the dense jungles of Asia following their nation’s surrender, we continue to man our foxholes all alone in the wilderness, biding our time, whilst one nail after another is hammered into the coffin of our careers.

My refusal to sign on the dotted line ultimately meant I had to give up on my dream of becoming an anaesthetist, as well as a guaranteed place in training.

*

However, it was not the end of my career in politics. I had developed quite a taste for it, and I decided I wanted to become more directly involved. Like the vast majority of my city, I had always voted Labour. We were not overly concerned about things like policies and manifestos; it was more of a cultural thing – they were our side, our team, and they automatically got our vote. But as was the case for many others on my side, Blairism had gradually worn me down. The war in Iraq had disillusioned me, and by the time the hapless Ed Miliband came along, I had truly given up on the Labour Party, so I went in search of a new political mistress and found the Green Party.

At first, I was reluctant to make the switch. I had a persistent nagging doubt, a burning guilt in the pit of my stomach, a sense of shame even, over the betrayal of my long-term love in favour of a newer, flashier model. I rationalised it was my old love who had actually cheated on me, and on millions of other Labour voters. They had betrayed us by waging an illegal war on Iraq and engaging in all kinds of other nefarious and shady activities that had become less palatable and more difficult to ignore in the years before I eventually jumped ship. These people no longer represented me. I didn't want any part of what my party had become, and the Greens were the only mainstream party in the UK that now represented my moral values.

I officially joined the Green Party and tentatively decided to attend a meeting. As progressive as the new Green manifesto appeared to be, I found that the majority of my new party members very much fitted the old stereotype of a "Green voter". The group was a mixture of scatty, middle-aged art-teacher-types donned in the obligatory home-knitted woollen cardigan and well-worn Birkenstock sandals, the eco-warrior, middle-class student, and the occasional smartly dressed, out-of-town professional-type who seemed to be completely uninterested in the meeting and everybody else in it – I later found out they were there to represent the serious seats, and by that, I mean the very few seats in Liverpool that the Greens actually had a chance of winning.

I sat in the plush meeting room in city-centre Liverpool with my dad, who had come along as moral support, in the hard plastic chair next to me, as we silently listened to the outlining of multiple battle plans for the upcoming council elections. I have to admit I felt completely out of place as we debated cycle paths and the environment. I didn't really get involved in the meeting at all and was surprised when I was asked to stand for election in the Speke/Garston ward at the end of the meeting. The Greens had never gained more than a handful of votes in these areas. I got the distinct impression they had absolutely no hope, or interest, in making any further advances in these "backward seats" and simply needed a stooge to put their name on the ballot paper.

However, the leaders of the local party had massively underestimated my bloody-mindedness and determination, as well as my connection to both areas in my allocated ward. As we have already well and truly established, I was born in Speke, but I had also lived in Garston for many years. My wife's family were, and still are, from the area, and we were very well known there. I was told that I wasn't expected to actively campaign, and there would be absolutely no budget available at all, not even to produce flyers, as they were going to concentrate investment on the "greener" areas. I could have a poster for my window if I so desired, though.

As you can imagine, this didn't sit well with me, so I completely ignored the advice and wrote a stirring campaign letter. Using my home computer, I printed off hundreds of copies which were then promptly posted all over my campaign area. I spread the word over social media and had friends and family members campaigning tirelessly for me in the weeks leading up to the elections, and when the big day finally arrived, I found myself standing in the counting depot in Wavertree tennis centre in the south of the city, flanked by my wife and an ever-proud mum and dad. We went in search of the other Green candidates and found them in one corner of the room.

I had been communicating with the secretary by email and had not seen most of the others since the initial meeting, some I didn't recognise at all. I was given a lukewarm reception, to say the least. A couple nodded and half smiled at us, almost pityingly, before quickly turning their backs, whilst the rest either barely glanced in our direction or contemptuously looked down their long, thin, bespectacled noses at the poor relations, before quickly falling back into the orbit of their out-of-town star candidates – the big guns who were standing in the serious seats. We awkwardly stood on the periphery of the group, slightly embarrassed, for a few minutes, before I suggested we go and get a coffee.

We quickly drank the weak and tepid machine coffee and found ourselves with literally hours to spare and not much to do. We unanimously decided we were giving the stuck-up Greens a wide berth, so we went for a slow stroll around the centre, observing the scene developing around us as we went. It almost felt like my first day of university. I was a complete outsider, yet again. As such, I watched the social experiment in human behaviour that is politics from the very fringes of the crowd.

I observed the arrival of the city's big hitters – Mayor Joe Anderson and the celebrity Labour MPs, Steve Morgan, Luciana Berger and the Eagle sisters – and witnessed first-hand the sycophantic gaggle of Labour candidates from the middle-class areas of the city instantly swoon around them, champagne flutes in hand. But then I noticed the local Speke and Garston candidates standing well off to one side of the hall – like us, the poor relations, very much shunned and ignored by the political elite of the city. I decided right then and there that this kind of politics wasn't for me.

We walked over and introduced ourselves to the other Speke candidates, and I was surprised that most had already heard of me from my time as chairman at Speke Parklands JFC, the junior football club my wife and I had started in 2007. We had initially started with a handful of my son's friends and eventually developed it into a successful junior football club that had four teams spread across multiple age groups, with well over sixty kids playing for us. We had many initiatives over the years to promote healthy eating and often gave out menus, cooking instructions, and even boxes of fresh ingredients to the parents, all kindly funded by my wife's catering business. They had heard about our community support and been impressed, so they eagerly and warmly welcomed us into their gang.

They were an amazing group of people, passionate about the community and dedicated to the betterment of the area, selflessly sacrificing the majority of their spare time, often to the detriment of their own families. They were excellent advocates for the local Labour Party and everything I expected from local politicians. The same could not be said for their colleagues from the better-off areas – blatant social climbers who would change allegiance at the drop of a hat, depending on who sat in power.

The Speke/Garston ward was staunchly Labour, and I never realistically stood a chance of winning, but I was glad to see the ripple of shock amongst the Green Party candidates when I beat the Lib Dem and Conservative candidates, eventually coming narrowly third, just behind the UKIP candidate – this was at the height of the anti-EU propaganda campaign peddled by Nigel Farage and his cronies – obtaining a respectable seven hundred votes in an area in which the Greens had previously achieved less than ten votes.

In the days following the election, I was contacted by both the Greens and the Labour Party asking if I would be interested in standing for local council again in upcoming elections, to which I replied, thanks, but no thanks. My career in politics was over, as was my interest in politics in general. I had lost faith in the lot of them… until a certain Mr Jeremy Corbyn came along and swept us all up on a short-lived wave of optimism that was quickly and brutally stamped out by a ferocious right-wing UK national media.

As an aside, I actually met Jeremy Corbyn years later, outside the hospital up north to which my career would become inextricably linked, and I can honestly say that the old adage of "never meet your heroes" has never rung more true. But that's a story for another time.

Dog Eat Dog

As mentioned in previous chapters the time I spent at the cardiothoracic centre was the happiest of my career so far. But although I really enjoyed it there, I certainly had my fair share of challenges and, shall we say, "difficult" situations. As you can probably imagine, a world-renowned cardiothoracic centre attracts the very best doctors, and surgeons, and whilst the cardiologists could occasionally be difficult, they were mostly decent and well-rounded human beings. The surgeons, on the other hand, were a whole different ball game. We had some giants of cardiothoracic surgery, and as always, many of these big personalities came with giant, world-class egos.

It could be a ferocious environment, and it was often a case of "if your face fits", which fostered a sycophantic culture amongst the trainees and a god-like aura around many of the senior consultants, who could make or break a career with a simple turning of a thumb, like twisted twenty-first-century Roman emperors. This level of nepotism inevitably led to the progression of some pretty average registrars, and to the complete destruction of some pretty impressive ones – such as the registrar of my first firm, who we shall call Albert.

He was a rather bizarre character who stood at well over six foot tall with a broad frame that was probably once muscular but was now bordering on the heavy side, and although Chinese in origin, he had the strongest Australian accent I have ever heard. His accent was in such strong contrast to his appearance that it often caught people by surprise when first introduced. He was around forty-five years of age and, in his previous life back home in Oz, had already achieved the dizzy heights of consultant in both emergency medicine and ITU. He was one of – if not *the* – most knowledgeable doctors I had ever worked with, even to this day. He had decided upon a total change of career and started off again as a junior surgeon, steadily working his way up that greasy pole. By the time our paths crossed, he was at the level of senior registrar in cardiothoracic surgery, and as I am sure you will have already deduced, he was a bloody good surgeon as well.

Unfortunately for Albert, however, he was almost too good, and he never really learned to play the game. He rather naively believed that being diligent, hard-working, and good at your job was enough, but in a field as competitive as his, people are always looking to take your place, and there was also an undoubted level of jealousy around his extensive medical knowledge. This all led to a stitch-up on a scale I have never witnessed before in Medicine. Unfortunately, I had a part to play in both events that led to his downfall and eventual dismissal back to sunny Australia, tail very much between his legs.

The first incident involved a lady who had been flown down from the Highlands of Scotland with a leaking thoracic aortic aneurysm, which in layman's terms is very bad news. This occurred over a weekend, and I just so happened to be on call. As a result, I "clerked her in" and requested a CT aortic angiogram, which is basically a scan of the aorta to establish the severity of the thoracic aneurysm.

The scan was quickly reported by the radiologist, who bleeped me to verbally hand over his report and opinion that this lady needed urgent surgery before the aneurysm ruptured and killed her. I immediately passed this information on to the other registrar on our firm – an Indian gentleman, who must have been in his late sixties or maybe even early seventies, possibly the nicest and most pleasant man I have ever had the pleasure to work with, though I wouldn't want him repairing my aorta, or even putting a cannula in me for that matter. We shall call him OB.

I documented this report and that I had handed the information over to OB, in the electronic clinical notes and never gave it another thought until I returned to work on Tuesday – we were always given the Monday off after a weekend: told you it was a cushy number. Anyway, on my return, I was setting up the ward round and noticed that nothing seemed to have happened with the patient, which slightly concerned me, and as I couldn't find OB on the ward, I informed good old Albert, just as the consultant burst onto the ward with OB and one of the new young registrars trailing behind like an overeager Labrador puppy. Albert waved a dismissive hand at me and told me not to worry about it, assuring me that it would be sorted out on the ward round. So, I dutifully grabbed a COW (computer on wheels) and took my place in the ever-growing entourage that orbited around our superstar boss, Mr S.

We arrived at said patient's bedside just as the unfortunate Albert had peeled away from the ward round to discuss the previous patient with a radiologist. I elbowed my way to the front of the throng and started to present the patient to a half-interested Mr S, who casually glanced between the nervous-looking lady propped up in the hospital bed and the clock that hung above the door of the four-bedded bay, undoubtedly eager to get scrubbed in for his morning surgery. I wasn't a hundred per cent convinced he was actually listening to me until I highlighted the findings of the CT report.

He suddenly and explosively turned toward me and angrily demanded why I hadn't informed anyone of this report earlier. I felt the familiar surge of adrenaline course through my body, the butterflies fluttering in my stomach, the pulse pounding in my neck, and my cheeks instantly warmed with a mixture of embarrassment, humiliation, and anger. I tried to hold his gaze as the rumbling undercurrent of side conversation amongst the entourage abruptly stopped and every pair of eyes in that crowded bedspace suddenly swivelled in my direction and fixed on me.

There was a deathly silence, only broken by the ticking of the second hand on the wall-mounted clock as I composed myself and replied from a suddenly bone-dry mouth, a slight nervous tremor to my voice, that I actually had highlighted the results of the report to the on-call registrar, who was currently standing to the left of me conspicuously silent, way back on Sunday, and only this morning I had also tried to inform Albert, who was currently on the phone to a radiologist.

Mr S glared at me for several long seconds with a look of utter contempt on his face, before turning to an unsuspecting Albert just as he rejoined the ward round. He unceremoniously marched Albert out of the bay, past a sheepish OB, and straight into the corridor where he instantly unleashed a furious tirade, fully audible from our position in the bay, heavily laden with words of the four-letter variety, a "beasting" that would have made Sergeant Bastard proud.

Albert limped back into the bay, trailing behind our consultant like a scolded schoolboy, crestfallen. I looked around the faces of the shocked surgical team, and the even more shocked patient, before I finally fixed on OB, the man who had initially been provided with this crucial information three days ago. He half smiled at me, but he couldn't hold my gaze, quickly looking down and feigning interest in the iPhone permanently cradled in the palm of his hand, uncomfortably aware of my continued scrutiny.

Mr S slowly and rather dramatically turned on the heels of his surgical clogs and walked out of the bay like the greatest of Hollywood divas, shouting, "Prep her for theatre, cancel my nine o'clock, and consent her, Albert," over his shoulder as he left, without saying a single solitary word to the poor patient. She turned and looked at me. I shrugged my shoulders, my facial expression simultaneously apologetic and mortified, as she laughed ironically and almost sang in a soft Scottish lilt, "I guess I'm going to theatre then."

The second incident occurred just a few weeks later and proved to be the final nail in poor old Albert's coffin. Once again, it occurred whilst I was on call, but this time, I was with the condemned man for the unfolding of the whole dastardly plot.

We had finished our work for the day and were taking a leisurely stroll through the old Victorian corridors of the hospital at around eight fifty p.m., heading toward the evening handover, both in good spirits and sharing some light-hearted banter. We were suddenly and rather rudely interrupted by the harsh sound of Albert's bleep and took a short diversion to the nearest phone so that he could return the call. I overheard him conversing with the Labrador puppy introduced in Act One of this Machiavellian plot. We shall call him Rich. He was currently in the first year of his registrar training and was about as green as they come but very keen to impress. He was covering the Post-Operative Critical Care Unit (POCCU) and had been struggling to site a surgical chest drain into one of his patients, who now had low oxygen saturations and "seemed to be struggling slightly".

I would place my hand on a bible and attest to any court in the land that I was standing next to Albert as the following conversation transpired, witnessing it from his side, as he asked Rich if this was an emergency situation, or could it wait for half an hour until handover had concluded? If so, he would come over immediately after and site the drain, which incidentally, would have been after he had finished a thirteen-hour shift. He was assured there was actually no great rush, and so we continued on to handover, the conversation put to the back of our minds.

Handover was good-natured with no significant issues to pass on to our evening colleagues, other than the chest drain, which Alfred forthrightly stated to all present he would happily do straight after this meeting. We were about fifteen minutes in, rapidly emptying a couple of bags of mixed Haribo jellies whilst laughing at an unfortunate story from one of our colleagues, when the heavy door to the handover room flew open, flooding the warm and stuffy room with a blast of cool refreshing air as our superstar consultant dramatically burst onto the stage, with crazed eyes and a facial expression well known to me from my days in the boxing ring. He demanded a word with a rather confused-looking Albert.

Albert stood up slowly, a giant of a man, shoulders stooped, collapsing in on his own body, head hanging low, subconsciously trying to make himself a smaller target, whilst dragging his feet to delay the inevitable. They had made it less than five metres out of the now jammed-open door, when Mr S unleashed his absolute fury.

Apparently, the ladder-climbing Rich, recognising an opportunity to kick a man whilst he was down, had phoned the consultant and complained that Albert had refused to review a critically unwell patient, prioritising handover above immediately siting a chest drain, so that he could finish nice and early for the day. Our little eager beaver had also, rather helpfully, requested that the consultant come in from home and site the drain himself, as it was now an emergency, and the anaesthetist was already busy with another unwell patient, and the second on call was currently in theatre. Game, set, and match.

It appeared, however, that there was still some fight left in the old dog. Albert, having finally had enough of his regular verbal beatings, decided to fight back, and fight he did. A ferocious and vicious argument ensued that got more and more heated as it went on, and the last thing I heard before a rather embarrassed hospital manager closed the heavy lead-lined doors of the handover room was a strong Australian accent angrily shouting, "Fuck off, Mr S. Just fuck off, you stupid pompous c**t."

And that was the last time I ever saw, or heard from, Albert. I was later reliably informed that he was suspended for three weeks and told his upcoming contract would not be getting renewed, so he had cleared out his little one-bed room in the hospital accommodation, packed his bags, and headed back Down Under.

It was not just unfortunate Australian registrars who experienced the sharp edge of the consultants' tongues, however. We were all occasionally subjected to the odd bollocking from one massive ego or another, and not many egos come bigger than that of our surgical director, who had a famously bad temper to go with his famously massive ego.

I was present at one of the more bizarre incidents that will, no doubt by now, be just one more tale amongst the collection of insane incidents that have entered into surgical folklore to be eagerly recounted whenever Mr F is mentioned in certain circles. It happened during one of the national audit days, which were highly competitive events held at our hospital, in which the brightest and best from all four corners of the United Kingdom, and often further afield, would compete for a prestigious fifteen-minute slot to present the findings of a curriculum-vitae-enhancing audit or quality improvement project.

Mr F had rather generously decided to award himself a prime mid-morning slot to share a photo slide show of himself and his friends driving old motorbikes around northern India and Nepal. I watched incredulously as the shocked and mildly confused audience, made up of hundreds of guests, was essentially treated to a budget version of the UK TV show, *The Hairy Bikers*.

I had briefly witnessed the wrong end of his foul temper on a couple of occasions, earlier in my surgical rotation, but had managed to mostly avoid him by keeping a relatively low profile, spending as much time in the hospital gym as I had in theatre or on the surgical wards. I was not a surgical trainee, and I had absolutely no interest in becoming one. As I was coming to the end of my second year, I was psychologically winding down and looking toward my next step into the unchartered waters of the professional locum, and I needed no reference from, and was in no mood to take any shit from, surgeons.

Mr F was an out-and-out Geordie, who was extremely proud of his working-class roots. The only thing he seemed to enjoy more than telling us how great he was and how far he had come from such humble beginnings was humiliating junior doctors, especially if there was an attractive female nurse, or an attractive female junior doctor, or an attractive female HCA, or an attractive female domestic, or in fact, any attractive, or even half-attractive member of the opposite sex present. I had managed to stay well out of his way most of the time, and on reflection, he had given me just as wide a berth, leaving me to my own devices, which was how I had managed to get away with spending so much of my surgical rotation in the hospital gym.

Unfortunately, though, all that changed when Mr F decided to give me a lesson about TTOs (medicines for patients to take home with them on discharge). I was on call for the wards and, as usual, was pumping iron in the gym, when I was fast bleeped to attend one of the surgical wards, which was extremely unusual during working hours, because each ward had their own allocated doctors. I gave it a little jog across the hospital, as it was the furthest possible point away from where I currently was, and I suspected this was probably an emergency situation – there was no other reason I could fathom that I would be fast bleeped.

I arrived on the ward a little flustered and facially flushed from my exertions in the gym followed by a steady jog across the whole length of the hospital, and on entering the ward, I found Mr F sitting, or rather, lounging at the computer on the main reception desk. He was leaned as far back as humanly possible in the computer chair, head cocked to one side, legs spread wide apart, manly bulge on full display in the ultimate power pose. His long, grey hair was draped behind his shoulders, and he was surrounded by a couple of young nurses, a young female ANP, and one of his sycophantic registrars. Just off to one side, slightly out of the group, stood an older ward sister, who looked thoroughly unimpressed by what she knew was coming, having undoubtedly witnessed it many times before.

"Did you fast bleep me?" I asked the ward sister calmly, deliberately ignoring the knock-off Kris Kristofferson who was so clearly revelling in his role as orchestrator of this whole pantomime.

"I did," replied Mr F tersely, not even glancing in my direction. "Did you fucking cancel all Mr M's medications?" he spat with venom, looking directly at me now, a smug self-satisfied look on his face. He was about to take me down, the only other working-class doctor, and the rival to his imaginary "toughest doctor" crown.

"No," I replied, again calmly, not an ounce of fear or even the slightest tremor showing in my voice.

"Well, it's got your fucking name all over the TTO, and you've cancelled all the fucking medication." He was leaning forward in his seat now, glaring at me as he flicked his long, grey bangs out of his eyes. He was on a roll, performing for his crowd, the star of his show, steadily building up to the crescendo. "Who the fuck do you think you are—" he started in.

"Do you know how to use this system?" I said, cutting him off, much to his annoyance – this was his show, who the fuck did I think I was to interrupt him.

"Of course, I fucking do." He was exaggerating his Geordie accent now, emphasising his tough roots, trying to intimidate me whilst playing up to his young crowd. He was still fully in control.

"I don't think you do," I replied, staring straight into his eyes for the first time, unflinching.

He was absolutely furious, his face instantly flushing as he leaned even further forward in his seat in an aggressive pose, body tense and rigid, hands clamped tightly on the arms of the computer chair, skin stretched tight across white knuckles, eyes pure steel.

"Because if you did know how to use it," I continued, a subtle smile on my face, eyes never leaving his, "then you would know that you are actually looking at the discontinued medications section. If you want to see the TTO, then you click here." I leaned over him, forcing him to retreat in his chair slightly, and casually pushed the cursor over the TTO header and clicked, revealing all of the medications I was currently being accused of discontinuing. I stood up, straight-backed, chest pumped out, face serious now, but still completely calm, again looking directly into his furious grey eyes, as I asked, "Is there anything else?" I continued to hold his firm and furious gaze for a few more seconds, catching the young nurses desperately trying to keep straight faces in my peripheral vision.

I spun on my heels and looked directly at the ward sister who smiled and gave me a slight nod as I walked off the ward, down the stairs and straight back to the gym. That was thankfully the end of my surgical rotation and the last time I have ever worked in surgery.

A Very Personal Arrest

When I arrived at the cardiothoracic centre, I already had a decent amount of experience in cardiac arrest situations. In all such situations, I had never hidden away in the background, never tried to blend in. I have already documented my first arrest. It was pretty daunting, but I believe I handled myself well, and overall, it was a confidence-boosting experience. However, the second certainly wasn't. That one was even more memorable, and for all the wrong reasons.

I was bleeped to an overflow ward to find a patient mid-cardiac arrest with a young female SHO leading what was the very definition of the old military phrase "a complete shit show". She was certainly no acute medic, and I walked into absolute pandemonium, with no set roles for the team members, no structure, and zero communication. After five minutes of shirking all responsibility whilst unsuccessfully attempting to site a green cannula, she gave herself a needlestick injury and, a little too eagerly, dismissed herself down to A&E to get her bloods tested.

Relieved, I took control of the situation as best I could, and after almost a quarter of an hour of bumbling through the resuscitation algorithm amid varying levels of confusion, the cavalry eventually arrived, after having to deal with another arrest that had occurred simultaneously. Although we hadn't exactly covered ourselves in glory, the patient was still just about alive.

I learned a lot from the chaos of this arrest, which had highlighted the importance of being organised, structured, and having the right people in the right jobs, and I put these lessons to good use throughout the rest of F1, so I was pretty confident in both participating in and leading an arrest by the time I started second year. I honestly thought I was pretty good. But little did I know that I was about to enter a completely different league. The cardiothoracic centre dealt with the third most cardiac arrests in the entire UK, annually, and as a result of this, it had a dedicated arrest team. The team was highly organised, made up of a consultant anaesthetist, a cardiology registrar, a cardiac or thoracic surgical registrar, a specialist critical care ANP, and at the very bottom of the pile, a designated dog's body (SHO), which just so happened to be my level of seniority.

We could have multiple arrests in a single day, and they ran like clockwork once the arrest team arrived on scene. The ward doctors and nursing staff were usually dismissed, and the team would quickly take over with minimal fuss. Everything was calm and everyone knew their specific role. A patient would be quickly intubated, pacing wires placed in a matter of minutes, and the chest opening kit was even utilised in the direst of circumstances. It was a phenomenal environment to learn how to run a cardiac arrest, or even just be part of one, and the consultants would often push the SHOs to take a supported lead role, especially if you were the up-and-coming blue-eyed boy of the anaesthetic department, as I was.

As I gained more experience throughout my second year, the continued exposure to the most harrowing of situations desensitised me somewhat, and I found I could often emotionally detach myself from the tragedy unfolding in front of me. I suppose it was self-preservation. I rarely questioned my decisions or took problems home anymore, leaving the shift behind me as I walked out of the sliding hospital doors.

However, no matter how detached you become, there will always be occasions when a patient gets to even the hardest of us. Every doctor has some patients who stay with them for the rest of their career. This is usually because the patient is relatable in some way, or they remind us of a family member or even a good friend, and during my second year, I encountered just such a patient – one of the few who will stay with me for the rest of my life, who I still feel as raw about today whilst writing this, as I did all those years ago.

She was a youngish lady with Down syndrome who had recently had a pretty severe MI and, as a result, had had a couple of stents fitted and had initially done really well. We had all been concerned about putting her through the procedure, due to her severe learning disability and her limited understanding of what was happening to her, wondering whether it was really in her best interest, but we took the chance, and she had handled the situation remarkably well and seemed relaxed on the CCU on which I was working at the time.

I had actually been on call when the patient was brought in, working with the interventional registrar, who had become a good friend during my time on cardiology and who had allowed me to assist with the stents. I met the patient immediately before the procedure, to consent her, and we had instantly developed a good rapport. I have a younger cousin who has a congenital development disorder called Smith-Magenis syndrome, and we are very close, and this lady very much reminded me of her. So, I made it my mission to make the situation as comfortable for her as I possibly could, and over the following days, I really won her over and we were getting on like a house on fire.

I will pick up the story from day three post MI. I had just completed the ward round and was very much minding my own business whilst casually perusing social media at the beacon of calm that was the nurses' station, when the sister suddenly asked me to "take a look at your mate in room four". I entered the room with a sense of impending doom and could immediately see she was in distress as I quickly noted the ventricular tachycardia (VT) on the monitor. Most non-medics are probably unaware of why VT is such a dangerous condition, so I will attempt to lay it out as simply as I possibly can.

The heart is basically a muscular pump that is made up of four chambers, two little ones at the top called atria and two big ones at the bottom called ventricles. The heart is also split into a left and right side, meaning we all have a left atria and a left ventricle and a right atria and a right ventricle. Oxygen-rich blood makes its way to the left side of the heart from the lungs, and deoxygenated blood that has already had its nutrients and oxygen taken by the muscles and organs, makes its way back to the right side of the heart for pumping back to the lungs. All blood initially enters the heart via the atria and is funnelled through the small chambers of the atria and down into the large muscular pumping chambers that are the ventricles.

This all occurs whilst the heart is at rest, and if the heart stays in a relaxed state with a nice controlled rate of contraction, for example, sixty beats per minute, this allows the ventricles plenty of time – in this case, one second – to fill with blood. On contraction, the deoxygenated blood is forced from the right ventricle to the lungs to drop off the waste product (carbon dioxide) and pick up oxygen, whilst the left ventricle simultaneously pumps the oxygen-rich blood, that it has just received from the lungs, out and around the rest of the body to deliver the oxygen needed to keep the muscles and organs healthy. As the blood is ejected out of the left ventricle and into the body's main artery, the aorta, some of that blood is redirected into three vessels that are situated at the very base of the aorta, the coronary arteries, which double back and supply the heart muscle itself with oxygen and nutrients.

If the patient is suffering from VT, then the ventricles are essentially beating a lot faster than normal, usually around four times faster. As the heart is working harder, it needs more blood delivered to its own muscle tissue to stop those muscles cramping up and failing. The problem, however, is that the ventricles are contracting much faster now and are no longer beating sixty times per minute but closer to two hundred and forty times. Therefore, they no longer get a full one second to completely fill up with blood, but around a quarter of a second, meaning only a quarter of the amount of blood is pumped out into the aorta with each contraction of the heart and not enough of this blood will make it out of the aorta and back into the coronary arteries. This lack of blood starves the heart muscle of oxygen, and the heart weakens as a result and is unable to generate enough force to pump sufficient blood around the rest of the body to supply all the other organs, quickly resulting in multi-organ failure and death. This is why VT is such a medical emergency and why it needs to be corrected as quickly as possible.

Anyway, back to my little friend in room four. As treatment for the VT, I asked a nurse for my standard 4 g stat dose of IV magnesium and a loading dose of IV amiodarone – which is a medication that can slow down the heart rate sufficiently to allow the ventricles time to fill up properly – and instructed another nurse to put on the pads, in case the amiodarone failed and we needed to quickly shock the heart back into rhythm with electricity.

Suddenly, I noticed my patient had developed a bluish tinge to her skin, and as I looked at her, she was looking back at me with pleading childlike eyes. She reached out and squeezed my hand hard, begging me to "make the pain go away". I assured her that I would make her better as I tried my best to explain what was happening to her. Remarkably, she appeared to take it all in and, with a trembling voice, asked me if she was dying. Trying to remain professional and focused on the job at hand, I promised her she was definitely not dying. I squeezed her hand back in reassurance, forcing a hollow smile onto my face, whilst the cold hand of fear strangled my intestines with a firm relentless grip, and I struggled to swallow back the lump that was forming in my throat.

Her blood pressure continued to drop, and I asked the nurse to put out an arrest call. I was finding it really difficult to maintain composure now, as every time I looked at her, I visualised my cousin's face. I could not stop myself from thinking about how she would be feeling, how frightened she would be in this situation. I asked the nurse to administer a sedative, whilst as slowly and calmy as I could manage, I explained to my patient that we needed to give her a shock.

She was absolutely terrified, gripping my closest arm with both hands and pulling me forcibly toward her with amazing strength. I could feel her warm, wet tears on my cheek as her body wracked with sobs. I tried my best to console her, but I was just about holding it together myself. She kept repeating, "Is it going to hurt? Is it going to hurt?" over and over again. All I could think as I choked back the tears was, *Where the fuck is this arrest team?*

They eventually arrived and made the decision to instantly shock, as her blood pressure was now barely recordable, whilst simultaneously injecting a strong sedative into her cannula. I had to physically pull myself away from her grip to allow the shock to be administered, and she continued to grasp out toward me, her eyes huge with terror. I took a step back as we shocked, and she screamed out in agony, I quickly stepped back in toward the bed, ready to start chest compressions, pleading with the anaesthetist to give more sedative, as those terrified eyes burned deep into my soul.

She lost output, and we alternated between chest compressions and electric shocks, whilst she intermittently wailed and cried out, despite huge doses of sedatives, until she finally succumbed to propofol and became worryingly silent. I watched her face as I pushed deep into her chest with the palms of my hands, her unseeing eyes rolled upward toward the anaesthetist who held an oxygen mask tightly against her face, skin white around the knuckles as he pumped life-preserving oxygen into her lungs.

Despite our best efforts, I watched the life slowly drain away from her, and I knew she was gone. I eventually looked up at the anaesthetist, who half nodded at me and looked toward the rest of the team. "Anyone have any objections to calling it?" Total silence. I watched the fingers relax and loosen on the mask, and I stepped away from the bed and staggered backward, hitting the wall hard on increasingly unsteady legs.

"Are you okay?" the anaesthetist asked me, with a look of genuine concern on his face, and I snapped back to the present moment.

"Yes," I managed to murmur, but I wasn't okay. I would never be okay again. I was absolutely devastated, a broken man. I had promised her she would be okay. I had promised her I could take away the pain. I had promised her she wouldn't die, and she had fucking died. Not only had she died, but she had suffered a horrific, terrifying, and painful death. All alone in that oppressive room, with the only person she trusted holding her down and pressing hard and painfully into her chest. I had lied to her. I had failed her.

We tidied away our equipment in total silence. There is normally a gallows humour around an arrest, and someone, usually me, cracks a few jokes in an attempt to diffuse the dark atmosphere, but not this time. I couldn't speak; I would have broken down in tears, and I'm not sure I would have ever stopped. We had all taken it hard. I looked around at the others, and it was like looking into the faces of Somme survivors. The debrief was a solemn affair, but thankfully quick, as we all just wanted to get away, to leave this place and scrub the screams from our ears, scrub the images from our eyes.

I sat at the nurses' station and started to write up the arrest on complete autopilot, unsure how I was even holding a pen. The sister looked at me with pity in her eyes and opened her mouth. "Please, please don't ask me," I said, before she could say anything, and kept my eyes focused straight down at the notes, holding back the tears, as we sat in silence for a few moments. I eventually stood up and walked out without a word, a part of me changed irrevocably.

Unchartered Seas

Over the years I have been fortunate enough to work in some world-class specialist centres with some of the best in the profession. However, I have also worked in some real shitholes and shared handover meetings with colleagues who I had more than a sneaking suspicion may not have held a valid licence to practice Medicine. I have gone from being figuratively wrapped in cotton wool, a cocoon of safe practice, to flying by the seat of my pants and playing Russian roulette with my GMC registration on a daily basis, and back again. I have plied my trade, far and wide, from the Scottish borders down to the beautiful valleys of South Wales and pretty much everywhere in between. I have worked in massive city-centre hospitals, highly specialised tertiary centres, and small district general hospitals (DGHs). But the hospital in which I undoubtedly earned my stripes was a surprisingly modern DGH set in an isolated and impoverished corner of northern England. It was here that the real story begins. This was where I cut loose from the safety of training and set sail into the vast unknown.

The junior doctor strikes had finished me off. There was no way I was going to sell out and work under the hated new contract, so there was no way I would be taking up a training place on anaesthetics. How could I have held my head up high, looked my family in the eyes, or myself in the mirror, for that matter, if after campaigning so strongly against the contract for well over a year, I had completely folded and signed it. That kind of capitulation just isn't in my makeup – this lad is not for turning.

I had joined the A&E Agency for locums whilst working as an F2, and had long since been allocated my first agent, Ragen, who was as strongly Manc as I was Scouse. Unlikely as it had seemed to me at first, we'd really hit it off, and she had successfully kept my head above water by finding me regular weekend work. We formed a highly successful partnership, and so it was only logical that it would be her I turned to when starting out on my long and winding road. However, she passed me straight over to her colleague, one of the two famous Wesleys in the trade, who found me a high-paying long-term job within an hour.

I'd already glimpsed the dark underbelly of the locum world and understood exactly why most medics decided early on in their careers that training was a much safer and more stable option than entering into the world of the mercenary doctor. I had experienced some pretty ropey situations in that first year of weekend locum shifts, but the one that stands out above all others and is enough to still send shivers down my spine, even after all the craziness of the years that followed, was a set of weekend nights that I picked up in a Greater Manchester hospital in the mid-twenty-teens.

It was a glorious early summer's Friday evening, and whilst most of my colleagues were several pints into their weekend, I was heading off in my pride and joy, the little white BMW 1 Series I had recently treated myself to. I had just indulged in an hour's post-dayshift battle kip and a quick cold shower to blow away the cobwebs, and was now driving way too fast up the M62 in order to arrive at the alien hospital site nice and early, giving me plenty of time to pay for parking and avoid yet another hospital parking fine (believe it or not, hospital trusts actually pay private parking companies to financially persecute their own staff), and drag my exhausted arse to the night handover.

With no prior knowledge of the hospital layout, I did what I'd always done in similar circumstances and headed straight to the switchboard, the fount of all hospital knowledge and the saviour of many a young doctor. I knocked a little too loudly on the rather unimpressive chipboard door and was buzzed in to a cramped and dark room that was essentially a glorified broom cupboard. In the centre of the space, behind a cluttered desk, sat a stick-thin middle-aged woman, undoubtedly a heavy smoker who wore every knock life had given her in the form of deep wrinkles creasing the thin, leather-like skin stretched taught as canvas across the prominent bones of the skull beneath.

She lazily looked up from her screen, its light giving her face an eerie glow in the low light of the room, and, after the most cursory of scans, looked back at her computer and casually informed me she had been expecting me. There was a spare bleep available on the rack located behind me, but unfortunately, nobody had left me an induction pack, which would have contained a temporary password for the IT system, and a security pass to access the wards, which, of course, would all be locked overnight.

So, essentially, I could not access the IT system because I had no log-in details, but even if I could, I wouldn't know what I was looking at as I had no induction booklet to guide me through the multiple complex systems I would need in order to review GP records, blood results, and imaging. And to top it all off, I also couldn't access any of the wards, as I had no key pass. Welcome to the world of the locum.

Okay, so we were off to a good start, and in all honesty, I probably should have left then and there, but as you have probably guessed by the fact that I was working a night shift straight after a day shift, I desperately needed the cash. I left the switchboard with the most rudimentary of directions and wandered the ghostly corridors, not passing another soul until I eventually, and rather fortunately, stumbled upon the small office that was utilised for the night handover, which was handily located next to the AMU. I opened the door and was greeted by the briefest of head nods from a rather uninterested medical SHO who was leaning way too far back in a creaking computer chair, belly stretching the well-worn, royal-blue scrub top to its very limits. Standing next to this top-knotted indie kid was a small, chubby registrar with patchy overgrown stubble wrapped around a childlike face that contrarily contained the eyes of one who has seen far too much at far too young an age. He greeted me warmly in a friendly sing-song Scottish accent, whilst simultaneously fidgeting nervously with the crumpled outstanding jobs list in his left hand.

Rather bizarrely, and despite Tony Blair wasting billions of pounds trying to connect them in the late nineties, most UK hospital trusts have their own computer systems, which tend to be completely individual, often differing greatly, even from those of their closest neighbours, so navigating each system is usually the first challenge of the short-term locum. The pleasant Scottish reg sat me down and gave me a whistle-stop tour of the IT system and, upon hearing of my induction pack woes, immediately tore off a jagged corner of the job list and wrote down his username and password, whilst rather dramatically hanging his security pass over my head, as though awarding a gold medal at the Olympics. I thanked him with genuine gratitude and more than a little relief. *Maybe it wasn't going to be too bad, after all.*

Not surprisingly, I had relaxed too soon, my positivity angering the fickle hospital gods. I left handover with a list as long as my arm, thanks to my top-knotted friend, and an ensuing shift that could only be described as the night from hell, culminating in one of the most bizarre incidents I have experienced as a doctor, even after all my years of nomadic wandering from hospital to hospital.

I had somehow managed to muddle my way through the night, clearing one hurdle after another, and now found myself sitting at a deserted nurses' station half-heartedly writing up a drug chart that had been left incomplete by the day team, one eye on the beams of sunlight forcing their way through the fat-bellied lilac clouds sitting astride the hills and mountains of the Peak District, framed like a Turner painting by the large window immediately opposite me. I was hungry and tired, yet to take a break, doggy-paddling against the tide but head still just about above the waterline, when the obligatory early morning drug round arrest call went out.

The six a.m. drug round nurses are the healthcare equivalent of the early morning dog walkers in every true-crime story ever written, uncovering the gruesome fates of the unfortunate victims of the witching hours, the hours when patients are left to their own devices by a workforce who make a living from plying their trade whilst the rest of the civilised world sleeps in their beds. As a result, the first checks of a morning often uncover patients in varying states of deterioration, occasionally stone-cold dead.

I was instantly awake, night-shift fatigue slipping from my shoulders like a heavy woollen shawl, the old butterflies dancing in my stomach as I followed the instruction from my bleep and headed for the side room in the darkest recess of the AMU. There I found a couple of nurses gathered around an unresponsive ancient Asian man's bed, red crash trolly half in, half out of the small doorway, unopened and doing nothing other than getting in the way. I squeezed past and asked the closest nurse for a handover. Neither nurse even looked up as they mumbled something or other between themselves about chest pain and not being able to feel a pulse.

I asked one of them to hook the patient up to the defib pads and the other to start CPR, whilst I forcibly pushed an orange Guedel airway into his gaping mouth and put together the green self-inflating bag mask ventilating system, sealing the mask over his mouth and nose with my left hand, whilst quickly checking for a pulse in the neck with my right, simultaneously eyeing the chest for signs of respiration between the pumping of the tired-looking nurse. In the absence of a detectable pulse, I started to count the nurse's compressions out loud and gave two good squeezes of the firm plastic bag between every thirty thrusts, settling into my role whilst I waited for the arrival of the anaesthetist.

After a minute or so, I realised the tiny, withered old man had become noticeably floppier and seemed to have sunk through the flat, plastic hospital mattress, almost folding in on himself as the rapidly tiring nurse, who was now red in the cheeks and puffing and panting, performed each compression. I looked up from the patient and around the room, suddenly realising we were alone, the second nurse nowhere to be seen. I shouted loudly for some help, no reply. I shouted again, louder and not as politely, for some "effing" help.

I was slightly startled by the sudden appearance of a stern-looking nurse who popped her head through the door and, in the broadest of Mancunian accents, asked me what I wanted.

"A bit of help wouldn't go amiss," I replied.

Her face instantly granite, she tersely replied, "Sorry, I'm on my drug round. Can't you see the red vest?" pulling at the front of the red cotton apron, with a sarcastic smirk. And as quickly as she had arrived, she was gone from the doorway.

I was lost for words, for one of the few times in my life, as I looked across at the equally baffled and increasingly fatigued nurse who continued working away on the chest in slow motion. Regaining my composure, I shouted after the departed nurse, "Get me some fucking help then, immediately," with the emphasis firmly on "immediately". She never replied, or returned.

The shattered nurse and I soldiered on alone for the best part of ten minutes before the anaesthetist and an ODP finally arrived on the scene. I quickly took over the chest compressions before our physical wreck of a nurse had a coronary of her own. But despite our best efforts, the unfortunate old gentleman passed away a short time later. I have no idea if he could have been saved if I had received help earlier, if the chest compressions had been rotated through a fresh team. I suspect the hand of time had finally caught up with this old gentleman, and a DNAR should have been in place, but a bit of help certainly wouldn't have done him, or us, any harm.

*

As soul-destroying an experience as locuming could be, I revelled in the freedom that an out-of-hours hospital provides a junior doctor. I actually enjoyed the lack of senior support and the experience of independently managing and prioritising my workload and my list of patients. I had been self-employed for the majority of my working life, outside of the forces, essentially my own boss, and as frustrating as being bleeped to prescribe fluids in the early hours of the morning could be, it was also exciting being removed from the routine day-to-day of the wards. As much as I loved the learning opportunities, prestige, and support provided by working in a world-renowned tertiary centre, cardiothoracic surgery had started to become tedious. I was not a surgeon and the novelty of spending all day in the hospital gym had worn off. I was in physically good shape but was bored and desperate to get my teeth back into a bit of proper medicine.

When the day finally arrived to leave the tertiary centre, I was ready. With more than a little bit of nerves, I accepted the six-month contract offered to me by Wes. The job was in a hospital way up north, not quite north of the wall but not far off. Little did I know at the time how much this spur of the moment, rather blasé decision would change the rest of my life, or how much it would eventually push my physical and mental health to the absolute limit.

I had visited the hospital four weeks prior to accepting the offer, as part of a weekend recce with my wife, and discovered it was located in a beautiful part of northern England, a part of the country the locals proudly referred to as “God’s Country”, and I could fully understand why. I had initially set off with a sense of apprehension, after a quick Google search of the local area had flagged up multiple news reports about a local supermarket worker who had been covertly filmed by shocked partygoers drunkenly staggering around a nightclub then pulling his trousers down to his ankles and squatting so he could empty his loose bowels onto the highly polished dance-floor of the town’s most hip and happening hotspot. Even worse, as I delved deeper into the story, there he was, proud as punch, on the front page of one of England’s most popular red-tops, tucking into a plateful of steaming vindaloo curry – the culprit he claimed was responsible for the unsavoury incident.

The next story I uncovered was a lot more sinister. A crazed gunman had gone on a murderous rampage with rifle and shotgun. I actually remembered watching the police chase unfold live on Sky News many years before but didn’t realise it had occurred amongst such beauty, the contrast of nature in all her glory with depraved evil making the heinous act seem somehow even worse, an affront to all that is pure and good. I had decided that was enough research for one day, and as I snapped the laptop closed, I don’t mind admitting I was having serious doubts.

But that had been before I found myself in the passenger seat of our little white 1 Series, winding our way past mountain after mountain on endless, winding single-laned roads, flanked all the way by miles of cobalt-blue lakes that were flat as glass, a literal visualisation of Wordsworth, and when bathed in high definition sunshine, as it was on that day, a rival in beauty to any place on God’s green earth. As our route led us seductively toward the little coastal town that was our destination, I was sold. I was in.

When we approached the old fishing port, the lakes and mountains receded to become but a distant blip in our rear-view mirror, and the sun seemed to retreat behind the safety of a lonely wandering cloud. As we entered the town centre, a gloom enveloped the boarded-up side streets of a place that had well and truly seen better days, a place in which I could well imagine a local shitting on the dance-floor of a tacky nightclub.

The town sat like an ugly wart on the end of a beautiful nose, and I was once again deflated, and rather depressed about making the move from my beloved Liverpool. I was itching to make a break for it and head back home, back to civilisation, as we pulled up outside a coffee shop on a pretty high street in the very heart of the town. The high street was at complete odds with the derelict and decrepit arteries that fed into it. We decided to go in for a "cuppa", just as the heavens opened and soaked us through to the skin. After a quick dash to safety, we sat, sodden, at a window table, both in quiet contemplation whilst we watched the heavy raindrops fall outside, exploding like transparent bombs on the York-stone flags.

The rain eased off, and with a belly full of Americano coffee and rocky road cake, and with the sun breaking through the grey clouds, the sense of impending doom slowly receded. We decided to explore more of the town, walking through the market square and along the beautiful marina before eventually stopping for a burger and a pint in the one and only chain-pub restaurant. After my initial hesitance, I was feeling more positive again. The first impression had been a brutal contrast to the beautiful lakes, but the town did have its charms, and if I could survive Speke, Bosnia, and Northern Ireland, then I was sure I could handle a few dance-floor dumpers.

We drove up the hill leading us out of the town centre, which was lined by attractive Georgian-style villas and elegant townhouses, and passed the golden arches of the one and only fast-food-chain restaurant, continuing toward the hospital, which was an old, imposing Victorian building, sitting proudly on its hilltop perch, the giant grey housing estate wrapped around it no doubt providing the vast majority of its customers. My wife pulled up outside and left the engine running as I popped in through the glass sliding doors to check out the interior. I was unsurprised to find it had that mental asylum kind of feel to it, with low ceilings and thick, bunker-style walls coloured in the familiar shades of apricot, meadow-yellow, pastel-blue and magnolia, that I swear have not existed anywhere outside the NHS or prisons since the seventies.

I had seen enough. It wasn't ideal, but not only had I made my bed, I had also convinced two of my friends, Mark and Tim, to jump in with me – more about that later. I walked back to the car, now resigned to my fate, ready to head home. Ever the diplomat, my wife encouraged me to continue exploring and at least check out the rest of the hospital, so we drove the loop road that led us toward the back of the building, first passing an old mortuary that wouldn't have looked out of place in a Sherlock Holmes movie. Swinging around a sharp bend, the pothole-riddled road dipped steeply before unexpectedly widening out into a smooth, perfectly level and freshly tarmacked road surface. And there, revealing itself to us, like a glorious phoenix rising from the dullest of ashes, stood a massive and impressively modern steel-and-glass construction awkwardly sandwiched onto the old original hospital building. The distant mountains were perfectly reflected in the huge mirrored windows that sat within beautiful panels of bright cladding – this was pre-Grenfell – and the sun dazzled us as we circled the roundabout and parked in the drop-off bays immediately outside the A&E department.

A brief inspection revealed that, not only did this building house A&E, but also the other acute departments, as well as ambulatory care, the surgical wards, the general medical wards, the maternity ward, and outpatient clinics. The old and crumbling Victorian hospital only contained the elderly medicine wards – ironically, crammed full of old and crumbling patients. I later found out that the new hospital was supposed to have been built in two phases. The first phase to replace the acute areas of medicine had obviously been completed, but the older building remained because the trust had run out of money. It was such a shame, but the least of the problems facing a population that has since had its services stripped away, one by one, to finance a parasitic PFI hospital located a rather inconvenient sixty minutes' drive away – another legacy of Tony Blair's New Labour.

I spent the next ten minutes or so exploring my new stomping ground, which was as modern a hospital as I had ever set foot in, and which I will call East from now on. I got back into the car with a renewed sense of optimism, and as we drove back through God's Country toward my Liverpool home, it all suddenly became very real.

East's a Beast

When I signed on the dotted line at East, I managed to convince my buddy Mark, of cardiothoracic centre fame, to join me, before he embarked on the well-trodden, chlamydia-ridden pathway of the elephant-print, baggy-trouser-wearing, polaroid-photo-taken-with-a-drugged-up-tiger, gap-year student. You know the one, the standard "finding yourself" backpacker trek through Thailand, Vietnam, and Cambodia, before disregarding all pretence of "travelling" with a glammed-up month on the piss in Australia, followed by a prolonged period of convalescence in New Zealand. Amazingly, Mark also managed to convince his university mate and upcoming travel partner, Tim, to come along for the ride, and so there were three – the Musketeers, or "Spice Boys" as we would rather annoyingly be christened by the nursing staff on our arrival.

The day arrived for me to pack up my bags and leave my family behind, making the two-and-a-half-hour journey north on a bright Sunday in early August 2016. My wife had found us Musketeers reasonably priced accommodation that was in the process of being renovated, and even though I was the last to arrive, she had ensured the owner saved me the best room in the shared house. It was a huge double bedroom with large windows that gave it a spacious and bright air, situated next door to Mark's single room, which overlooked the alleyway and brick wall of the rear neighbouring house, and directly beneath Tim's room, which could only be described as a slight upgrade on Harry Potter's under-stairs boudoir, with ceilings so low that even

Tim, standing at just over five and a half foot, had to constantly stoop, and rather hilariously didn't even contain enough space for a wardrobe.

We sat in the tatty communal living room with its freshly painted magnolia walls barely masking the damp stains seeping through from the outside wall separating us from the overgrown yard, on mismatched and uncomfortable faux-leather chairs, enjoying a Chinese takeaway and a couple of Tsing Tsao beers to celebrate our first evening. I listened whilst the terrible twosome regaled stories of the previous couple of days, in which they had caused a few ripples amongst the local community, to put it mildly. I was amused by the tales but homesick, missing my family, and my beautifully decorated and comfortable house in Liverpool almost as much.

We awoke early the next morning and had breakfast together before cadging a lift in Tim's battered old Renault car that absolutely stank of skunk, despite him claiming to have never smoked in his life. I wound down the window to avoid a contact high, enjoying the fresh air on my face. It was a cool morning, more akin to autumn than summer, as we drove an identical route to that of my wife and I just a few weeks previous.

Arriving with plenty of time to spare, we parked at the back of the hospital on a large, loose-gravel car park and walked the short distance to the business suite, which was a small, sparsely furnished room next to the front door of the old half of the building. Waiting in the doorway for us to arrive, whilst impatiently glancing at his watch and then back at us, even though we were ten minutes early, was our inductor. He was a serious-looking little fella, bespectacled and balding, ruddy-cheeked and middle-aged. He stood about five foot three in height and was slight in build, weighing around nine stone, but looked like he meant business.

He gruffly instructed us to come in and take a seat, without making any attempt to move from the partially obstructed doorframe, ensuring that we had to squeeze past him to get inside. We gave each other a quizzical glance as we took a seat at the island of tables that dominated the centre of the room, sniggering like a group of naughty schoolchildren. I got the impression this annoyed him even more because he aggressively threw double-sided A4 questionnaires at us, with a flick-of-the-wrist motion, each one rather impressively and gracefully landing on the table and sliding into perfect position in front of us.

We quickly completed the paperwork and were informed that this wasn't our official induction – that had been booked for four weeks' time at the sister hospital, a mere hour's drive away. We were then impatiently marched down to the security office, which was situated a level below the ground floor, amongst the laundry, supply rooms, and storage facilities deep in the bowels of the hospital, the three of us lagging behind as he forged ahead relentlessly, like an overeager geography teacher on a field trip. He walked through the security room door and returned a couple of minutes later with a digital camera in hand.

"Fucking hell! Is there only one person working here?" Mark muttered under his breath, as we struggled to contain our laughter.

"Stand against the wall," he ordered, more like the commander of a firing squad than a man who oversees NHS inductions and takes ID badge photographs for a living. We stood against the plain wall, whilst he took three quick snaps, denying each of us the opportunity to review our image before quickly moving on to the next person. We were then provided with an ID badge and security passkey conveniently slotted together either side of a plastic holder attached to a blue cotton NHS lanyard, which had a rather handy white plastic safety clip situated at the opposite end from the plastic holder.

We thanked him and turned to walk away.

"Whoa, where are you going?"

We turned in unison. "To work," Mark said.

"What about the breakaway training?" he replied.

"You don't do that as well, do you?" Tim chipped in, with more than a hint of sarcasm.

"I do actually, yes," he stated proudly, whilst pumping out his chest.

"I'm okay, thanks," I replied.

"Well, what would you do if someone grabbed your badge, like this?" He leaned forward and snatched at the lanyard I had just placed around my neck. Instinctively, I reached behind my head, firmly gripped either side of the safety clip and quickly pulled in opposite directions, freeing the lanyard from my neck whilst causing him to stagger backward a couple of steps, ID badge still in hand.

"Isn't that what the clips are for?" I asked him, as I put out my hand, indicating for him to give me back my badge. He passed it back, turned on the balls of his feet and silently walked away. And that was pretty much our induction. We never did get that jolly boys' outing to the sister hospital four weeks later.

We headed to the emergency assessment unit (EAU), which was to be our base for the next four months, and met our consultant, who kindly showed us around the department, which to my surprise was pretty impressive, having twenty-nine beds, of which only eleven were occupied that morning. The layout of the emergency areas, as a whole, was planned to perfection. It was based around the simple principle of L-shaped corridors, one leg of EAU leading directly to A&E, whilst the other led to the doors of CCU, concurrently leading through those doors and past the first four single rooms before turning ninety degrees left and heading straight to the ITU department, thus completing the reverse L-shaped corridor of CCU. The continuous corridor design meant that, in an emergency situation, an unwell patient could be wheeled into CCU or ITU in seconds. It was ingenious planning by the architect, and I benefited from the time saved transporting sickies many times over the years that followed.

The department also had excellent staffing levels for providing the appropriate level of care to the steady stream of patients who rotated through its twenty-nine beds, which, to be honest, was not that unusual in the glory years before the enforcement of the new contract, Brexit, and COVID. The staffing was made up of at least one consultant, a registrar, four SHOs, a GP trainee, and at least one ANP, but usually two. There were also three nurses and three HCAs.

All was not rosy in this garden, though. The hospital was in special measures and, as a result, was not allowed foundation or other grades of training doctors on site, but the overstaffing using locums made this almost irrelevant. We were essentially all locums, with the exception of the GP trainee, ensuring there was none of the stigma or animosity attached to the status that I had experienced in most other hospitals in which I had worked so far, no snide comments about our pay. And best of all, the worst jobs couldn't be specially reserved for the "mercenary" doctor, because we were essentially one big army of mercenaries.

It was a great introduction into the life of a full-time locum, and even though I was working away from my family and regularly suffered from bouts of homesickness, it was one of the happiest times in Medicine for me. I was living with two doctors, who became really good friends – we worked together virtually every day, went the gym together every morning – and the atmosphere was so laid back and relaxed on EAU, with its young and enthusiastic workforce, that most days would just be one long laugh.

I remember early on in the job, the female consultant, who had obviously read my CV, asked me how I had ended up at East and how it compared to some of the bigger hospitals I had worked in. She was genuinely surprised when I informed her that it was the safest I had ever felt whilst working as a doctor. She couldn't believe it, but at that time, it genuinely was. We had the odd dodgy locum, who would come and go, but on the whole, we had excellent junior doctors. Most of the SHOs had been doctors for over five years and, as a result, were very experienced, and two of the registrars had been qualified for over twenty years, whilst most of the others had well over ten years under their belts. Added into the mix were us Spice Boys, who despite our relative inexperience, occasionally casual nature, and tendency to joke around, were actually very good doctors. We had all been trained in and had worked in proper centres of excellence, and we were knowledgeable, clinically excellent, and loved nothing more than a good arrest. We hit the ground running and fit in immediately, proving to be very popular members of the team.

But alas, all good things must come to an end, and after Christmas, Mark and Tim went off on their travels, and life was never quite the same for me again. I miss those glory days, and despite us talking about getting the band back together on several occasions, it never happened. I stayed at East for several years. Following their travels, Mark went to work in London for a year before taking a training post in Manchester, whilst Tim took up a labouring job in Australia – I shit you not – before realising how hard life can be in the real world and accepting a GP training placement back home in Manchester. I have unfortunately lost contact with Tim, but still check in with Mark, now and again, to see how he's getting on.

After two thirds of the Spice Boys deserted the band, it all became much more of a chore because I now travelled back and forth to Liverpool a lot more frequently. It unfortunately coincided with a monumental shift in the world of locum medicine as the UK government implemented a new system called IR35, which rightly or wrongly changed the rules for locum doctors and, added to the uncertainty of the upcoming Brexit, led to a mass exodus of overseas doctors and a gradual spiral into the devastation of the post-COVID healthcare service in which we work today. But all that was still a long way off, back then.

Bumped Up

I had been an SHO for just eight months, when my consultant first suggested I step up to become a registrar. The landscape had shifted monumentally with the introduction of IR35, and locums were looking to the future, many long-termers simply calling it a day, whilst others returned home or decided to move to countries that were financially more appealing. All of a sudden, doctors from India and Pakistan were looking toward Australia, America, Canada, and the Middle East as much better options than the UK. Most European doctors had one eye on Brexit and were hatching escape plots, and a lot of career registrars had decided to finally take that step up to consultant as a way to bridge the lost wages.

Two such doctors looking to advance into consultant roles were our very own night registrars, who had both been qualified for well over twenty years, and had worked in our hospital for more than ten of those years. Within a couple of months of IR35, one had taken a job as a consultant down south, which was actually something of a Hobson's choice, because he was being investigated by the trust and local police for fraud, as a result of "overclaiming" hours, whilst the other had stepped up in our hospital as an elderly medicine consultant. This left two big holes in the night-shift registrar rota, and endless opportunities for an opportunist like myself. Our consultants had decided to look more closely at their own SHOs for potential step-up candidates, and despite being one of the least experienced, I found myself top of that list.

After discussing it with my wife, we decided I would do it, as it not only meant a massive step up in responsibility but also in wages. I had worked a lot with the night team over the past eight months, and I had no doubt I could fill those boots – despite being massively inferior in experience, I was by no means inferior as a doctor.

I have a very good memory for detail, but for some reason, probably PTSD related, I can't actually remember my first registrar night shift. I can't remember driving in or how I felt about the situation. I remember the first month as a blurred period of time rather than individual nights. I remember genuinely believing I was cursed as I stumbled from one disastrous shift to the next, increasingly stretched to my physical and emotional limits.

Around this time, we had lost a lot of doctors and were heavily reliant on the remaining reduced number of staff, boosted by junior ANPs, most in the first year of training due to a massive internal recruitment process in response to the loss of said doctors and the increasing difficulty in recruiting medics of any real experience or quality. This meant we were noticing a significantly increased workload on the night shift as EAU stopped working like the well-oiled machine it had once been. Patients were not being reviewed in a timely manner during the day, so we arrived onto a battlefield most nights.

Discharges were also becoming delayed, and beds remained blocked for longer, putting extra pressure on A&E where patients waiting for beds in our ward were backed up, resulting in an increased workload for the A&E nurses who were having to manage patients requiring a very specific type of specialist nursing care, usually provided by medical nurses on the wards. This type of care required a different skill set to that of an emergency nurse, which, in turn, led to us receiving a higher number of deteriorating and sicker patients and so resulted in more transfers to HDU and ITU.

Added into this perfect storm, the medical wards were also struggling to cover shifts, meaning patients all across the hospital were not only having discharges delayed but were not being reviewed in a timely manner, so they were "going off" overnight in disproportionate numbers. The wards were also heavily relying on ANPs to cover doctors' shifts, and as a result, the hospital was actively recruiting the best and most experienced nurses from across the wards into the new role, essentially weakening their own workforce, as most of the senior nurses were replaced all at once by a very junior and inexperienced nursing force. In turn, this meant patients were often deteriorating for much longer before the signs were picked up by the relatively junior nurses, signs that would have been quickly pounced on by the older heads who had once made up the main body of the ward sisters, but who were now being employed as very green and cheap alternatives to doctors.

It was a disaster in the making, and this was the environment in which I started out life as a medical registrar. My role was to liaise with A&E and discuss all medical referrals, supervise the SHO who would be based in EAU (front of house) and who would be responsible for clerking in any new patients who had been accepted overnight by myself, supported by two ANPs, after they had walked around the wards (back-of-house) and picked up the F1-type jobs of prescribing and replacing cannulas etc. I also supervised these two ANPs, providing support for any difficult patients and reviewing any patient with a MEWS score of seven and over. I also led the arrest team with the support of the on-call anaesthetist, and the critical care outreach (CCO) nurse who would manage her own job list that had been handed over by her colleague covering the day shift and would also assist me with the sickest of patients. In addition, I was expected to review any patient who required assessment for non-invasive ventilation (NIV), admission to CCU, HDU, or ITU. And lowest down the priority list, I was expected to help out with the clerkings if we were being overwhelmed. Finally, I had to write the handover list, meaning I had to be aware of the clinical condition of every single patient on EAU in order to hand this information over at the morning meeting.

My first set of nights were an absolute disaster. In fact, I would go so far as to say the whole first month was an absolute disaster. It was a baptism of fire, and everything that could go wrong did go wrong. For the first time in my career, I really started to doubt myself, and I found myself wondering if I had bitten off more than I could chew. I was walking from arrest to arrest, and we were losing quite a few patients. I was getting very little support from the anaesthetist and was meeting nothing but resistance when attempting to admit patients to ITU. I felt I was being continually tested by the ANPs, who were usually very senior nurses and, as such, had been around the block a fair few times and knew how to handle a young upstart registrar like myself. They would walk the wards in pairs for company and spend hours doing the jobs that most decent F1s could knock out in minutes. They would often linger on the wards, chewing the cud with their former colleagues whilst drinking tea and neglecting the clerkings, causing them to quickly stack up and overwhelm the SHO. This meant I was spending a lot of my time whittling down the list of clerkings, often walking straight from an arrest to EAU and getting stuck in.

Added to this chaos, the A&E staff sensed new blood and began referring completely inappropriate patients, slipping them in between arrests, so that I couldn't question the referring doctor thoroughly enough, just accepting the patient in order to save time and get back to my sick patient. But this attempt to save time was having the negative effect of adding a lot of extra work to our already unbearable workload.

Around three weeks into the job, it all came to a head, and I decided it was make or break time. I had been handed over the now customary six patients to clerk, which meant the SHO was going to need help tonight, unless we had a miraculously quiet A&E department, which was highly unlikely. I was asked by hospital management, via the bed manager, if I could do a "quick" ward round for "potential step downs" on CCU to free up beds, as there were no CCU, HDU, or ITU beds available in the hospital. I was about an hour into the shift when an arrest call went out over the bleep system, for one of the elderly medicine wards, which were located literally as far away from where I was currently standing as it was possible to be. I jogged from CCU and bumped into the CCO nurse, who was also from Liverpool, and we went up together.

The two ANPs were in attendance, looking busy but not really getting anywhere, whilst one of the ward nurses was performing CPR. I shouted in the direction of a group of health care assistants, "Could someone please get me the patient's notes?" and asked one of the ANPs to rotate on the chest with the fatiguing ward nurse whilst the other took on the role of record-keeper. The CCO nurse waltzed straight into the thick of the action without any prompting and set up the defibrillator, whilst I took control of the airway.

Quickly scanning the medical notes whilst the record-keeper held them open under my nose and helpfully turned the pages as I tried my best to keep a good seal on the face mask, I decided that this patient really should not have been for resuscitation, as he was in his late eighties, had multiple significant medical comorbidities, and was very frail – testified by the space his collapsed and fractured ribcage had once occupied prior to us starting the chest compressions. I asked the CCO nurse, Les, what rhythm was showing on the defib as we took a brief pause in the compressions.

"PEA," she informed me, after digging her fingers into the patient's groin to feel for a femoral pulse whilst I simultaneously felt for one in the neck with my spare hand, essentially meaning that the electrical activity shown on the monitor should be resulting in a pulse, but wasn't. This often has a poor outcome, even in younger patients, but in an elderly man like this, who is clearly not responding to resuscitation, it is almost always associated with a very poor outcome.

After several minutes of heroics and a couple of minijets (pre-filled syringes) of adrenaline, I solemnly informed the team it was my opinion that we should stop CPR and asked what they thought. It was unanimous, and I called it, instantly leaving the room and phoning the patient's wife to inform her of what had just happened. I completed my call and was sat at the nursing station writing up the events of the arrest in the clinical notes when the anaesthetist casually strolled past me, with not a care in the world. It really was the straw that broke the camel's back.

I sprung to my feet and, struggling to keep my cool, asked, a bit louder than intended, "Where have you been? The call went out twenty minutes ago."

To which he casually replied, "I went to the wrong ward," without even glancing in my direction as he continued straight past me and into the now dead patient's room, asking Les what had happened as he entered. I immediately followed him into the room and informed him in no uncertain terms that he should be asking me what had happened as I had led the arrest, in his absence. I also informed him of what I thought of him turning up twenty minutes late. He attempted to snap back, but seeing I was more than ready for this argument, he wisely decided against it.

The frustration of the last few weeks had caught up with me, and I'd had enough. I was drawing a line in the sand and taking no more of this nonsense. I had torn him to shreds, and I had done it publicly to let the ANPs and the CCO know things were going to change from now on. They had been feeling me out, and I had tried to be nice. I had tried to make friends and influence people, but they were all about to find out I was no pushover.

I walked out the room and Les followed. "Fancy a coffee?" she asked.

I nodded, and we slowly walked back down the long corridor that led from the Victorian half of the hospital to the new half, chatting as we went, the arrest we had just attended scrubbed from our minds already. As we walked through the large automatic double doors of EAU, we were immediately accosted by a young nurse who looked in a mild state of panic. She blurted out, a little too quickly, "Lee, will you have a look at this patient? He doesn't look very well," clearly relieved to have found someone she could hand over the burden of responsibility to.

We turned immediately left into the first bay off the corridor, directly opposite the reception desk, and instantly noted a youngish male, who looked to be in his early forties, sitting up and clutching at his chest whilst he struggled to catch breath. Immediately, I could clearly see he had a navy-blue hue to his lips and surrounding skin, and a cursory glance at the monitor next to his bed showed his oxygen saturations to be in the sixties, which to the non-medics amongst you is low enough to start seriously worrying. I tersely shouted at the nurse to put out an arrest call, whilst Les ran to get the crash trolly and I cranked the patient's oxygen up to the maximum. He was obviously struggling as I went through the ABC approach and Les hooked him up to the defibrillator.

After a couple of minutes, I shouted, "Where's that fucking anaesthetist?" just as he entered the bay, looking a little flustered. He slowly walked up to the patient and, after what seemed an age, said, "He looks like he's breathing effectively."

I snapped back, "His O_2 sats are in the eighties on fifteen litres of oxygen, and he's fucking navy-blue."

Les immediately piped in with, "And he's forty-four years of age."

"What do you want me to do?" the anaesthetist asked.

"Your fucking job," I replied, glaring at him.

That's when Les snapped and stormed out of the bay. The anaesthetist had just started his dithering assessment of the patient when she returned and said, "Come on, I've spoken to the anaesthetic consultant and got him a bed."

We quickly wheeled the patient around to ITU, utilising that clever L-shaped corridor to great effect, and never saw him again. Although, I did hear he had sadly passed away a couple of days later after being treated for a massive clot on his lungs. I'm not insinuating that the elderly anaesthetic registrar on duty that night was incompetent, but in an attempt to make peace as we settled the patient onto the unit, he randomly and rather bizarrely asked me where I had been when I found out that Princess Dianna had died. I told him I had just returned from a night patrol in Bosnia when I was given the news. He nodded slowly at me – he did nothing fast – looking slightly impressed and told me he had been working in the newsagents he had owned. Things suddenly started to make sense…

From that day on, I was as thick as thieves with the CCO team. There were five of them who rotated through nights and every one of them was excellent, all very senior ex-ITU and CCU sisters. Three of them were particularly good, much better than most of the SHO doctors I worked with, and over the following months, we developed into a formidable team. In fact, at the risk of sounding big-headed, I was one hundred per cent confident we could turn any patient around, if we got to them early enough.

As the staffing levels worsened, the hospital was forced to rely even more heavily upon the ANPs, but many did not appreciate the extra responsibility, and we were losing as many nurses as we could recruit. Therefore, the decision was made, by hospital management, to cast the net further afield, and the role of advanced clinical practitioner (ACP) was introduced. Dropping the word "nurse" essentially meant the hospital could recruit anyone, including therapists (physios, OTs, etc.)

and paramedics, into the role, replacing highly skilled and experienced doctors and nurses with practitioners of varying levels of clinical experience. These ACPs were to be supported by a new influx of overseas doctors, recruited freshly from Africa, as the looming Brexit was impacting more and more on our ability to recruit and retain European doctors.

The hospital had been spiralling out of control for a while, but this latest management decision, whilst understandable, ensured East was now both a dangerous place to work and be a patient. We noticed we were dealing with a massive increase in peri-arrest and arrest situations, and it was not unusual for us to have more than one cardiac arrest a night. Everything was falling apart around us, but on the flip-side, dealing with this much acute pathology meant I was becoming better and better at my job. I was unbelievably confident at this time and would have put myself up against any medical registrar in the country. Not only had I developed into an excellent leader, but I was fast, decisive, never hesitated, and had absolutely no tolerance for fools.

Although developing a good working relationship with the CCO team had become a high priority of mine during those dangerous times, it was by no means my only priority. I had several other goals, including sorting out the day team, plugging the steady stream of inappropriate referrals coming my way via the A&E department, and attempting to gain some control over certain members of the ACP team, who were becoming a problem for both me and the clerking SHO, with the number of outstanding clerkings being handed over by the day team continuing to increase week on week. To be fair, we had some excellent ACPs who had been very senior nurses and who were hard-working and essential to keeping the hospital afloat during those dark days, but the skill mix was variable to say the least.

Each new referral made by the A&E doctors to the med reg needs a medical clerking, which involves the completion of an admission document, including a thorough history and assessment, diagnosis, management plan and, ideally, a medication reconciliation, and the completion of a drug chart. This takes a good SHO anywhere from half an hour to an hour to complete, depending on the complexity of the patient, but can take hours if the patient requires admission to a higher level of care.

All of the patients referred to the day registrar should ideally be distributed amongst the much greater workforce that is present during daylight hours and clerked before the night team arrives to ensure they are starting with a clean slate. However, it's inevitable that some patients referred around the handover period will be missed. In my SHO days, it was normal to have one or two patients handed over. This increased to around six in my early registrar days, as staffing levels began to be negatively affected by IR35 and the looming threat of Brexit, but by the time the influx of inexperienced African doctors combined with the over-reliance on unqualified ACPs, the numbers had increased to around twelve each night.

Twelve clerkings could equate to twelve hours, without a break, essentially the entire length of the night shift, which was a lot of work to start off a night with, and it could be a lot worse. It certainly was not unheard of to have twenty handed over, which completely hamstrung the night team, especially if the ACPs were sitting back-of-house drinking tea, and I was away half the night dealing with sick patients, leaving a single SHO working their way through twenty odd patients, and that was before the night referrals had even started to come in.

Obviously, this was unsustainable, so I decided to start the fight back. My first tactic was to kick up as much fuss as possible during handover, deliberately making it uncomfortable for the day doctors by openly questioning their productivity and asking how many patients they had clerked and at what time they had seen their last patient. As awkward as this made it for everyone present in that meeting, and as much of an arsehole as it made me look, it was effective, and the numbers gradually started to reduce. I combined this tactic with being an absolute nightmare referral option for the A&E doctors.

Don't get me wrong, if a patient was sick, I was there in a flash and would get stuck in straight away with no questions asked. But if another doctor wanted to palm me off with a dodgy referral then I was going to make them work for it, and by God, did I make them work hard. This may not have endeared me to the A&E doctors, but again, it was effective. As any experienced medical registrar knows only too well, an

A&E patient's journey takes the path of least resistance, and I simply made it much easier for a doctor to do the extra bit of work necessary to get a patient home than to inappropriately refer to me.

I managed to gradually stem the tide over the next eighteen months, and although I readily acknowledge I could be difficult to work with at this time, to say the least, I also know, for a fact, that the vast majority of my colleagues would have wanted no other doctor to be the one on call when the shit hit the fan, no matter how much of a pain in the arse I could be. We would often have nurses and other staff members phoning EAU to check if I was on duty before deciding whether they would risk admitting their relative to East or embark on the hour-long journey inland to attend our much better staffed and serviced sister hospital.

I could handle anything that was thrown at me during this time, the more the better. I was absolutely thriving, but I was taking on far too much responsibility, as I was still relatively junior, and I was becoming obsessed with work. I never stopped whilst I was there, and I never stopped thinking about it when I wasn't. I suppose I had developed a form of Stockholm syndrome. I was on a one-man mission to save the hospital. And then it happened, after fifteen years of trying for another baby, my wife was pregnant with twins, and I instantly knew my time at East had come to an end.

It was with a heavy heart but an enormous sense of relief that I handed in my notice. Although I couldn't see it at the time, I had given everything I had to give and was physically and mentally exhausted, stretched to my very limit, and I badly needed a break from that pressure cooker environment. I accepted a combined acute medical/acute stroke job in a hospital located in deepest darkest South Wales, which although very busy – being the national stroke centre – was so well staffed with trainee doctors that there were always more than enough bodies to distribute an even share of the workload, no matter how much of it there was.

I settled in quickly, revelling in the more supportive and relaxed atmosphere of the large teaching hospital, nestled amongst the beautiful green valleys of Cymru. Quickly becoming a popular and key member of the team, I was offered a twelve-month rolling contract by the senior stroke consultant. This would not only provide stability but would also provide a route to completion of training, as he offered to support me through the CESR programme, which is basically an alternate pathway to becoming a legitimate consultant and having my name added to the specialist register – the dream ticket, meaning I could work anywhere in the world, if I so desired.

I informed him I would consider the offer over the weekend and give him an answer on my return to work on Monday. I set off for home, excited by this opportunity, high on the potential of another new beginning. But this euphoria quickly dissipated when I found myself stuck in heavy traffic on the M6, arriving well over six hours after setting off, and I knew then that I could not commit to South Wales whilst my wife was pregnant. I could not risk her going into labour whilst I was potentially six hours away.

So, with regret, I turned down the offer and decided to change tactics by picking up ad-hoc shifts, allowing me to remain flexible with minimal commitment to any trust or organisation. It allowed me total freedom, and again, I was excited, this time by the prospect of becoming a lone ranger. However, the best laid plans of mice and men oft go astray, and I eventually found myself back at East. And somehow, in the few short months I had been away, things had managed to get even worse.

The Other Side of the Fence

This is the chapter I have been dreading writing the most. I've put it off for as long as possible, but now is the time.

We had been desperately trying to provide a sibling for our son for well over fifteen years, and due to a rather unfortunate set of circumstances, including extreme endometriosis, multiple ectopic pregnancies, and the surgical removal of one fallopian tube, I had started to believe it wasn't going to happen for us.

We had burned through all of our savings and every penny we could borrow on a combination of redeveloping our Victorian terraced house and years of ongoing fertility treatment, and we had a half-finished house and three failed attempts at IVF to show for it. But by a stroke of luck, we still had two embryos sitting in a freezer somewhere in Liverpool Women's Hospital and the possibility of getting them both implanted for the princely sum of £1,500. We decided to put ourselves through the emotional wringer one last time, and after much deliberation and scraping together the necessary cash, we decided to have both embryos implanted.

After the implantation, one anxiety-riddled day followed another, until D-day finally arrived, and I once again found myself in the rather undignified setting of a cramped bathroom, watching my wife hesitantly urinating on a white plastic stick. We were both nervous and holding our breath as we watched the urine slowly spread up the litmus-like paper, revealing two little red lines perfectly contained between the test and positive notches situated at either end of the tiny viewing window that housed the paper. Pregnant. We stared at the test for several seconds in silent ecstasy, not daring to believe. We had been in this situation many times before, and knew only too well that what can go wrong, often does.

We attended the first scan and, unbelievably, both embryos had taken. This was alien territory. Despite our initial caution, we were ecstatic, spending weeks on end fantasising about the amazing life our little twinnies were going to have. We had picked out a double pram and even had matching names; it was a truly glorious period. I had let my guard down. After losing faith many years before, I was actually allowing myself to believe, and then… bang.

Twin Two had stopped progressing, and eventually, the heart stopped beating. All that hope, all that joy and belief was gone. I was back in familiar territory, filled with deep uncertainty and anxiety. I had opened myself up to pain and disappointment, and I felt foolish. The scab formed from all the years of false hope had fallen away to reveal the open festering wound that lay below. I pushed it all deep down and stopped myself from feeling. I blocked it out as well as I could and spent the next twenty odd weeks trying to prepare myself for the bad news I knew was coming.

But it never came. Twin One (T1) had continued to progress and was positioned lowest in the uterus, essentially blocking the exit for Twin Two (T2). As a result, the pregnancy continued without being spontaneously aborted – as it would have been if T2 had been in a position to make their way out through the cervix so pulling the rug out from under T1 and leading to a total abortion of all foetal products. As time passed, T2 became enveloped and incorporated into the placenta of T1. I cautiously allowed myself to believe this was really going to happen, and all the years of disappointment would finally be over. But before we all get carried away and start crying into our hankies and slapping me on the back, I am going to skip forward to just under six weeks after the delivery.

The day was Thursday, 23 November 2017, the place, Liverpool, England, and I had just flown in from Seville where I had, only the day before, watched my beloved Liverpool Football Club blow a 3–0 half-time lead at the Estadio Ramón Sánchez Pizjuán, to draw 3–3 with

Sevilla. My wife called me up to the bedroom as soon as she heard me drag my hungover and physically exhausted arse through the front door to tell me she was severely concerned about the physical condition of our tiny baby daughter, who had been born less than six weeks previously. She asked me to check her out. I immediately noticed something was wrong, the three-day break having allowed me to see her through fresh eyes, and I'm not going to lie, I was pretty freaked out by what I was seeing.

Our beautiful daughter had been born on the morning of 12 October 2017, after a long labour that had initially started on the afternoon of the eleventh and continued through the night, lasting around four seasons of the UK comedy, *Peep Show*. It sounds crazy, and admittedly I wasn't the one attempting to push a melon-sized object out of my privates all night, but it really was a pleasant experience. It was so relaxing watching comedy and just enjoying the rare opportunity to spend some time together… that was until dawn approached and the multiple tricks employed by the midwives to coax out our little angel finally started to work their magic.

My wife had handled the long night like a trooper, with the minimum of fuss, but eventually, she succumbed to the excruciating pain that the gas and air was no longer touching, and after holding out for as long as she possibly could, she requested diamorphine, which unbeknownst to her, as our son had been born within an hour of onset of labour, she was very sensitive to. She was given the opioid at seven centimetres dilated, with the baby looking in no rush to see the outside world. However, no sooner had the effect hit her, leaving her looking like a character from the nineties film *Trainspotting*, then our little cherub unexpectedly decided to make a break for freedom.

Suddenly, a crown of jet-black hair emerged, and with a bit more coercion and one last big push, the tiniest and skinniest little human being I could ever have imagined was pulled roughly out and dangled upside down in front of me. Time stood still whilst the room remained silent, worryingly silent. I stood rigid and paralyzed with fear, a sudden wave of shame and embarrassment washing over me. *What a fucking idiot*. I had allowed myself to believe again. I had opened myself up to hope again… And then she opened her eyes, and she looked at me, emitting the quietest little cry, barely audible in the large room, but the most beautiful sound I had ever heard in my whole life. I broke down in tears of pure joy and relief, as the midwife told me our baby was safe and she was a girl – I think I may have had just about enough medical training to have worked that out for myself, but I let it slide – before thrusting her into my arms. I looked into her little almond-shaped, navy-blue, alien-like eyes, and she looked back at me calmly and inquisitively, and I was instantly and deeply in love.

I slyly wiped the tears from my cheeks with the sleeve of my T-shirt, suddenly aware of our surroundings and ashamed of the public display of weakness. I turned to congratulate my long-suffering wife, who smiled back at me dozily with heavy eyes, as I held up our daughter, our little miracle. However, one look was enough to tell me my wife was seriously sedated, which meant I was all alone. The midwife quickly took my daughter from my cradling arms to give her a quick once over, weigh her and then wrap her in a lilac hospital blanket, before almost tossing her back to me and rushing off to handover.

My daughter looked so small and delicate in my arms that I don't mind admitting I was absolutely terrified. I had been through some shit in my life, and I had faced some pretty harrowing situations, but this topped them all. I held her lightly, like the most fragile of glass ornaments, petrified of damaging her. She was by far the smallest baby I had ever held in my arms. I sat in silence and stared at her beautiful little face, held her tiny hand, stroked her translucent doll-like fingers, fingers that seemed too small to belong to a real human, and I felt a knot of apprehension deep in my stomach. I wished my wife was present enough to tell me what to do, how to act, how to feel.

My seventeen-year-old son suddenly entered the room, and I have never been more relieved to see him. I gladly handed over this precious, tightly bound bundle, and we both just sat and stared at her in silence, neither of us having a clue what to do. She was very quiet and calm, almost too calm, and as the three of us just sat staring at one another, my son asked, "Is that normal? Aren't babies supposed to cry or make some noise?"

I tried to look at her through the eyes of a doctor and not a shit-scared new dad, and agreed that maybe she was unusually quiet and, thinking about it, she may have been "slightly dusky". I asked my son to quickly find a midwife, which he seemed glad to do. I got the distinct impression he was relieved to be absolved of the shared responsibility of protecting this tiny little girl.

A new midwife entered the room, older than the previous one, and gently plucked her from my arms without a word, calmly placing her on a table she had just unfolded from the wall, and simultaneously pulling the red arrest button situated just above the table.

The shrill and deafening alarm pierced the tranquillity of the room, and I instantly realised what was going on. Rooted to the spot with terror, everything seemed to slow down around me, and the world was suddenly silent as the room filled with medical staff of all designations. They shuffled about in slow motion like an old Charlie Chaplin film. A mask was placed over my daughter's perfect little bow-shaped mouth, whilst a faceless, slightly blurred figure pressed a gloved finger into her pale chest. Watching on from the sidelines, numb, in complete shock, I felt an arm wrap around my shoulders, but I didn't look to see who it was. I couldn't take my eyes from the horror unfolding before me.

It suddenly ended, people drifted away, one by one, and the baby was once again swaddled and placed in my arms. The loud buzzing in my ears confirmed my hearing had returned. And we were alone once again. I slowly looked down at my daughter, gently resting in my arms, and then looked back up at my wife, silently pleading for her to wake up and help me. She sluggishly opened her eyes and looked at me with concern before drifting off back into her own world. *Please wake up. Wake up and help me. I need help.*

We sat there, my son and I, in that dull, cool room, both terrified and desperate for our family rock to wake up. We took turns to hold my daughter. We attempted to feed her, and we watched my wife like a hawk, praying that she would wake up soon – she would know what to do. Thankfully, she eventually came round, and as soon as she was lucid enough to take care of our baby, I found an excuse to get away, to remove myself from that room as quickly as my legs could carry me. I couldn't deal with the situation. I needed to compose myself. I drove the relatively short journey home from the hospital, which took about fifteen minutes in light traffic, using the excuse of getting a shower and a change of clothes.

Standing under the hot shower, I tried to block it all out, tried not to think, just focus on the droplets of water that ran down my chest and fell to the floor like mini waterfalls. It suddenly hit me: what the hell was I doing? I had to stop feeling sorry for myself. I had to man up and be there for my family. I had an overpowering and irresistible urge to get back to the hospital, filled with panic and guilt.

I jumped out of the shower and quickly dried off in the bathroom, panic and guilt replaced by a new urgent determination, a flush of excitement, euphoria even. I needed to get back. Grabbing my phone from the shelf above the sink, I noticed six missed calls from my son. I instantly called back, but it rang out. I quickly redialled, and again, there was no answer. It hit me, the fear. I instinctively knew something was wrong as I ran, stumbling and sliding, into the bedroom and quickly dressed, falling backward and landing heavily on the bed as I thrust my hips forward and aggressively pulled up my tight jeans, before pushing my foot into my Balenciaga runners, rapidly twisting my foot forward and sideward into the snug space like my life depended on it.

I ran down the stairs, taking two at a time, and jumped the last few, landing with a heavy thud that reverberated around the empty house, before swinging open the front door and slamming it heavily after me. I pulled open the driver's door and squeezed into the tight gap behind the steering wheel, guilt, shame, and fear overwhelming me and burning deep in my stomach. *What the fuck was I thinking*? Why did I leave? I dialled again, and again, but still no answer.

I made the fifteen-minute journey in less than ten minutes and abandoned the car in the drop-off area outside the front entrance. The security guard moved toward me as though to say something, before looking into my face and stepping aside to let me pass. I ran to the lift and pressed the button – nothing. I hopped from foot to foot, before deciding to take the stairs. I sprinted up to the second floor and burst through the door and out into the corridor, quickly getting my bearings before heading to the maternity ward. I buzzed impatiently, and buzzed again. The door opened, and I headed straight to the nurses' station and blurted out my newborn daughter's name.

The midwife looked at me and paused for a second, then said, "She's been moved to NICU," which is the neonates intensive care unit. I instantly felt cold, panic flooding through my body as every worst-case scenario simultaneously tried to play in my mind, causing a traffic jam that was suddenly interrupted by my son's voice. "Dad."

I turned around. He looked worried. I asked him what had happened as we walked to NICU together. He informed me the baby had gone dusky again, and they had called the arrest team who arrived and quickly pushed an oxygen mask over her tiny face before literally running her out of the room without saying another word to either him or my now compos mentis and extremely shocked wife.

My daughter ended up staying in neonates for a few days but remained stable. After a whole raft of investigations and reviews by very senior neonatologists, it was decided the issue had been neonatal respiratory distress syndrome. She had suffered from a condition called intrauterine growth restriction, which essentially means she had grown very little from thirty-two weeks until birth and was, therefore, technically classed as a premature baby. As a result, like many prem babies, she had not produced enough surfactant in the lungs to allow her to breathe independently.

Surfactant is an oil-like substance, produced by specialist cells in the lungs, which coats the outside of the air sacks that are responsible for the exchange of oxygen and carbon dioxide. This substance increases the surface tension of the alveoli (air sacs) and stops them collapsing as the pressure rapidly changes within the lungs during the action of breathing in and out. It's a rather complicated system, but the relevant information, in this case, is that, if surfactant is not produced, it's difficult to get oxygen into the body through the lungs, hence the continued dusky episodes and respiratory arrests.

She was given antibiotics as a precaution and steroids to help mature the lungs, and after a few days of observations, we were assured she was fine and could be discharged from hospital with regular home visits by the transition care (TC) nurses. And life pretty much settled down. As the initial nerves receded, we very much enjoyed the first few weeks with our precious little miracle. My wife, however, continued with her doubts and would regularly ask me, the TC nurses, and various GPs if our daughter's breathing was normal. She was continually assured that it was perfectly fine for a prem baby and that she should stop overthinking and worrying herself about it, leave it to the professionals. But the nagging doubts persisted, and luckily, she would not let it lie, and refused to just leave it to us professionals.

And so, we found ourselves, just over five weeks later, back in the bedroom of our Victorian terraced house in Wavertree, with me having just returned from Seville, my daughter lying flat on her back, hands above a head that was bobbing side to side rhythmically, like that of a Bollywood dancer. And I had to agree with my wife – this did not look normal. Looking back at it now, I can't believe I hadn't picked up that something wasn't quite right. I suppose I had limited experience in either neonates or paediatrics, and I had blindly put my faith in the neonate consultants who I had worked with as a student and who I trusted implicitly, but I should have picked this up. Maybe I hadn't wanted to see it because I was so scared about what it could mean, the classic head-in-the-sand scenario.

First thing next morning, we found ourselves sat in a large, bright, and airy consultation room in what had once been the bank next door to the barber shop in the famous Beatles song, "Penny Lane", whilst a puzzled-looking GP tried to alleviate our concerns about the weird breathing pattern currently being displayed by our five-and-a-half-week-old baby. He listened to her chest, studied her with his head cocked to one side in the classic display of concentration, and then listened again, and after a few minutes of umm-ing and ah-ing, he suggested we take her to Alder Hey Children's Hospital. He would phone ahead and have one of the paediatricians ready to take a look at her.

We arrived and reported at reception and were quickly shown into a brightly painted triage room by a young nurse who unclipped our daughter from the portable car seat and expertly unbuttoned her onesie whilst initiating a set of observations and cheerfully engaging us in the most trivial of conversation. Suddenly becoming more serious and businesslike, she stood up mid-blood pressure reading and hastily informed us that she would "be right back". *Was that a tremor in her voice?* We looked at each other with escalating levels of concern and then simultaneously back at our daughter, just as the door burst open to reveal a team of doctors stood outside, armed and ready to go. *Fuck, not again.*

We were quickly ushered into a resus room, and our baby girl was snatched from the arms of my wife and placed in the centre of a massive bed, whilst being stripped of the last vestiges of clothing. It was all happening so fast that it didn't seem real. Just like the episode in the Women's Hospital, not even six weeks previously, time seemed to slow down as everyone buzzed around this tiny, naked human being who looked so small and lost in the middle of the hospital bed. It suddenly hit me – she was grey and mottled, almost marble-like. She was in cardiogenic shock. *How the fuck hadn't I noticed?*

Now I was scared, really scared. Not "freaked out", not "overly concerned" – I was fucking terrified. I was more scared than I had ever been in my entire life. I looked at my wife, who smiled at me and told me our little girl was in safe hands. She had faith in the doctors. I did not. I had spent a large part of my career working in cardiology, acute cardiology and acute medicine, and I knew how these situations could go down. I knew how this type of shit could pan out, and often it was not good news, often it was very bad news.

The hand of fear squeezed my guts so hard I could almost feel each icy finger as they strangled the soft loops of warm intestine. I was gone, completely gone. Panic had set in, and I didn't know what to do. I felt so helpless. I wanted to run in circles, scream, cry, pull at my hair, scratch at my face, hit something, hit someone, get out of that room. Instead, I stood paralysed, as they hooked my little angel up to a defibrillator.

A middle-aged, female A&E consultant dressed in dark-green scrubs and sporting a frizzy grey bob, whose name has long gone but whose face I will remember until my dying day, had been leading the situation until a youngish anaesthetist and an older man I recognised as a cardiologist, who was flanked by two young female doctors, entered the fray. The A&E consultant took a slight step back and seemed to notice us for the first time, instantly embracing my wife in a warm and genuine hug, before taking a step toward me. She looked into my eyes and smiled sadly, and I simply shook my head at her, incapable of finding any words.

She took my hand and asked me to follow her into a side room, where she filled a waxed paper cone with ice-cold water from the cooler and handed it to me.

"You know what's happening, don't you?" she enquired. I nodded slowly as I still couldn't speak. She asked if I was a doctor. Again, I nodded. She looked down toward the floor, her eyes filling with tears and said, "I'm so sorry."

I couldn't hold it in any longer, and I cried solidly for what must have been about a minute. I was completely inconsolable as she hugged my limp body tightly. I eventually pulled myself back together, wiped the tears from my cheeks, dabbed at my eyes with a paper towel I found in a holder above the sink, and silently walked back into the room.

I was more composed now. I was still in a state of blind panic, but I was ready to fight back, to fight for my little girl. I looked at the monitor. Her heart rate was just below three hundred as the anaesthetist struggled to place a cannula in the back of her tiny hand. I asked to look at the ECGs, which one of the young female doctors was discussing with the other. She looked up at me, glanced across toward the consultant who nodded, and hesitantly passed them across to me as I informed her I was an acute medical registrar.

"What are you thinking?" I asked.

"SVT," she replied.

"It looks more like VT," I reasoned. "Are you thinking of starting amiodarone?"

They both nervously looked toward the cardiologist again, who was standing on the periphery, just outside of the ensuing chaos. He looked at me for a second, seemed to weigh up the pros and cons of his next sentence, and then informed me they were thinking of adenosine, which is a medication used to treat SVT and has horrendous effects on the patient, often described as bringing about a sense of impending doom by some patients, or feeling like an elephant sitting on your chest by others.

I watched my beautiful little girl being poked and prodded as she just lay there silently, smiling up at the team frantically working around her like a swarm of bees, despite the discomfort she must have been in. I watched her little face change as they injected the fast-acting adenosine into the tiny cannula which had finally been placed after multiple failed attempts. I watched the fear grow in her eyes as she seemed to jump through the mattress, and my heart shattered into a million pieces. I was a completely broken man.

They repeated this process twice more, and I stood back and watched helplessly as my wife leaned across the bed and comforted our little angel both times they injected the adenosine into her veins, watched as, each time, she gave out an almost animal-like murmur and instantly looked up at my wife with a look of sheer terror on her little face, eyes pleading for protection, far too young to comprehend what was going on, but instinctively knowing we were the ones who should be stopping this from happening to her.

I turned to the consultant again and almost pleaded, "Are we thinking about amiodarone yet?"

He couldn't look at me as he slowly shook his head and quietly asked for more adenosine. We normally only give three doses; he gave five. It never worked, but she was now managing to maintain her blood pressure, which I suspect was as much from the fluids as any other medical intervention, and it was deemed safe by the arrest team to transfer her up to CCU on the cardiology ward. As the porters arrived, I quickly slipped out to the front of the hospital and phoned my consultant at East to explain I wouldn't be attending my shift later that evening, just about holding it together as she asked me if I was okay.

Our daughter was taken up to the ward and put in the green section of CCU, barely filling a corner of the cot in which she was placed by the cardiology nurse, so tiny in body, yet a giant in spirit, fighting to cling on to life with the strength of a lion. We pulled the single sofa bed up to the cot and rested our heads against the wooden slats, pushing our hands through the gaps to offer a finger of comfort for her to wrap a perfect little hand around, and there we stayed for the whole night, not daring to move or sleep, never for one minute taking our eyes off our precious little girl.

There were multiple touch-and-go episodes throughout that first night, and the on-call registrar attended our room on a couple of occasions. However, our little scrapper somehow managed to make it through Friday, and we eventually found ourselves in Saturday as the early morning daylight worked its way through the large window behind us, flooding the room with dazzling sunlight that reflected from every high-gloss finished surface in the ultra-modern room and announced the start of the ward round. I once again enquired about amiodarone, and the consultant informed us he was considering it but would like to give beta blockers a chance first – she had apparently been started on atenolol. He also said he would like to try one final dose of adenosine.

An exhausted-looking registrar suddenly appeared from behind him, as if by magic, syringe of adenosine already in hand, and my heart sank at the thought of the discomfort once again heading my daughter's way. The reg quickly and expertly injected the drug into the cannula, and my little girl once again jumped from the mattress like a startled animal, was silent for a few seconds before loudly screaming in protest. She had been pushed too far. She'd had enough of this game, and so had I.

"For fuck's sake, the adenosine is clearly not working. Can you just fucking leave her alone?" I exploded.

My wife cradled the baby lovingly in her arms, and our little girl instantly settled, leaving an awkward silence in the room as the cardiologist lingered in the doorway for a few seconds, looking guilty, slightly embarrassed, and unsure of his next move, before silently walking out, night reg in tow. The day continued in that vein, and I was becoming more frustrated and agitated as my baby's heart rate remained in the late two hundreds. I knew it couldn't stay like this – her heart would eventually fail, and I wasn't going to let that happen.

I asked to see the doctor on call, who just so happened to be a young SHO who I knew from university. I told him I'd had enough. I had spent a year working in cardiothoracics, and around thirty per cent of our post-surgical patients developed a similar rhythm to what my daughter was currently displaying, and we had always used magnesium first, followed by amiodarone, which remained my first line of treatment for my own patients. I informed him I wanted her started on it now, before she went into complete heart failure, and I was not taking no for an answer. If the boss had a problem, then he should tell him to come down and speak to me. He informed me he would phone the consultant and discuss it with him. Around fifteen minutes later, a nurse walked into our funky lime-green room with a bag of amiodarone infusion in her hand.

For the first time since Friday morning, I started to feel some level of control. It was a huge relief, but not as much of a relief as when I watched the heart rate start to drop down on the monitor, first to the low two hundreds, then the late one nineties, one eighties, and then, bang, it was in the one thirties and forties, which is where it stayed throughout the rest of the evening and well into the night.

Sunday arrived, as did our dithering consultant, completing his final ward round of the on-call weekend. He was accompanied into our room by one of the female doctors who had been present on the Friday, at the start of all this insanity, and my SHO friend. He never looked at me once, kept his eyes focused straight ahead on the monitor, exclaimed to his entourage, "That is better, much better," and turned to walk out. Pausing in the doorway, he raised his voice slightly to ensure we could clearly hear him and said to the female doctor, "Maybe we should have tried amiodarone earlier," and then he was gone.

I never saw him again, and still haven't to this day, but from Monday, we were handed over to the young electrophysiology (EP) cardiology consultant, who was absolutely amazing throughout the rest of our journey. He explained that my daughter had a condition called junctional ectopic tachycardia (JET) which meant her heart was beating from the middle, and not from the SA node at the top, like a normal heart. He explained that, if we could keep her heart rate down with the amiodarone, then she would have around a thirty per cent chance of making it to her first birthday, and if she made it to her first birthday, she would have a further thirty per cent chance of eventually developing a normal rhythm, though it was likely she would require amiodarone for the rest of her life.

I already knew this information following a quick Google search the previous Saturday night, but I had not shared it or allowed myself to face up to the reality of the situation until that moment. I was crushed. My wife, on the other hand, appeared relieved. Astonished, I looked into her eyes, and I knew she genuinely believed, one hundred per cent, our daughter would grow out of this condition. She would, without doubt, be one of the thirty per cent who survived to one year of age and who then grew out of JET. It wasn't an act; it wasn't a show of bravado – she genuinely believed it. I did not have my wife's faith or her mental strength, and I set out on a downward spiral that would take me dangerously close to oblivion.

My daughter was back home within a week, but I never fully left that hospital.

The Wilderness Year

I found the last chapter very difficult to write. It brought back memories I've tried to avoid over the last few years, and it took me to a place I never wanted to return to. It was an episode in my life that has undoubtedly changed me as a person and was extremely stressful for me and my family to live through. The feelings associated with this time in my life and the time that follows in this chapter are particularly difficult to commit to print, because by writing them down and publishing them, I am creating an indelible record of my spiral into darkness and the deterioration of my mental health in the year following my daughter's diagnosis, which exposes my vulnerability and lays open my weakness to a wider audience than those trusted few, including people who may know me personally. If I'm completely honest, I find it both uncomfortable and embarrassing to allow people to see me in that light.

Where I come from, being "weak" was frowned upon. Growing up in Liverpool, any sign of weakness would be pounced upon as something to be exploited. You certainly didn't talk openly about your feelings, not unless you wanted your sexuality and manhood seriously questioned and ridiculed. The military was a very similar environment. Right from the start, we were reliably informed that pain was simply "weakness leaving the body", and the admission of pain, whether it be mental or physical, would mark us out as weak, and weakness would not be tolerated. It would be punished, either personally or, worse, collectively.

As unlikely as this probably sounds, considering how much time I have spent telling you my feelings about the events documented in this book, I'm usually a very private person, and I don't often talk about my problems. I tend to keep things to myself, bottling them up, locking them away, and rightly or wrongly, this is the way that I have always handled my emotions. It's probably not the wisest way to handle them, as I'm sure my wife will readily attest, but I have always dealt with things in my own way. It is what makes it particularly difficult for me to open up about the feelings I experienced during the aftermath of my daughter's hospitalisation. My fragile mental health and vulnerability during this period in my life is hard for me to admit. It's hard to admit that, as a man, I was weak… I *am* weak.

The thought of people I know – my family, friends, and colleagues – reading this chapter is extremely uncomfortable for me. I have always prided myself on being such a strong person. It really goes against the grain to admit I may not be as tough, or as resilient, as I portray. It's just not who I am. But something changed in me on that day my daughter was diagnosed with JET, living with the realistic high possibility her heart could go into an unusual rhythm at literally any moment, day or night, causing her to go into cardiac arrest and die… I was no longer the confident, positive, happy-go-lucky person I had always been. All of a sudden, I was anxious and on edge all the time, frightened. I felt very little happiness or joy. I became introverted, hiding away, a shell of the man I had been previously. I may have looked the same on the outside, but inside, I was empty and hollow.

In retrospect, even before my daughter's illness, my mental health had started to suffer from the pressure. Becoming a registrar and working a rota of permanent nights, away from home and separated from my family, coupled with the devastating effects on staffing levels of IR 35 and Brexit, had been slowly but surely taking its toll, undermining my mental and emotional resilience.

The lack of staff and over-reliance on career locums and foreign doctors, who were often new to the UK and our way of working, meant patients were not receiving the same level of care throughout the day that they once had. So, by the time I came on shift of a night, many of our patients would either not have been seen by a medical doctor at all or have only received the obligatory bag of IV fluid and stat dose of Tazocin whilst in A&E, which may have been many hours before handover. Even most of those who *had* been reviewed had only been seen by a relatively inexperienced doctor and would then be lost in the endless list of jobs, review of sickies, and new patients to clerk, that would inevitably have been handed over by the day team. This had all resulted in a sharp increase in my workload, which, rather than improving on my return to East, had only got worse. Added to this complete shitstorm had been the loss of one twin and the non-progression of the other, making the long-awaited pregnancy as stressful as humanly possible. All of this had left me in a state of permanent uncertainty and anxiety, but I had been managing, just about, to hold it all together… until we got my daughter's JET diagnosis. That's when it changed.

I was still the joker in work, still laughed my way through night shifts, always quick with a witty anecdote or a sarcastic put-down, and I was still just as good at my job. In fact, I was getting better by the day thanks to all the practice I was getting in peri-arrest and arrest situations. I think I hid my problems pretty well, at first. I glided effortlessly across the surface, but below, I was frantically paddling away, trying to hold everything together, struggling badly.

This manifested initially in the guise of poor sleep. I just couldn't sleep when I was back home. I was terrified of missing some change in my daughter's condition and would lie awake all night watching her like a hawk, checking she was still breathing, leaning across to check her pulse at the wrist every hour or so. Even when I did sleep, I was plagued by nightmares of waking up in the morning and finding her in the cot she slept in next to my side of the bed, cold and stiff. I lived in a constant state of fear, bordering on terror, and could not enjoy or take normal parental pleasure in being around my daughter.

My wife was so much braver, more positive and philosophical. She always believed our little girl would pull through, that she would be one of the thirty per cent who completely outgrew her condition. My wife's attitude was: even if something bad did happen, at least we would have had the pleasure of being her parents, no matter how short that time might have been. I tried to adopt this attitude, but I couldn't, and after a few months of persistent mental torture, I had become a ghost, a mere shadow of the person I had been.

My outlook was bleak. I was obsessed with my own mortality, continually plagued by dark thoughts – initially, once or twice a day but escalating rapidly. My answer was to just push my problems deeper down inside and throw myself wholeheartedly into my job. I became distant from my family, and I put everything I had into East. It was an escape from the reality of my home life. Everything was spiralling out of control at the hospital. The staffing levels were critically low, and as a result, I walked into a war zone every night, facing arrest after arrest. It was taking its toll on everyone, except me. I was absolutely thriving, throwing myself into it with vigour.

The only time I could think clearly and push away the dark thoughts and horrendous images that tortured me for most of my waking hours, only to return and torture me some more in my sleep, was during an arrest. I could be confident, decisive, brave, and good at something again for that brief period of time, no longer the terrified little boy who couldn't sleep for fear of nightmares. I was a man again. I was me, the whole me, not the ghostly shell. But I was becoming progressively more detached.

I had always been able to shake off a shift and remove myself from whatever clinical situation may be unfolding around me, but this was different. The curse of human emotion barely touched me anymore. I was becoming a machine – cool, calm, and collected. I was unshakeable, unfazable. I could walk from one arrest, straight to another, and did exactly that, on several occasions. There were exceptions, some of which I will highlight in later chapters of this book, but it had become very rare for me to give the patient a second thought or put myself in their situation. Dealing with an unwell patient had become nothing more than a way for me to distract my mind from the perpetual torture, a brief period of respite, a tantalising connection to the person I had once been.

I could recall observations, tell you exactly what the blood gas had shown, how much adrenaline we had given, how many shocks, and the precise time at which I had called the arrest, but I could not for the life of me tell you the patient's name. I could tell you who was the duty anaesthetist, and I could recall the argument I'd had trying to get the patient into ITU, word for word, but I couldn't tell you what the patient looked like. I had lost all interest in such trivial details.

I would walk away from the mind-numbingly monotonous morning handover at the end of each night shift, jump straight into the new white BMW 4 Series, and feel nothing at all as I sank deep into the soft leather seat and blasted Gerry Cinnamon at full volume all the way back to my shared house. I could have just witnessed the most unimaginable human tragedy, but I would be completely unmoved. I would do this for weeks on end, feeling absolutely nothing, nada… apart from the gut-wrenching fear of going back home. The fear of finding my daughter, cold and lifeless, in the cot next to my bed. The fear of falling asleep and missing the signs that she was just about to deteriorate. Those fears were always lurking in the deepest recesses, crouching in a dark corner of the hospital room, just out of the light, waiting to pounce on me as I walked away from yet another arrest.

I was supposed to work twelve-and-a-half-hour shifts each Monday to Thursday night, from nine in the evening until nine thirty in the morning, and then drive straight back to Liverpool on Friday morning, following my last night shift – air-conditioning and music turned up to maximum, a strategic stop at Lancaster services for a double espresso, followed by some intermittent face-slapping from Charnock Richard onward to get me over the finish line. But I would happily volunteer to do extra shifts over the weekend, using the excuse we were struggling for cover to justify it, working myself to exhaustion with eleven consecutive nights, mission accomplished as I took a red-hot shower to wash away the chaos of each shift before collapsing into bed and instantly falling into a deep, black, dreamless sleep, free from the nightmares I suffered at home.

I had taken to the habit of staying in bed constantly whilst away from home. I moved out of the shared house and into halls-of-residence-style accommodation. I stopped training in the gym. I stopped running. I even stopped attending the canteen or halls restaurant for meals and would buy the same food every single night, existing on a diet of pre-made chicken and stuffing sandwiches from Morrisons, pot of pomegranate seeds, protein yoghurt, large bag of roasted peanuts, and litres of strong coffee. I mixed with no one outside of work and did absolutely nothing other than sleep and obsessively watch series after series on Netflix from the safety of my bed.

I continued to be plagued by dark thoughts. My mood was black. My outlook was black. I felt as though I was wrapped in a heavy veil of black, swimming in a vat of black oil, struggling, but somehow managing to just about keep my head above the surface. I had started to believe my family might be better off without me. As a committed atheist, I had never been comfortable with the idea of death, but suddenly, it held no fear for me at all. I almost welcomed the prospect. I had a good life insurance policy, and with our ongoing debts and a house renovation that still required completion, I convinced myself my death would be a blessed relief and probably the best outcome for all involved.

I was suffering from extreme emotional lability and could swing from a cold and distant disposition, with absolutely no empathy whatsoever, to being inconsolable over Michael Scott moving to Colorado. This escalated to the point where I was waking up most days I was away from home in tears. I would actually sob my heart out from a combination of self-loathing and self-pity. I just couldn't deal with the emotions I was going through at the time. I was either avoiding my family and immersing myself in chaos and death at work or self-medicating by numbing myself with alcohol at home. I would arrive back in Liverpool and drink constantly from the moment I arrived until the night before I had to leave for East. Drinking myself into oblivion had become the only way I could achieve nightmare-free sleep.

I was thoroughly miserable and probably not much fun to be around for my family or work colleagues. I thought about suicide incessantly, fantasised about how I would do it. I had a slow puncture in one of my car's tyres, and I deliberately didn't get it fixed for months. I would let it go flat and then pump it up before setting off for home, and I would drive as fast as I could back to Liverpool, flooring the car and often reaching speeds of up to 140 mph. I was just waiting for the tyre to blow out, imagining losing control, the car swerving across the motorway and hitting a tree, the deafening impact, the split-second explosion of pain as my organs exited my body and disintegrated on the dashboard… and that would be it. Nothingness, blessed peace, and my family would be set for life with the insurance money. But it never did blow out, my family never got their pay out, and I continued to live in misery, persecuted by the ongoing dark thoughts.

I had compensated well at work, initially, but the mood swings started to affect my working relationships. I was stretched to the limit and hurtling toward full-scale emotional burnout. I was regularly losing my cool as my temper got quicker. I would start a run of night shifts my normal amiable self, but as the shifts progressed, the mask of normality would slip, and I would become pedantic, patronising, aggressive, and angry, falling out with everyone and deliberately picking the pettiest fights with the emergency department doctors and my own medical team. Then I'd go home to Liverpool and drink myself into oblivion, only to return and start the cycle all over again.

I felt like an alien, no longer a part of the human race, and I found colleagues and friends nothing more than an annoyance. I felt no desire to be around people. I became a loner and kept my circle very tight. However, as much as I was unravelling, I continued to excel in my work. I remained focused, knowing that the only time I could feel remotely like the previous version of myself was when dealing with a sick patient. I would suddenly come alive with this almost euphoric high, my humour would return, and for a brief time, I was me again.

I forged a closer working relationship with the CCO team as I began to lose trust in, and was probably pretty obnoxious to, everyone else around me. I felt invincible, as though I could face any situation. As long as I had a CCO with me, I knew we could turn anyone around. We didn't need any other help. I had an extremely delicate relationship with the on-call anaesthetists who were often the barrier to getting my patients onto ITU, but I fought tooth and nail and usually got my own way, as even the most workshy anaesthetic registrar – and there was certainly a few of them at East – knew I would only refer genuine HDU/ITU patients.

As hard as this period was, and as lost as I felt, I managed to retain an element of insight, and I knew that none of this was right. I was fully aware I had become a very unpleasant person to be around and my mental health was spiralling dangerously out of control. I knew I was hiding from the reality of my home situation by burying myself in work and pickling myself with alcohol. I also knew I needed to try and wrestle it back, to regain my sanity, but as described earlier in this chapter, when not writing a warts-and-all memoir, I am actually a very private person, and I don't like to share my problems, not even confiding in family or friends. I couldn't face the embarrassment and shame of opening up to people, telling them how I was suffering and how low I felt, showing weakness and forever changing their perception of me as a man, and so I decided the best course of action was to continue to struggle on alone.

I did, however, turn to Google for some coping strategies and, after much research on the subject, decided the tactic I was going to employ in the fight to win myself back was to focus on the root cause of my anxiety, the root of all my issues. If I could conquer the fear of losing my daughter, then I might just be able to dig myself out of the emotional and psychological hole I had fallen into. So, I focused on the only positive piece of information we had been given, the only ray of hope we had: thirty per cent of patients with JET survived to one year of age. This was going to be my line in the sand. This was where I would dig in and make my last stand.

I decided, if my daughter made it to her first birthday, I was going to host the mother of all parties, the party to end all parties. I would give myself permission to feel sad about the situation I currently found myself in, allow myself to wallow in self-pity, if that's how I needed to handle it, but once that birthday party was over, there was to be no more of it. I would man up and stop torturing myself. I would relax and allow myself to enjoy being her father. This was my plan, and I focused on it constantly. Every time I started to feel the darkness spreading over me, I would force myself to think, *When she gets to one, I will be okay*. I would even say it out loud if alone, or mutter it under my breath if in company. It became my mantra, my obsession. And as the weeks turned to months, and we got closer to D-day, I actually started to feel a little bit better. I felt slightly more positive, and the dark thoughts started to recede. I began to feel my death would not be the most beneficial outcome for my family, after all, and I finally decided to get that pesky tyre changed.

The day of our daughter's first birthday eventually arrived, and as promised, we held a party that was more befitting of an eighteenth than a first, one that went on into the early hours of the morning. I can honestly say that a switch flipped in me that night, and I finally started to relax around her. I gradually forced myself to stop the hourly checks during the night and, with the help of my wife, developed a much more positive outlook, even agreeing with the plan to move her back into the cot that had remained empty in the little bedroom next door to our own since the fateful night I had returned from Seville. My next focus would be on seeing her grow out of the condition and getting behind my wife's plan of freeing her from the chains of the particularly toxic medication she currently depended on. The next phase, the next battle in a long war, had begun.

I still had my moments, and the dark thoughts and nightmares continued for a long time after, but they became much less frequent over time. I allowed myself to start to relax, and I finally felt I could be a proper father to both my children, as I had also severely neglected my eighteen-year-old son during the last year. I could finally look at my daughter and feel only love, rather than the heavy sense of impending doom. Light had begun to break through the darkness that had enveloped my mind for the last year, like rays of sunshine bursting through the heavy rain clouds of a subsiding thunderstorm. I was far from fully healed, and it would take a long time to get back to anywhere near my old self. Even to this day, I go into her room most nights, long after we have put her to bed, to perform my safety check under the pretence of a goodnight kiss. But the healing process had definitely started.

I have found it extremely difficult to face up to how I felt during this, the darkest period of my life, and believe me when I tell you, I have agonised over whether to include The Wilderness Year chapter in this book, rewriting and removing it on several occasions. Eventually, I decided it had to be included for two reasons. The first being authenticity, as an integral part of my story, essential in understanding who I am and why I react the way I do in certain situations, finally offering a long-awaited explanation to those who may have suffered the heat of my temper during those darkest of days. The second is to offer some hope to others who may be going through a similar period in their life, to show them that things can change and brighter days do lie ahead.

I was well into my late thirties and had never suffered with depression or anxiety before this happened to me. I considered myself a well-rounded, mentally tough, and extremely resilient person, one who had served in warzones around the globe as an infantry soldier and had consistently remained composed under enemy fire. A man who had run a successful business in his early twenties and smashed down all educational barriers to become a doctor after leaving school with barely two GCSEs to his name. I honestly believe I am a strong person. I must be to have fought my way back from the very brink of oblivion in the way that I have. But if this can happen to me, at the age it did, with the experience I had, then it can happen to anyone, at any stage of life.

I started this chapter off by admitting I do not handle emotional situations well, admitting I bottle things up and try to remove myself or detach myself from such situations, rather than face up to their emotional consequences. A prime example of this attitude is my approach to funerals. I actually prided myself for never having cried at a funeral, as bizarre as that sounds. That was the mindset I had developed over the years. But it's not a good mindset. It's not tough, and it's not a healthy coping mechanism. Belief in this macho bullshit is the exact reason why so many young males commit suicide every year. Pain is not weakness leaving the body; pain is a warning sign. It's your body telling you you're damaged and need to stop immediately and address the situation before that damage becomes irreversible, whether that be emotional or physical pain.

Bottling things up and burying your head in the sand doesn't make you a man – it makes you a high suicide risk. If you are struggling, then please talk to somebody, ideally someone who is trained in dealing with such situations – the Samaritans, for example – but there are many other avenues of help, from friends and family to your own GP. Don't struggle on and suffer in silence. Don't do as I did and push yourself to the very brink of a mental breakdown or even suicide for some outdated notion of masculine pride. Be honest about how you are feeling. People would rather you cry on their shoulder than carry your coffin. You are not alone. Always remember, no matter how bad you are feeling, the world is a much better place with you in it.

Till Death Do Us Part

I may have been improving in the grand scheme of things, but I was still only at the start of a long and tortuous journey, with barely a foot on the pathway to redemption. It probably seems obvious that I would never fully heal until I left the pressure cooker environment of East and moved back home to the bosom of my family, but at this stage, I remained blissfully ignorant to that reality, still pretty much surviving on a combination of strong coffee and pure adrenaline, temper continually stretched to breaking point, in a permanent state of fight or flight, almost always choosing to fight, as I'm sure many an A&E doctor – and on the odd occasion, even a fellow medical registrar – would testify.

This particular night was one such "odd occasion". I arrived in handover, fast approaching the end of a long run of horrendous nights, and I was tired, dead tired. I was not in the best of moods, currently sitting at that fell-out-with-everyone stage in my perpetual cycle, and I, along with everyone else, was desperate for me to return to Liverpool for a bit of R & R. I sat in the doctors' office at the front end of EAU and waited impatiently for the obligatory list of fifteen unclerked patients to be handed over, like a condemned man awaiting the noose to be lowered over his head.

But it never arrived. I sat fidgeting in a hard plastic chair, flanked by patient flow on one side and my night SHO on the other, for thirty long minutes, and still, no sign of the day registrar. I could feel pressure slowly building inside my head, the warmth spreading across my cheeks, heartbeat pounding in my ears. I was restless and agitated, and I could wait no longer. I walked out of handover, a man on a mission, to find my colleague.

And find her I certainly did, located in a side room of the A&E department, with two concerned-looking CCO nurses, Les and Nic, and one very sick-looking patient. She was intently studying the monitor to the side of the patient's bed, which appeared to show atrial fibrillation at a rate of around 120 beats per minute. Her back was to me as I walked through the door, and I overheard her asking one of the CCOs for 2.5 mg of bisoprolol.

"What?" I snapped loudly, as I dramatically burst through the door. "Why are you asking for bisoprolol? The patient has a systolic blood pressure of 80 and is clearly septic. Why are you arsing around with bisoprolol?" All three in the room instantly turned toward me, both CCOs looking relieved, one flustered registrar not looking quite so relieved.

"Give me some fluid, please, Les, and run it through fast. Why don't we forget about the bisoprolol for now, hey? What antibiotics is he on? What are his bloods showing? And where do you reckon this infection is coming from?" I rapidly fired at Les, as I cut across the day reg and focused full attention on my team. She tried to cut in, and I turned to her and said, "I will take it from here, if that's okay. I'm on the clock now," instantly turning back to the CCO nurses. "Stat of gentamicin with that Taz, please, Nic. Let's move him to resus as well. Hey, and get on to the anaesthetist, please. He needs stepping up." I didn't see the day registrar leave the room.

I know the above transcript probably sounds quite arrogant and could even be construed as bullying. Reading it back even makes me feel slightly uncomfortable, but I was in a very different place back then. I had a different mindset and a different focus. I was there to save that patient's life, to give him the best possible opportunity of survival. I was the last line of defence in a hospital that was falling to bits. I was surrounded by incompetence, and I had seen enough patients die as a result of it. I certainly wasn't going to stand by and watch this man die through politeness and good old-fashioned English manners. So, I acted inappropriately, but I acted fast. I acted decisively, and I gave that man a chance.

Also, as an aside, the day registrar had been at the hospital for around a year, after leaving another UK hospital under a particularly grey cloud, following involvement in a national scandal in which she had been implicated in a number of serious cases of bullying and was only allowed to continue to practice if she fulfilled multiple criteria placed on her registration by the GMC, most of them involving not managing seriously unwell patients, such as this one, and avoiding bullying. She had failed to comply to both and had already been accused of bullying at least two junior colleagues that I was aware of by the time of this incident. Even so, two wrongs do not make a right, and I acknowledge that I was probably not a very pleasant person to be around during this period in my career. Although, strangely, I remained popular amongst my colleagues.

Back to the patient. What I didn't realise at the time was this patient actually had no chance at all. When I had first arrived in A&E, abruptly standing on the toes of the day reg, I noticed a small area of the thin hospital sheet appeared to be stuck to his upper left thigh, and a pinkish fluid had begun to ooze through the bright-white material. I pulled the sheet back to reveal what looked like a pretty decent haematoma (blood clot under the skin) of around four centimetres squared in size, that had a black crust over the surface and was situated just below his left groin.

We had allowed an exhausted Les to go home for the night after her prolonged day shift, and I asked Nic to bleep the on-call anaesthetist for an urgent review. Meanwhile, the patient rapidly deteriorated whilst I settled him on resus. As if by magic, a rather fed up on-call ITU consultant, the anaesthetist, suddenly appeared at my left shoulder. Unbeknownst to us at the time, he was only attending us to cover his registrar who was in the process of intubating this poor patient's wife.

I pulled back the sheet to obtain a second opinion and was taken aback by the horrific sight that now lay beneath, as was the highly experienced consultant who instinctively took a couple of small steps away from the patient. The haematoma had spread its ugly black fingers deep into the poor gentleman's leg and appeared to be opening up the thigh muscle in front of our very eyes, creating deep ravines spreading in both directions toward the knee and up into the groin, progressing from what had essentially been a decent-sized blood blister to chunks of flesh falling away from the leg, in less than an hour. It was the most shocking infection I had ever seen in my career. The leg was literally falling apart as we watched.

The anaesthetist shook his head solemnly and muttered, "He's not for us, my friend," and I knew we were losing an unwinnable fight. I had a hard decision to make, and I wanted his family to be aware of what that decision was going to be, so I asked his A&E nurse to find me the next of kin's details. It turned out his next of kin was a daughter, whose mobile number was currently being scribbled onto a yellow Post-it note in front of me. I dialled the number and was caught slightly off guard when it was answered on the second ring.

"Hello, this is Dr Keegan calling from—"

"I'm already here in ITU," she said, cutting me off.

"You are in ITU… Why?" I was confused. Had someone already informed her?

"I'm here with my mum," she said.

"Your mum." I asked, slightly bemused.

After an initially confusing conversation, I realised that both of her parents were in hospital and both were unwell, so unwell, in fact, that she had been called in to say a final goodbye to her mum. And I was just about to tell her that her dad was in the last hours to minutes of life. She was about to become an orphan. I asked if I could meet her in the family room next to ITU, and she agreed.

The daughter informed me her parents were farmers, and she had no other family to speak of and was probably at the wrong end of the age scale to start one of her own now, so she had decided to take up the offer of running the farm and occupying an old converted barn situated on the land, whilst the elderly couple took a step back and enjoyed semi-retirement. She had left her parents' farmhouse late the previous evening, after making them a cup of tea and ensuring they were ready for bed, and both had been very well at the time, with neither complaining of any medical symptoms.

The next time she entered the house, at lunchtime the following day, she had walked into a scene of utter chaos, her dad sprawled out confused on the kitchen floor, and her mother unresponsive in the marital bed upstairs. She had phoned an ambulance, and I already knew the rest of the story. Her poor mother had been admitted straight onto ITU, where she was intubated, whilst her father had drawn the short straw and been handed over to my registrar friend, who had been treating his raging sepsis with bisoprolol.

I explained to the daughter that her father was extremely unwell with what looked like a severe necrotising fasciitis, and it was my opinion, and also that of the anaesthetic consultant, that he was likely approaching the last hours of his life. She paused for a second, looked straight ahead, and calmly thanked me, before informing me she would be staying with her mother for the time being, as the ITU doctors had decided to take her off the ventilator. I asked her if she was okay, and she calmly shook her head.

I headed back to resus and swiped through the magnetically locked door as an anxious nurse hurried toward me, calling out, "Quick, I think he's going." I walked toward the bed, just as the man took his final breath, and instantly spun on my heels, heading straight back to ITU to break the bad news. I arrived at the viewing window and peered through the half-closed blinds, just in time to witness a private moment between a mother and her recently bereaved daughter. Turning to the visibly distressed nursing sister who had sidled up beside me, I asked if we could make use of this larger room, and the more serene environment of ITU, to lay the husband and wife together for viewing, and she instantly agreed.

The daughter went for a coffee, and we took the opportunity to wheel her father's covered body over from resus and place the beds next to each other in the ITU room. We then invited the newly orphaned daughter back. She was completely silent for a moment or two as she stood at the foot of the beds, and I was greatly relieved when a tall, elegant lady, who appeared to be in her mid-forties, entered the room and lovingly embraced the daughter whilst gently taking her hand in hers. Thank God for that. She had someone in this world who clearly loved her, someone who she could lean on in the difficult weeks that lay ahead.

Suddenly feeling awkward standing in the doorway, hands behind my back, head bowed slightly, an intruder on this very private moment of grief, I slowly and silently turned to leave the room, hoping I had not been noticed, when I heard, “Thank you, doctor,” from behind me.

I turned back around to face the daughter and her partner, who was now supporting her with an arm around the shoulders. She appeared completely calm, had not shed a tear, did not look in shock, was almost serene.

“I am only sorry I couldn’t do more. I am so sorry for your loss. I really am,” and for once, I genuinely meant it. I may have become a hollow vessel, but you would have to be made of solid stone not to be moved by the absolute tragedy that had just unfolded in front of my shocked night team.

“They had a good life and they had each other, right to the very end. I am a farmer, doctor, and this is the circle of life, nothing more. We are born, we live, and we die, and that’s it.”

I was genuinely in awe of her bravery and her resilience. I held out my hand, and she shook it firmly. I felt the rough, calloused palm contrasted against my own soft hand. “Again, I am really sorry for your loss.” I nodded slightly, and she nodded back and gave me a hollow smile that didn’t quite reach her eyes. I turned and walked out of the room.

Both parents had officially shuffled off this mortal coil within a couple of minutes of each other, according to the verification of deaths. However, I like to think they took their final breath at the exact same time.

The Burden of Responsibility

Anyone who knows me will know that, if I believe in something, if I get behind a cause, I am the ultimate team player. I will literally fight to the death for my people. I am stubborn, and although I was thoroughly miserable at East, I had well and truly bought into the hospital. I had fallen in love with the people and the area, and I had decided I was going to save this hospital, or I would die trying.

The downside of this mentality is that I expect everybody else to respond in the same way, to push themselves as hard as I push myself, to sacrifice everything for the cause, like I do. I completely lose perspective. I dig in hard, and I come out fighting. You are either with me, or you're against me, and if you are against me, I give no quarter. I take no prisoners.

Luckily for me, the CCO team was just as committed to the cause as I was. We had formed a tight unit over the past year or so and trusted each other implicitly. On reflection, we could be a pretty closed circle at times, and I was often reluctant to allow others to join our personal war against the incompetent functioning of the hospital's day shift. We would firefight every single night as the hospital continued to spiral out of control.

The latest cost-cutting plan devised by management had been to offload most of the expensive locums, and staff the whole hospital with twenty-two African doctors, almost all of whom had never worked in the UK before. These doctors had variable skill sets to say the least and did not receive the required support or bedding-in time to effectively adapt to the new systems and ways of working. As a result, the hospital had become an even more dangerous place to be sick or to work. I was constantly being advised to leave East by friends and family who were increasingly concerned about my mental health and the realistic prospect of me getting struck off by the GMC for making a fatal mistake due to exhaustion or time pressure.

I became more insular the more the hospital deteriorated, and I trusted fewer people as I circled the wagons ever closer. I was suspicious of people, and I had lost respect for a lot of colleagues who I had previously been very close to, resenting them because they didn't meet my exacting standards, standards that were becoming increasingly unrealistic and impossible to fulfil.

It was against this backdrop that I finally imploded and left East for good, unfortunately under a cloud and not on the best of terms, which I regret, but it was only ever going to end that way. With all of the personal issues and stress of the last few years, I had completely lost perspective. I had well and truly fallen down the rabbit hole, and I was madder than the infamous mentally fragile Hatter.

*

It was well after midnight on that fateful last night shift, and deep into the witching hours, when my trusty red bleep rudely interrupted my nightly CCU ward round that I had recently decided to take upon myself, ramping up that pressure by yet another notch, adding a bit more work to the already unbearable load. It announced that my presence was required at an arrest on A&E. *Okay, this is unusual.* I headed straight to resus, which was just across the corridor, to find the staff-grade doctor, a very experienced and competent GP – we'll call him Nigel – with over twenty years' experience as a GP consultant under his belt, pumping away on the chest of a disturbingly young woman, who was currently being intubated by a not-so-competent, notoriously workshy anaesthetist.

"What's the script, Nige?" I immediately enquired.

"Forty-one-year-old lady, non-smoker, no alcohol excess or drug history, in fact, no medical history whatsoever, phoned 999 with chest pain. Was thought to be anxiety-related but took a turn for the worse in the ambulance. ECG showed a tombstone STEMI, quickly followed by a VF arrest. Multiple shocks and unresponsive with no output, intubated by paramedics and tube was found to be placed in the stomach on arrival, had at least twenty minutes down time," replied Nigel.

To the non-medics amongst you, the beautifully succinct summary above can be translated into very bad news, very bad news indeed. The young lady was in trouble from a heart point of view and her brain had likely been starved of a sufficient amount of oxygen for around twenty minutes. She was in serious trouble, and despite her young age, the prognosis was very poor.

"So why am I here?" I asked, without a trace of irony. The medical registrar was not usually called to arrests in A&E – we had enough on our hands covering the rest of the hospital, never mind the A&E department.

"Tom isn't answering his phone. We've left multiple messages, and we're alone here, mate. We need some help." Tom was the on-call A&E consultant that night.

"So how long do we continue, team? What are we hoping to achieve here?" I asked frankly, as I slowly looked around the room, gauging the mental and emotional state of the attending resus team.

The first problem we faced as a team was that both nursing staff covering resus knew the patient, and her family, really well. One of them, a very junior and very emotional nurse, had even worked with the unfortunate woman, whose cold and clearly dead chest she was currently and enthusiastically pounding away on, in her pre-nursing days. As such, both voiced the opinion that we should continue.

Nigel was a veteran who had been there and done it all, and as a result, he was a realist at heart. He could see the writing was on the wall for this poor lady, but clearly didn't want to upset the nursing team, who he had an excellent working relationship with. The anaesthetist, on the other hand, was eager to get back to his bed and would agree to anything that avoided an admission to ITU and, consequently, further work for him. At that moment, I realised why I had been called. It was blatantly obvious – I was going to have to be the bad guy.

"Okay, let's be realistic here—" I was abruptly interrupted by a loud ringtone.

We all briefly stopped and looked at each other, attempting to locate the source of the sound that had so rudely cut into my sentence. The non-chest-compressing nurse picked up a small, not very smart type of phone that must have been haphazardly discarded on the white work surface next to the bed by the paramedics when the patient was initially wheeled in, along with the ambulance sheet and a large fob of keys. She held the phone in the palm of a trembling hand and, with glazed eyes and a quivering voice, stuttered, "It's… It's her daughter."

The reality of the situation seemed to hit us all simultaneously whilst the patient's phone continued to ring, none of us having the courage to answer it. This lifeless figure lying sprawled out in front of us, in the most undignified of positions, likely severely brain damaged, was not just a patient – she was a young mother. A young mother who had a family sitting at home somewhere, undoubtedly worried sick about her. The sentence I had been just about to utter suddenly stuck in my throat. This wasn't a game anymore. This wasn't about my ego, about me pitting my wits against the Hooded Claw. This was real life.

So, we got our heads down, and we carried on. We carried on until we were exhausted.

"Rhythm check, please," I asked for the umpteenth time.

"PEA," casually stated the anaesthetist.

I'd finally had enough. "Listen, guys, what are we doing here? Seriously, what are we hoping to achieve, man?"

Silence. No one wanted to be the first to speak.

"Nige, come on, mate. It's been an hour. She had a down time of twenty minutes before we even started, she's been shocked seventeen times now, mate, and we are currently going through the hospital supply of adrenaline like no one's business. It's time, man. Why don't we have a vote on this?"

"Can we at least try the consultants again?" replied Nigel.

"Or thrombolyse?" piped up the younger nurse.

"Right, the consultants are not answering. We need to face up to that reality, and we need to make a decision here, and now. Thrombolysis is out – we have well and truly missed the boat on that. She's been getting resuscitated for almost ninety minutes. Does anyone here honestly think we are doing this in the patient's best interest? She has no electrical activity of the heart. I know we all feel terrible here, but we need to make a decision. We're only continuing because we aren't brave enough to stop." There was a deathly silence. "I'm calling a vote. I vote to stop." I looked up at the anaesthetist, and he gave a faint nod. "That's two. Nige?" He looked up slowly and nodded silently. I looked across at my CCO who nodded sadly. "That's four. Let's stop."

I never asked the nurses. They undoubtedly believed I was being an arrogant prick, not valuing their input, but I actually did it in their best interest. I didn't want them to have to be any part of that decision. I didn't want to put it on their conscience.

We stopped, standing perfectly still in a semi-circle around the bed, in total silence, and watched as the anaesthetist pulled the tube from her throat. She made no effort whatsoever to breathe, having clearly already left this world some time ago. I looked around at the others, a rag-tag bunch, dishevelled, pale, exhausted, and shocked, each one of us deep in private reflection. It seemed the world had stopped for a few seconds, and I observed from the periphery, detached. I was snapped back to full presence by the deafening sound of the patient's phone ringing again, and I felt a deep, gut-wrenching sense of guilt.

It was all too much for the young nurse. She walked out of the room, clearly distraught, but none of us had the energy to follow her out. We were all too broken in our own different ways. We were not going to walk away from this unscathed, and we knew it. Each one of us would carry a scar. I turned and walked toward the door. "I'll leave it to you from here, Nige."

He nodded, shoulders heavy, eyes downcast.

I walked out of resus with the CCO. "Fancy a cuppa, Nic," I asked.

"Of course," she replied.

We walked back toward the staff room on the EAU and passed the SHO standing guard at the nurses' station, looking as rough as we were feeling.

"Have you had a break?" I asked. He looked up, exhausted, and shook his head. "Fancy a coffee?"

"After this," he said, indicating the clerking proforma he was currently filling out.

I walked into the staff room and couldn't believe my eyes. The two ACPs, whose main role of a night was to support the SHO and act in the old-fashioned house officer role, were lounging across the fixed metal chairs that lined the outside wall of the staff room, in semi-darkness. Paula, who I had previously had a lot of respect for, had her shoes off and appeared to be snoozing, whilst Adam, who I'd had considerably less respect for and who had been in the role for less than a year, was watching Netflix on his phone. An almost empty plate rested perilously on his knee, a few brown smears and the occasional grain of rice marooned upon it, testament to the curry that had once occupied the space.

"What's going on here?" I didn't even attempt to mask the anger in my voice.

"We're entitled to a break, you know," said Adam defensively, as he stood up and walked to the sink to rinse off his plate, flicking the light switch as he went, which roused Paula from her slumber. She looked surprised as she swung her legs into a sitting position, whilst feebly attempting to stifle a yawn.

I took a seat in the corner, next to the sink where Adam was currently rinsing the remnants of the curry from his plate. I just couldn't let it go. "Been busy, have you?" I asked sarcastically.

"Yes, we have," he replied tersely.

"Not as busy as James out there. He hasn't stopped yet." I was rapidly losing patience.

"You don't know what it's like on them wards," Adam suddenly shouted angrily at me, whilst pulling himself to his full height and leaning toward me in an attempt at intimidation.

"I've worked as an F1 in some of the busiest hospitals in the country, you fucking idiot." I could hold back no longer.

Adam took another step, towering over me as I remained seated. He was glaring down at me, chest pumped out, angry grimace on his face, just about to speak again.

"If I was you, I would get the fuck out of my face, before I drag you out of this room by your fucking head and rip you to pieces, you cheeky bastard," I delivered calmly, yet with deadly intent.

The room was completely silent now, the atmosphere thick enough to cut with a knife. Visually taken aback, he stepped away from me, paused for a second, unsure how to respond, before deciding it was not in his best interest to continue this conversation. He turned and walked out the door. "That's not fucking cool," he shouted over his shoulder, as he went.

I looked across at Nic, and she looked back at me pityingly. She had watched me spiralling out of control over the past few months, and she knew I had gone too far, overstepped the mark. I knew it too. I looked at Paula. Her face had the exact same expression, and I knew it was time to leave East – for good, this time.

I completed the shift and went to my last handover. As I was about to leave, the senior consultant, the very same one who had shown me around on that first day and had given me the opportunity to step up, asked if I could stay behind for a moment. "Of course," I replied, as I sat back down and waited patiently for the room to clear.

"You know what I'm going to say," she stated calmly.

"Yes," I mumbled, ever the naughty schoolboy in front of the headmistress.

"You can't speak to people that way, Lee. You are a doctor, not a soldier."

"I know, but where I come from, if you stand over someone and front them in the way he did, then you've got to be able to back it up," I offered feebly.

She looked at me in the same pitying way Nic and Paula had done earlier. She knew, as they did, how much pressure I had been under for the last year, how much of myself I had given.

"I think it's time to go, isn't it?" I asked.

"That's your decision, Lee." Though, it was clearly the same one she had made.

I nodded and stood up without saying another word. I walked out the magnetic doors of EAU, saying goodbye to the ward clerk as I went, and headed straight out the back entrance.

I paused for a second, pulled out my phone and took a selfie with the hospital sign behind me, instantly uploading it to Facebook, with the caption "and then there was none" in reference to the other two Spice

Boys who had started this crazy journey with me. It all seemed such a long time ago now. I walked to my car, opened the door, and dialled my agent, Jamie, as I sank into the leather seat and started the engine. "I want out," I told him as he answered.

"Where do you want to work?" he asked.

"I want to come home," I replied, and by the time I arrived back in Liverpool that Friday morning, he had me a new job as a cardiology registrar in a prestigious Liverpool Hospital, working nine to five, and starting the following Monday. He was a legend, and I was out.

That night had been a watershed shift. I had known I needed to leave East for a while, and as sad as I was, I was relieved it was finally all over. With regards to the patient who had ultimately set off the whole chain of events, I completely forgot about her in all the commotion, and never gave her another thought, until just over a year later, when I was sitting at home alone in Liverpool and picked up my phone, opening the Facebook app. There, at the top of my feed, was a tribute post of pictures and memories from a son on the anniversary of his mother's death. It had been shared by the younger of the two nurses who had been present at the arrest. I vaguely recognised the young woman in the photograph, and I hesitantly clicked open the post and instantly fell apart, shattered into a million pieces. I was overwhelmed by heart-wrenching sadness at her tragic loss, and a deep-seated, suffocating guilt, a guilt I was not aware I had been carrying, until that moment. I sat for a long time and looked through that Facebook post. I looked at every photo and read every single one of those tributes, each word a dagger thrust into the pit of my stomach.

I guess I didn't have to worry about not being able to feel again, after all.

New Horizons

I was home for the first time in three years, and it felt good. I took to the role of cardiology registrar like a duck to water and was offered a year's extension on my contract after working just one shift with the clinical lead. I was put on the registrar trainee rota and staffed CCU most mornings, which left me free to wander the wards for the consultant reviews in the afternoon. We had complete autonomy, but there was always a consultant on hand for help and advice if we needed it. I actually felt supported for the first time in a long time and part of a team. I had gone from trench warfare to lunchtime teaching three times a week with a complimentary M&S buffet. I worked normal hours and actually had some semblance of a life again. I was even playing for the cardiology football team.

But it was too good to last. I had accepted a significant pay cut to come home, sure we could live on a more modest wage because we were in the final phase of selling our house, just about to stride over the last hurdle and clear our mountain of debts. And that was when I was hit by a double whammy.

The initial kidney blow to soften the legs and make me drop my guard came in the form of a devastating emergency tax situation, precipitated by a company notorious amongst locums for wage scams. After the Conservative government brought in the hated IR35 tax law, our industry had become much more tightly regulated, and we had to work through a handful of companies. One such company quickly capitalised and, completely out of the blue, took control of the whole market. Within a year, around ninety per cent of hospitals would only pay through them. But they were notorious for paying significantly reduced wages and blaming it on the taxman, despite HMRC assuring us the discrepancies had nothing to do with them.

Locums are normally paid weekly, and for my first eight weeks back home, I received a paltry twenty-six per cent of my wages. Every time I phoned to complain, I would be bounced from the umbrella company to HMRC and back again, with both completely absolving themselves of all responsibility. I was only getting by with the aid of overdrafts and credit cards, but as the house sale was imminent, I thought I could at least see a light at the end of the tunnel, a light that turned out to be a huge train rapidly hurtling in my direction.

Just as I was approaching the very limit of my last overdraft, the second blow took me right in the jaw. The house sale fell through, and I found myself with debt I had no way of paying back and a wage packet that barely covered my monthly bills. I was in trouble, but I'd signed on the dotted line for a whole year and the head of admin was adamant she was going to hold me to it, despite my protestations of imminent destitution. She even threatened to report me to the GMC if I didn't honour the full twelve-month contract.

I was in a deep hole and starting to feel the pressure again. I decided to swallow my pride and go cap-in-hand to the clinical lead who, barely a few weeks ago, had rather generously offered me a year's contract and a route back into training as a cardiologist. I explained the dire financial situation I found myself in, and legend that she was, she instantly called off the attack dog and terminated my contract whilst even offering me the chance to pick up where I had left off when I was in a more stable financial position.

Thanking her profusely, I found myself in the familiar position of being jobless and reliant on my overworked agent to find me a plum role. By the time I pulled up outside my house, a mere twenty minutes later, I had three solid job offers. East and South Wales had offered me my old jobs back, starting immediately, and I also had an offer from a hospital in which I had previously worked in Greater Manchester. Coupled with it all was a depressingly familiar sense of impending doom.

I asked for the weekend to make a final decision whilst he cast out my CV to see if any bigger fish were biting. Taking the phone from my ear and turning it over in the palm of my hand to end the call, I noticed an email notification from a name I instantly recognised. Olly was the business manager of a hospital nestled away on a beautiful little island, set like a sparkling emerald in the turbulent blue seas that surround the British Isles, in which I had accepted a three-week job at short notice a couple of years earlier.

*

That email had arrived almost exactly two years to the day after I first touched down on the runway of the quaint little airport located on the southern tip of the Island, following a short hop up and down on a bright-orange budget aeroplane. I had rushed through baggage claim and headed to the car hire desk, second in line behind a tall Scandinavian lady who had just secured the only remaining car from the only rental company with a physical presence in the now deserted foyer of the airport.

The young girl behind the desk suggested my next best option would be to take a taxi up to the hospital, and after thanking her, I exited through the sliding glass doors located at the far side of the old-fashioned lounge, straight into the complete silence of a beautiful early May morning. Taking a deep lungful of fresh air, I waited for my ears to become accustomed to the deafening silence, gradually able to detect the songbirds' faint dawn chorus.

I waited for half an hour, enjoying the serenity of the early morning, barely seeing another living soul before a battered old black Skoda noisily drove up to the rank, puffing out exhaust fumes as it pulled up sharply beside me. The boot popped, and the driver jumped out of his side and did a little half-run, half-shuffle around the car, taking the bag from my hand without asking and dumping it unceremoniously into the spacious boot.

He was a friendly, portly, middle-aged man who had lived on the Island for well over thirty years. I took the passenger seat up front next to him, and we engaged in easy free-flowing conversation, through which he quickly established who I was and why I was visiting the

Island, interrogating me with all the skill of a seasoned detective, before providing me with a brief history of the place and drafting a "must see" list. Suddenly and unexpectedly, he paused mid-sentence, muttering, "Hello, fairies," under his breath, as we passed into a dip in the road, gloomy and eerie beneath the heavy tree canopy, and crossed a small bridge littered with flags of all nations and multicoloured graffiti. Feeling concerned, it dawned on me that I had not seen a taxi sign on the outside of the car, nor had I been shown any form of ID. Was this legit? Had I been picked up by an escaped psychopath? The old salmon poaching episode from *Only Fools and Horses* instantly sprang to mind.

Now regretting taking the front seat, I continued to engage in polite but cautious conversation, not wanting to trigger this potential killer.

Suddenly, he laughed and asked, "Did I just say 'hello, fairies' out loud? You must think I'm bloody mental."

Laughing, I told him it had concerned me slightly, and he went on to explain the Island tradition of saying hello as you cross the fairy bridge. Perplexed by the quaintness of it all, but greatly relieved, I was much more relaxed as we continued on with our journey, eventually getting dropped off at… you've guessed it – the fount of all knowledge: the hospital switchboard.

*

I had a relaxing three weeks, travelling back to Liverpool every Friday afternoon, and returning to the Island on the early Monday morning flight, each time being driven by my new, non-psychopathic killer, taxi-driver buddy. I fell in love with the place and always hoped to return one day, so as I opened the email from Olly offering a job that paid similar wages to what I had been getting at East, with the added bonus of a maximum twenty-per-cent tax, I didn't have to give it a second thought. Barely a few weeks later, I found myself in that same deserted little airport at ten to seven on a bright and beautiful Monday morning in mid-spring.

Within four months, we had sold the house in Liverpool, and my son, now twenty, had decided university life was no longer for him. He moved back in with us, so that we were living together as a complete family for the first time since just after the birth of our daughter. We settled all our debts and were paying just over £800 a month to rent a three-bed semi-detached hospital house, which included all utilities and services. Despite it being old-fashioned with crumbling Artex walls in the kitchen, threadbare carpets throughout, old pine dining furniture, and a burgundy faux-leather three-piece suite, my wife worked her magic and turned it into a family home in no time, and I was happy for the first time in a long time. The nightmare of the last few years was finally behind us as my daughter went from strength to strength, coming off the amiodarone, just as my wife had said she would, and I gradually began to heal as a person, as we healed together as a family.

We owed nothing to no one, we had savings in the bank, and we were earning real money for the first time since my wife's business had gone bust, during the early years of my medical degree. Exploring every inch of the Island, we revelled in the great outdoors and travelled at every opportunity, visiting the USA twice, embarking on a mini tour of Canada, and taking eleven European holidays or weekend getaways in just under eighteen months.

Work was relaxed, we were well staffed, and life was good. In fact, life was perfect, and then along came COVID.

COVID-19

It's strange writing this chapter for a third draft of the book because the situation has changed so much over the past year. At the initial time of writing, I was very angry, which I can now see reflected in the raw emotion of my words whilst reading them back and editing. I faced an uncertain future over my refusal to be injected with a vaccine I did not want, or believe I needed, and at one point, I was only a few weeks away from unemployment, even enrolling on an accelerated law degree with the aim of leaving Medicine and becoming a medico-legal barrister, going as far as to complete the first two modules of the one-year programme before finally being handed my reprieve.

We live in such bizarre times that I know there will be many people who read the above paragraph and instantly think "anti-vaxxer". It will be the first word that pops into their mind, even after everything they have read about me so far, after knowing all I have been through, knowing all the clinical experience and medical knowledge I have amassed over the years. We have become so polarised as a society, and people are so fixed in their individual beliefs, so blinded by the cult of COVID, that they will simply not tolerate any opposing opinion, but I sincerely hope this chapter will give an insight into why so many medical professionals were prepared to walk away from a job that we love, a job that we were born to do.

When I started out on this crazy journey, way back in 2007, it seemed such a straightforward path to follow. I was under no illusions. I knew it would be hard work, but I figured I would pass my exams, graduate, become a doctor, forge a long and successful career, eventually retire, and all would be good in the world. However, as I have already recounted, there have been many serious unforeseen challenges along the way that have tested me to the absolute limit, but no challenge has been as strange as that presented by the COVID period, because none of it made any sense to me.

*

I had already lived through some pretty interesting times for someone who had been a fully qualified doctor for less than a decade, including the first strikes in the history of the NHS, the biggest change to tax laws, and the disaster that was, and still is, Brexit. Some start to a career in Medicine! I was beginning to feel I may be cursed, and just as I was settling down on my little Island and putting the dark days of the recent past well and truly behind me, just when I thought the strikes would be the pinnacle of controversy in my career, along came COVID and said, "Hold my beer."

I am writing the third draft of this chapter a full thirty-one months after the shock announcement made by Boris Johnson, on 23 March 2020, that the UK was going into a short period of "lockdown" in an attempt to disrupt the transmission of a respiratory virus that is now universally known as COVID-19. It feels strange to freely write that one single word without a warning message popping up on my screen offering me some free unbiased advice, or fact-checking what I've just written.

Those thirty-one months could be described as a period of communal insanity; there really is no better term for what happened. Yes, we really did stand on our doorsteps and rattle our pots and pans, put rainbow drawings in our front windows, grassed up our neighbours for spending too long outdoors in the fresh air, had Zoom quizzes every Saturday night, and spent a small fortune on home gym equipment from Amazon that we would never use. As mad as it all seems, looking back now, and as much as I sometimes question if it was just all a bizarre dream, it really did happen.

I could start this chapter with any of the heartbreaking stories of elderly patients left all alone to die in a strange room, terrified, calling out for a loved one, looking for some human contact as they entered the final moments of life. I could choose any anecdote, any witty story, and believe me there have been many of those during the handling of this pandemic, but I was always told it's best to start at the beginning, so that is what I am going to do.

*

My beloved Shar-Pei dog was approaching the end of her life, deep down I knew it, but I wasn't quite ready to face up to it just yet. We had recently been back home to Liverpool for a flying visit after being locked down for months, and our Island's government, in an attempt to block all "non-essential travel", especially for the unvaccinated, had decided to pluck a random number out of thin air and proclaim that all returnees must isolate in their own home for a period of twenty-one days. Failure to do so would result in a minimum fine of £10,000 or a custodial sentence for the most severe breaches, such as attending a supermarket to get the food I had to get in order to survive the twenty-one days of isolation.

As a result of these draconian rules, we had been forced to stay at home to keep our Island community safe, and during this relatively early period in the pandemic, we were not even permitted the one hour per day of daily outdoor exercise that would be granted later on. However, rather bizarrely, it was decided that, as I was a doctor and in great demand, I did not actually have to isolate at home during the hours from eight in the morning to six in the evening. Despite being deemed a great risk, I would be allowed to work and freely mix with my patients and colleagues during working hours, but had to head straight home and isolate with my family after six p.m. Maybe COVID was more contagious of an evening?

At the time of this madness, I had just been stepped up into a junior consultant-type role to independently manage an intermediate care unit that was located sixteen miles away from our base hospital and, as a result, was actually working with the most elderly and frail patients at the time, making the decision made by the powers that be even more bizarre. I was safe to continue working with my elderly patients, but heaven help me if I stopped off for a pint of milk on the way home.

Despite feeling like a First World War Tommy, I had followed the Kitchenesque restrictions that had been placed upon me to the absolute letter. We as a family had finally reached the end of our period of detainment, and I was already well into a nineteen-day stint of back-to-back shifts as we pick the story back up.

There I was, flanked by my wife and son, intently inspecting the physical condition of this once fine specimen of a dog, who had also not been allowed any exercise for almost three weeks, because as we have already established, her parents were in isolation and therefore not allowed outside to take her on walks.

"She looks thin," I agreed, noting the prominent ribs that poked their way through the tatty, waxy coat, which had once been thick and as smooth as silk. She looked old. I was pretty sure she hadn't looked like this when we first entered isolation. She appeared to have gone downhill fast. She was now severely frail, and it was clear her time with us was coming to an end.

Disheartened, I left for work, all thoughts of my rapidly declining dog having left my mind until I was interrupted by a rough vibration in my trouser pocket whilst mid-geriatric ward round. I noticed it was a grey overcast afternoon and the clouds outside my window looked heavy with the promise of rain as I answered the call from the private number that had rudely interrupted my ward round.

"Hello," I answered.

"Is this the owner of Penny?" asked a cheerful, young female voice.

"Yes," I replied, sounding not quite so young and definitely not as cheerful. I was informed that my wife had brought our dog into the practice for a consultation that morning. Penny had been very breathless and had become so agitated that the vet had been forced to sedate her for a chest X-ray, which had unfortunately shown cancer. They had phoned my wife to inform her of the results. My wife had requested that they phone me, and here we were.

"Cancer?" I asked, slightly baffled.

"Yes, cancer," she continued cheerfully, informing me that Penny remained sedated and asked would I like them to "quickly and painlessly" euthanise her, whilst she was still under.

"Cancer, euthanised, what…?" Even more baffled now.

The X-ray had apparently shown "a big round heart" and "shadowing on the lungs", so she "probably had cancer", and as a result, the vet thought it may be kinder to euthanise her.

"Is this a joke? Are you taking the piss?" I asked, now genuinely confused by the whole situation.

"I can assure you this is not a joke" she replied calmly.

"Okay then. Let me rein you in for a second. Firstly, how did we arrive at a diagnosis of cancer?" I asked, offering that I was a doctor.

Which she completely ignored, before proceeding to tell me that "shadowing on the lung" and a wide "mediastinum" – okay, getting a bit more medical now – "often indicate cancer, and we should consider euthanasia, without distressing her further by waking her up. It's the kindest and most cost-effective solution".

"Okay, so let's take a step back again, please. As I've just told you, I am a doctor," I informed her again, more curtly this time, "and I have experience of respiratory medicine, cardiology, cardiothoracics, acute medicine, and am currently working as an elderly medicine consultant, so I think I have a grasp of what you are talking about. Is the large heart not more likely due to heart failure? And could the lung shadowing possibly be pulmonary oedema secondary to a decompensation of the heart failure?" Basically, I was asking: *Has she just got a knackered old heart that is no longer working effectively as a pump?*

"I suppose that's a possibility," she replied.

"So, what's your evidence of cancer?" I countered.

"Errrmmmm, the shadowing on the lungs," she meekly offered, as more of a question than a statement.

"Haven't we just established it's more likely that's fluid," I cut in again.

"I suppose so," she replied.

"So, is the diagnosis not more likely just a progression of her heart failure, secondary to escalating frailty?"

"Erm, I suppose so," she repeated.

"Bloody hell, if I euthanised my patients every time their heart decompensated, I wouldn't have any bloody patients left. So can you please wake up my dog, prescribe some diuretics for her, and let me get back to my ward round."

Three weeks later, Penny was dead. She had developed a twisted bowel, and due to the weak heart previously described, the vet could not operate. I found myself crammed into a tiny room that smelled strongly of dog, with my son, our beloved family pet resting her large, wrinkled head on my arm, a head that suddenly became heavy as lead when the lethal solution, which had just been injected into her front leg, worked its wicked magic, and she was gone.

*

So why have I decided to start off my COVID chapter with a rather depressing story about losing a beloved family pet? Penny was old and she was frail, and although it was a twisted bowel that had finally finished her off, it literally could have been anything. A heatwave, a cold snap, a particularly long walk, or even a respiratory virus. We had been released from our house arrest just the day before that comical exchange with our veterinary practice. It had been a particularly warm day, and as we had been denied even the simplest pleasure of a walk in the fresh air for three weeks, we decided to take the dog on a country walk. The three-week period of inactivity had taken its toll on an old dog like ours, and she had significantly deconditioned over that period, to the point that a relaxed stroll through the rural lanes of our Island, at the pace of my two-year-old daughter, had proved too much for her frail old heart. And there we have the relevance. Frailty.

Frailty also effects humans, obviously. It's called old age, and just like animals, as we age, our bodies start to fail, our organs wear out. We lose muscle mass, which affects our balance, our mobility, and our functional reserve, as energy supplies are stored within these muscles, and without this stored energy, our ability to fight infection is severely reduced. Frailty is without doubt the biggest killer of humans, as the organs decompensate, and we go into heart, lung, renal, or liver failure. We may develop dementia as our brains age and shrink or become tangled up with string-like proteins, or we become a falls risk, as we lose core stability and strength, or our eyesight fades, our balance goes, or even, our feet become numb, secondary to diabetes or other chronic neuropathic disease. Just like Penny, there are hundreds of ways frailty can lead to the death of an elderly patient, from the devastating trauma following a heavy fall, to the extra burden on failing organs of a simple cold.

And this was my first thought as government after government announced lockdown measures, including forced isolation of the old. This did not sit right with me, and I am going to put forward the same argument I put down on day one, an opinion that hasn't changed at all, after over three years of working on the so-called front line of the pandemic, which thankfully now appears to be over. These measures were put in place to protect the elderly, but it was obvious to anyone with a medical background that lockdown would have negative consequences for the very people we were supposed to be protecting.

We indiscriminately locked away a whole generation of elderly people, lots of whom may have been advanced in years but remained young in spirit, healthy, and active. Many visited gyms regularly, enjoyed shopping, taking classes, visiting family and friends, and the right to undertake these social activities, which kept them mentally sharp, kept them sane, and gave them the motivation to get up every morning, was forcibly stripped from them when they were told to stay safe by staying at home. At the same time, it's important to remember, MPs in a similar age bracket were living it up behind the closed doors of Parliament and 10 Downing Street.

As anyone who has worked with elderly patients will know, they decondition quickly, and as a result, most hospitals have initiatives that encourage them to avoid remaining in bed or just sitting on their backsides all day. They lose muscle bulk quickly, and this very rarely returns. It amazed me, as Boris's government was issuing stay-at-home orders, that very few of the celebrity doctors reading out the daily doomsday predictions were acknowledging that a consequence of these actions would be the condemnation of hundreds of thousands, maybe even millions, from our elderly population to a rapid escalation in the natural ageing process and, as a consequence, an earlier death. This isn't even controversial. It's a long-established and well-recognised fact.

We were essentially making a large percentage of the population more frail, increasing their risk of injury and making them more susceptible to illness, to avoid them dying from a respiratory virus. And even more worrying, we were doing it to all of them at the same time, meaning vast swathes of our population would be at higher risk of hospitalisation, just as we were expecting our hospitals to fill up with COVID patients. I was concerned that, not only would we be destroying our elderly population's quality of life, but we would also be bed-blocking the wards with patients who are notoriously difficult to discharge, due to a limited social services budget and a lack of community beds in care homes.

These concerns turned out to be well-founded, and we find ourselves in precisely that position, even today. I had daily debates with colleagues and newly qualified non-medical social media experts as they pointed out the rising daily death toll, whilst I provided an alternative perspective to the one that has been commonly accepted. The pandemic hit not only this newly frail group but also the existing group who were approaching end of life at the time, the people who are, unfortunately, always the first victims of any adverse change in environment that places an extra burden on a rapidly failing body.

It's the low-hanging fruit theory. We have a population of patients imminently approaching the last days of life who hang heavy and ripe, like fruit on a tree, just waiting for the next gust of wind, the next heavy rainfall, or even the vibration from a passing vehicle to knock them off the tree. It was our existing group of end-stage frailty patients who provided the initial mortality spike at the start of the pandemic, for a variety of reasons, ranging from change in environment to disrupted routine management plans. This was to be expected. However, what happened next went beyond expected mortality rates based on experience from when we'd had spates of flu or severe cold weather, and the like. This time, we had a conveyor belt of elderly patients rapidly coming up behind the first spike, because they were prematurely hitting end-stage frailty due to lockdown restrictions, essentially rapidly filling our tree with low-hanging fruit. To make the situation even worse, a policy decision was made early on in the pandemic to follow China's strategy of denying intensive treatment to these patients, in an attempt to save beds for younger, healthier patients.

It's important to remember here that we were still being told all these measures were in place to protect the elderly, the very same people we had now decided were not going to receive invasive treatment, such as intubation. To be fair, this was normal advice for elderly and frail patients, but NIV was also now completely off the table, and not just for the elderly. NIV was part of the staple management for our chronic lung patients, but because it was deemed an aerosol generating procedure, these patients were no longer eligible either. This was particularly hard on our chronic lung patients such as the COPD regulars who attended hospital a few times a year, usually throughout the winter and autumn months, to get the bog-standard three days of NIV before being sent on their merry way with some oral antibiotics and prednisolone (steroids). As a result of us following Italy and China's management protocols, many of these patients were amongst the very first victims of COVID.

Our care home residents were also in for a rough ride, as it was suddenly deemed far too risky to allow anyone into these homes, even GPs. Many care homes collaborated with community-facing doctors to draft escalation plans for residents in the event of an outbreak on their premises, which usually involved "hospital avoidance" or, as was the case for thousands, including my own nan (who ended up in a care home due to progressive dementia during the pandemic, and sadly passed away leaving my grandad Bell as my only remaining grandparent), "treatment avoidance", and if not complete avoidance then at least severe delay whilst doctors were essentially barred from attending for face-to-face consultations. Again, it's important to remember that these measures were still being justified as benefitting the elderly. We were locking them away and refusing to allow GPs to attend to them, refusing them hospital attendance, and refusing them potentially lifesaving treatment, but remember: *It was in their best interest.* Obviously, it was all for their own good.

This care home policy added to the large number of deaths early on and explains why the average age of COVID mortality was early to mid-eighties. I continually pointed out this flawed logic to my colleagues and was frustrated by the lack of advocates for the elderly in the media. There was no alternate narrative, no one was balancing the risk versus benefit, and no one was asking the elderly what they wanted. Did they want to be locked away, separated from their loved ones and friends for the last months to years of life? Did they want to be denied the simple pleasure of a walk in the fresh air, or the warm embrace of a fellow human? Most I spoke to certainly didn't want to be held prisoner in their own home or be the reason their grandchildren were missing out on family holidays or education.

I felt I was a lone voice, adrift in a rough sea, bombarded and forcibly submerged by the overwhelming and irresistible power of the waves of insanity all around me, fighting my way to the surface to take a lungful of fresh air, whilst screaming, "Are you all fucking mad?" before being beaten down again and sucked back under. I felt hopeless, frustrated, but I kept going, and it kept getting worse.

Prior to COVID, I had had the unfortunate task of breaking the devastating news of end-stage cancer to two completely unsuspecting patients. Thankfully, this was extremely rare because of our excellent screening services. And then along came COVID. I think around halfway into the pandemic, the mainstream media was still reporting cancer deaths alongside anyone who had died within twenty-eight days of a positive test. I remember it being pretty much neck and neck, and then suddenly, they just stopped reporting on cancer deaths.

Many of these cancer deaths were avoidable with simple screening, which had been initially stopped to focus on COVID before briefly restarting and then pausing again for the NHS to concentrate on the vaccination of healthy young people. Many of these cancer patients were also young, children even, and many had young families, and we allowed them to die in their thousands, as policy. Remember, someone somewhere consciously made the decision to stop screening for cancer, to stop the two-week referrals, with full knowledge that people would die, all in order to protect the old and vulnerable in society – vulnerable groups such as cancer sufferers. The logic truly baffles.

These measures didn't only have a devastating effect on physical health. What was the effect on the mental health of the next generation, the youth? We normalised mask-wearing and social distancing to a generation of children. We taught them to fear fresh air, to avoid human contact, to distance themselves from extended family and friends, all because of a virus that had virtually no chance of making them seriously ill. Who knows what the long-term effects of that psychological trauma will be.

And then we stepped down the road of mandated vaccination. We actually sacked thousands of carers. The very people who were keeping the elderly safe, giving them medication, keeping them clean, keeping their stomachs filled, even wiping their backsides, were sacked for refusing to take part in the greatest medical experiment ever undertaken.

I will put it out there: I have not had any of the COVID vaccinations. I have worked for almost four years without a vaccine, often without correct or sufficient PPE in the early days. There were periods during the "first wave" that I worked continuously for nineteen days, before taking two days off and then heading straight for another nineteen-day stretch. My normal pattern was twelve on, two off. Throughout the whole first eighteen months of the pandemic, I had no more than six days off in a row, and those six days consisted of being locked down in Liverpool over Christmas. I sacrificed, I put my patients first, and I have suffered as much as anyone else throughout the insanity of the last couple of years, even missing my own nan's funeral because I refused to punish my daughter with another twenty-one-day lockdown before she had even finished the twenty-one days she was already serving as punishment for returning to Liverpool to spend Christmas with family. And after all that, they were going to sack me for using the knowledge and experience I had acquired over fifteen years of medical education and clinical practice to make a highly informed and personal decision.

I am not "anti-vax", which seems to be the current derogatory trope used to beat down anyone who chooses not to be vaccinated against COVID. I have done a lot of research on this subject, and I actually single-handedly devised the treatment protocols for my hospital trust at the beginning of the pandemic, researching every shred of evidence available on the treatment and management of COVID in the process, and I have several reasons for arriving at this decision, and none of them involve the wearing of a tinfoil hat. I initially chose not to get vaccinated because I am pro-science. I strongly believe in the scientific process of rigorously safety testing a medication before allowing mass inoculation, which makes sense really, as I am a scientist at the end of the day. I honestly don't believe this rigorous process was followed. I did not want to take part in a clinical trial, which is my right, therefore I chose not to participate in one, but that doesn't mean I am against anyone else being vaccinated, or any other vaccination. If you feel comfortable, and if you feel safer being vaccinated, then I fully respect your right to choose, because it's your choice and ultimately has nothing to do with me.

A vaccination for a respiratory virus will not stop me catching or transmitting the virus, and the likelihood of me becoming seriously unwell from COVID was very low, so I decided I did not require one. I believe that, after working for well over three years on the so-called front line, including running an acute COVID unit as a registrar, splitting a COVID ward with a respiratory consultant as an acute medical consultant, down to my most recent job which involves running the COVID side of A&E majors as an acute medical consultant, whilst suffering from nothing more than the odd sniffle or couple of days of cold-like symptoms, have well and truly borne out this belief. And to those of you who may be concerned about me spreading a respiratory virus as an unvaccinated acute medical consultant, there is absolutely no credible, and I repeat the word *credible*, evidence to support any disparity in transmission relevant to vaccination status, none whatsoever.

My second reason for not getting the vaccine is that I have strong morals and beliefs. As you will be aware by now, I will stand by my principles. I am willing to die for them, never mind walk away from my life's calling. I strongly believe in medical autonomy, and forcing any medical procedure or intervention onto a person by direct force or severe coercion, such as the loss of a career or refusal of entry into public buildings or sporting and leisure events or venues, is completely unacceptable to me.

The official statistics stated that up to a hundred thousand NHS workers in the UK chose not to get vaccinated, and each one had their own reasons for this, and every single one of those reasons should be respected, just as those people have respected you and your family's choices if you have ever been directly under their care. It's the thin end of a wedge for me, a slippery slope. If we allow mandatory vaccination, then what comes next? Forced sterilisation of the unemployed, refusal to treat the obese, or smokers, or alcoholics? It's a very worrying prospect for me, one I would not be happy to be a part of, and so, I decided to make a stand. Yes, another one.

I lost many friends and even fell out with family members over my beliefs on lockdown measures, health passports, and mandatory vaccination, and I have no doubt this chapter will have turned off a lot of readers, but it is a very important part of my career to date, probably the most important, so I could not simply gloss over it or be dishonest about my beliefs. I have been attacked on social media, ridiculed, called a conspiracy theorist, and accused of being mentally ill by people who have nowhere near my level of understanding of the pathophysiological process of a respiratory virus or the management of one, people who previously respected my opinion and held it in high regard, especially when seeking out a second opinion or confirmation of a diagnosis. I understand that this was driven by fear, and I hope these people have now learned to live with a virus that is endemic and looks to be here for the long haul. I am unsure what the future holds, and in some ways, I am terrified and intrigued in equal measures, but I believe we all must learn to live with the aftermath of COVID, and I hope that we can learn to live with each other again.

As I stated earlier, I could have approached this chapter from many different angles. I have so many stories from my time working during this pandemic. I have witnessed unimaginable levels of craziness and selfishness, but I have also witnessed compassion and love in equal measures. I have watched as nurses and healthcare workers volunteered to stay behind after a long shift and hold the hand of a dying patient. I watched on with immense pride as they ignored social-distancing policy to offer one final embrace, to provide one final act of love and comfort to a fellow human being in their last moments of life.

We have been fed on a diet of fear and division, but I have witnessed kindness and community spirit on levels unrivalled since the blitz spirit of the Second World War. This is what I would like to focus on as this book nears its end. As controversial as it probably sounds these days, following revelations about some dodgy relatives, I would like to focus on the Captain Toms of this world and the millions of other "little people" who carried out millions of selfless acts of endurance, kindness, and love, in order to make the world a better place. I would like to focus on those people who burned brightest, during the very darkest of days, and I would like to end this chapter by quoting a rather appropriate part of a very famous early Beatles lyric. An enduring sentiment so aptly linked to my hometown of Liverpool.

All you need is Love.

Retaining Humanity

And now, my friends, the end is near, and as old blue eyes would say, I face the final curtain. I cannot lie, it's been emotional, but it's also been cathartic.

When I started writing this book, way back in 2015, I couldn't have envisaged the challenges that lay ahead of me. It feels like a lifetime ago that I was asked to put together a presentation for the foundation doctors. As that slide show germinated into the idea for this book, the question I ultimately wanted to pose was: Can we, as doctors, retain any semblance of humanity in a career in which death is such a normalised part of working life? That is the exact sentence I wrote down, word for word, in the notes for the original slide show. That was it, the impetus for me starting this journey through my life in Medicine.

Looking back now, I was pretty naïve to believe that death was the primary challenge our humanity would face. Death is but the endgame, and as people far wiser than me have said, there are things far worse than dying. After reflecting on the last ten years of my life and career whilst re-reading and rewriting this book, it's clear to me that death is often a blessed relief for the person who dies. Most of the time, the real tragedy, the real story, comes from the emotion that surrounds it: the anticipation, the suddenness, the finality, and the impact on those left behind.

It's interesting for me to see how I have evolved from that relatively fresh-faced SHO, straight out of the foundation programme, into the bandana-wearing, battle-hardened Vietnam vet I have become.

Watching the whole process play out by reading through these chapters has been quite surreal. It's sometimes difficult to comprehend that it's actually me I'm reading about. I have changed so much throughout the journey, and I wonder what I would say to the SHO version of me, if I had the opportunity. What advice would I give him? Probably: "Run, run as fast as your little legs can carry you. Do not stop. Do not pass Go. Do not collect two hundred pounds."

I have been through hell at times, both in and out of work. I have faced everything that can be thrown at me, and I have just about made it out the other side… just about. I genuinely don't regret a single minute of this crazy ride, and I would say that, although I have been slightly eroded as a person, and may now be a bit tattered and frayed around the edges, bearing one or two scars from the many battles I have fought over the years, I am still a relatively happy person, even if, like everyone, I do have my moments. I have managed to climb that greasy pole and now find myself sitting on the uppermost platforms, with a fine view of where I have been and where I have come from.

As an acute medical consultant, I now find myself atop that hill Sergeant Bastard confidently assured me "shit rolls down". It's a long way to have come for a kid who loved nothing more than frogging on Hale field and sailing old sofas across the Big Daddy. I have been beaten and moulded into the person I am today by the direct or indirect influences of those I have surrounded myself with, some who I have lost contact with along the way, and some who are no longer with us, who I miss every single day.

After all that's happened in the world over the last couple of years, I think I need to expand my initial question. The question of whether humanity can be retained in the face of so much death is not just for the doctors of this world, not anymore. It is a question we all need to be asking ourselves. So, here is my new question: Can you, can I, can *we* retain humanity in a post-pandemic world?

I grew up in a very different world to the one we live in today. It was a world in which racism, homophobia, and sexism were the norm. Institutional racism was an everyday part of my childhood. We lived in a casually cruel and divisive society, one that threw bananas at footballer John Barnes, one that laughed hysterically from the safety of their settee as television comedians "blacked-up" and put on derogatory Jamaican accents. The few black people I knew in Speke had nicknames like "Chalky" or "Snowy". Victimisation of the weak, alienation of minorities, in fact, of anyone who may be different, was just a part of life. That was the reality of "the good old days". That's not to say there weren't some benefits to living in this very different era. There was a greater reliance on family, and a strong sense of community, within your own community, unless you happened to be "Chalky", of course. But overall, the undercurrent was more violent, less tolerant, or so I thought.

Pre-COVID, I genuinely thought times had changed. I thought we had moved on, progressed as a society, but I am no longer so sure. Over the past couple of years, I have noticed the same people who would smugly wave Pride flags are the ones calling for a medical apartheid on the unvaccinated, "the unclean". So-called tolerant, enlightened, and left-leaning people didn't want to be treated by or share a bus, stadium, shop, or even plane with other human beings who had chosen not to or couldn't partake in a mass vaccination programme. It was less than two years ago that people actually called for the unclean to be either forcibly vaccinated or isolated at home, shunned from society, forced to wear a yellow badge when shopping in Morrisons – yes, they really did choose yellow.

Does this sound like a civilisation that retained its humanity in a world gripped by pandemic? Has society changed, or has the focus for division simply changed? Has the hatred, the vitriol, the viciousness, the nastiness, the bile just shifted from the black player on the opposition team to the unvaccinated fella in the seat next to you? The very same people who once threw bananas at John Barnes got all jabbed-up and somehow seized the moral high ground.

So, back to the initial question posed by this book. Can a doctor retain humanity in a profession that regularly exposes them to so much human tragedy? I obviously can't speak for the whole of Medicine, but have I, as a single component, a small cog in an immense machine, an acute medical doctor who has witnessed hundreds of deaths, who regularly has to break the most devastating of news in the direst of circumstances to the most unsuspecting of victims, managed to make it out relatively unscathed? This is a difficult question for me to answer. I was carrying a lot of excess emotional baggage when I entered the role.

I remember returning from Bosnia, following months of being tasked with the job of hunting down war criminals, uncovering mass graves, and getting shot at almost daily, whilst living with a constant cycle of paranoia, fear, and violence. It had got to the point where I absolutely loved it. In fact, I lived for it. I couldn't wait for the rounds to come in so that I could feel the adrenaline rush again, unleash the animal within. And then, after almost seven months of living deep down the rabbit hole, they put us on a plush Lear jet and sent us home for two weeks' leave, and we were expected to simply slot back into civilised society, forget the violence we had lived and breathed for over half a year, flick off that survival switch, curb the instinct to kill, forget that lust for violence. But I couldn't just turn it off.

This was the kind of emotional and psychological baggage I had brought with me into the job of doctor, so it's hard to know how much of the damage I may have suffered over the years is from the trauma of a career in Medicine, and how much could be attributed to the trauma I had already taken on before even enrolling on the degree course. I would argue forcibly that I have always had a strong sense of community and humanity, and although I initially joined the forces to get away from the trainwreck my life was becoming in Liverpool, I was immensely proud of the peacekeeping and humanitarian role I played, particularly in Bosnia, where our job was to stop the ethnic slaughter of Muslims, who had been murdered in their hundreds of thousands, and to hunt down and arrest the perpetrators of that ethnic cleansing.

I also know that I went into Medicine and became a doctor because I wanted to help people. I genuinely wanted to make a difference, and I am capable of feeling overpowering, all-encompassing sadness and empathy for my patients. I can be seriously affected by tragic situations, and I suppose that's why I have learned to block it all out. It's a defence mechanism that I probably started to develop in my childhood, nurtured throughout my military days, and honed to perfection as a doctor.

So, personally, have I, as a doctor, retained any semblance of humanity, after two careers in which death is such a normalised part of working life? I will answer this question with one final anecdote.

On my last ever registrar job in early 2021, I had a patient who presented at A&E with ongoing pain in her right lower ribs. She was barely fifty years of age and had absolutely no medical history, but she had attended A&E multiple times over the past few months and had been fobbed off with the old "it's just musculoskeletal pain" line without any further investigations.

I was asked, by my rather junior SHO, if I would review the patient and make a decision on whether she needed a CTPA scan of her chest to exclude a clot on the lung, due to a high d-dimer (a blood test that can be a marker for clots) and concerns that the pain was escalating in severity and may actually be pleuritic (originating from the space between the lung and chest wall) in nature. I reviewed the bloods and noticed that her liver function was acutely deranged. After a clinical examination, it became clear the pain was originating from the territory of the liver, and I initially requested an ultrasound scan, which unfortunately showed a few suspicious "grey" areas. I told her as gently as I could what we had found on ultrasound and prepared her for the worst-case scenario, using all of my considerable communication skills, skills I had honed over many years. Then I requested a full-body CT scan to investigate further.

A couple of days later, the results were back and unsurprisingly showed cancer, but surprisingly showed that this cancer had progressed significantly. It was now widespread throughout the whole body and was likely end-stage, requiring palliation rather than active treatment. This outcome would have been very unusual as a primary presentation in a pre-COVID world, but sadly, it's becoming far less unusual these days. My consultant, who was not a native English-speaker, requested that I break the bad news. Due to the COVID regulations in place at the time, she had presented to the ambulatory clinic alone, meaning that my first task was to establish whether she had anyone outside waiting for her who could provide comfort and an emotional crutch after I had broken the devastating news.

She instantly started to panic when I posed this question. "Why do you want to know? Is it cancer? It's cancer, isn't it?" I was standing on a busy corridor, with staff walking back and forth, and I couldn't break such horrific news there. I had to think on my feet. She asked why again, and I explained that I wanted to discuss her results in more detail, and it may be better if someone was with her to help digest and retain the information. A poor excuse, but the best I could come up with on the hoof. She seemed to accept this, but it was pretty obvious she knew some life-changing information was heading her way, as she sank deeper into the hard plastic chair. She told me that her husband was outside, and she'd phone him to come and meet us both on the ward.

I grabbed a senior nurse, Jenny a fellow scouser, from the ward as a token hand-holder and sat them all down in the family room. The husband shuffled his seat closer to his wife's and tenderly cupped her left hand with both of his, whilst Jenny sat the other side and leaned in close, ready to provide a supportive arm around the shoulders as I pulled up a seat in front of the assembly, taking centre stage as I settled into my tried-and-tested technique for breaking bad news.

I emotionally detached myself from the situation, started slowly, presented the facts, plenty of pauses to let the information sink in, plenty of warning shots. I felt nothing. I could have been telling her that her pizza topping had been messed up. I was nothing more than an observer sitting in the corner of the room watching this very personal tragedy unfold. Suddenly, a strong sensation washed over me, and a thought popped into my head. It felt like an instruction, an order even: *Allow yourself to feel.* It was irresistible and overwhelming. I was instantly pulled from the corner of the room, no longer observing the tragedy. I was now part of it, and a key player, at that. Instantly, everything became sharper, the colours brighter, the sobbing of pure devastation much louder. I anxiously looked toward Jenny who I had brought in with me to provide the patient and her husband with some real human emotion, some genuine unpractised and unrehearsed empathy, and she was visibly upset. Her eyes were glazed, and she looked as though she was about to break down. I watched her for a few seconds, and then I looked back at the scene of devastation unfolding in front of me.

I watched this proud man, holding his sobbing wife tightly as she heaved against his chest, his shoulder drenched in her tears, and then I heard the words she was repeating over and over again. How could she die now, how could she leave her daughter, her only child who was currently seven months pregnant, how could she leave her without a mother, without a grandmother for the baby. I suddenly realised her pain, her devastation was not for herself, not for the situation she found herself in. It was for others, for her husband, her daughter, and her unborn grandchild.

It hit me hard. The barrier that I keep between myself and the patient, the dam that holds back the turbulent emotional tide was instantly smashed to pieces, and a large lump formed in my throat, eyelids suddenly heavy with unshed tears. I desperately tried to hold it together, tried to regain control, be professional, but it was too late. I hesitantly stood up on shaking legs and attempted to speak to the husband, to offer some crumbs of comfort, but I couldn't physically squeeze out the words, and tears were now threatening to roll down my cheeks. I looked back across at Jenny who was looking at me sympathetically, like it was me who needed a hug, like I was the one who needed that supportive arm around the shoulder.

It was too much. I put up my hand in a half apologetic, half waving gesture, and quickly walked out of the family room and into the ward kitchen next door. I poured ice-cold water from the cooler into a white plastic cup and gulped down large mouthfuls, allowing the freezing liquid to push back against the knot of emotion and shame that was sitting heavy in my upper chest.

I stood there alone for a couple of minutes whilst I pulled myself together and then walked back onto the ward, deeply embarrassed as I sat down next to Jenny. She once again looked at me sympathetically and gently touched my arm, asking if I was alright. I felt my cheeks flush red, and I couldn't look her in the eyes. Shrugging her off, I walked away, straight on to the next job. Trying to erase the tragedy playing over and over again in my mind's eye, but I couldn't shake it off. It was burned into my memory, and I kept feeling I was about to well up all over again.

I followed the patient's case over the next month or so, as she rapidly deteriorated and had a terrible time with her illness, suffering in the cruellest of ways possible, eventually passing away with her doting husband and heavily pregnant daughter at her bedside. The fact she never got to meet her grandchild absolutely broke my heart, and she is yet another patient who will stay with me for the rest of my life, another one I will take to the grave with me.

Maybe there's still hope for me yet.

Useful Terminology *(relevant to this book)*

Doctors' Grades

- Foundation Year 1 (F1). The first year as a doctor, directly following medical school, not fully licensed.
- Foundation Year 2 (F2). The second year post-medical school. Doctor is fully licensed and has GMC number.
- Internal Medicine Training 1–3. The first three years of training in the doctor's chosen specialty (the new version of Core Training, CT 1–2). Surgeons have ST 1–2/3.
- Senior House Officer (SHO). Junior doctor level that encompasses all of the above from F2 to IMT/ST 3.
- Specialty Trainee 4–8. Registrar level, sometimes known as SpR, StR, and SD, depending on hospital trusts.
- Consultant. Completed all training, most senior level of doctor.

Medical Pathology

- Chronic Obstructive Pulmonary Disease (COPD). A group of diseases that cause chronic irreversible inflammation of the small airways in the lungs, unlike asthma which is fully reversible.

- Myocardial Infarction (MI). Also known as a heart attack, blockage of a blood vessel/vessels by a clot within the vessel.
- ST-Elevation MI (STEMI). An MI with elevation present on the ECG, usually the bad one.
- Non-ST-Elevation MI (NSTEMI). No elevation on ECG, may be T-wave inversion, often not as bad.
- Primary Percutaneous Coronary Intervention (PPCI). Emergency intervention to unblock a coronary artery with stent or balloon, following MI. Also known as angioplasty/coronary angioplasty.
- Percutaneous Coronary Intervention (PCI). As above, but non-emergency. Can be done electively.
- Tachycardia. A fast heart rate, above 100 beats per minute.
- Bradycardia. A slow heart rate, below 60 beats per minute.
- Arrythmia. Irregular heartbeat.
- Atrial Fibrillation. An irregularly irregular heart rate occurring from disorganised electrical activity within the atria (top chambers of the heart). Can be fast or slow, but more commonly fast.
- Junctional Ectopic Tachycardia (JET). A rare syndrome of the heart in which a fast heartbeat is generated from around the middle of the heart (AV node) and not the top of the heart (SA node).
- Ventricular Tachycardia (VT). Arrhythmia that occurs when the lower chambers of the heart (ventricles) beat too fast to work as an effective pump.
- Ventricular Fibrillation (VF). Arrythmia that occurs due to disorganised electrical activity within the ventricles and prevents heart working as an effective pump.
- Pulseless Electrical Activity (PEA). There is electrical activity present, but it is so disorganised that it does not

generate any effective cardiac output (pulse). The heart is no longer working as a pump.
- Cardiac Arrest. Sudden loss of effective cardiac output, heart unable to function as a pump.

Medical Terminology

- Non-Invasive Ventilation (NIV). Pressure support to assist with breathing, can include continuous positive airway pressure (CPAP) and bi-level positive airway pressure (BiPAP). CPAP gives the same level of positive pressure when breathing in and out, whilst BiPAP gives a higher level when breathing in and lower when breathing out. CPAP tends to be used for obese patients (sleep apnoea) and heart failure management, whilst BiPAP is generally used for chronic lung pathologies such as COPD.
- Invasive Ventilation. When a patient is intubated and breathing is not initiated by the patient.
- Verification of Death. The process of a doctor confirming the death of a patient through an examination and set of clinical tests.
- Certification of Death. The issuing of a death certificate.

Hospital Departments

- A&E/ED. Accident and emergency or emergency department, as it's becoming increasingly known, is the gateway to the hospital. Patients are first assessed and triaged, and may require stabilising before moving to a ward.
- AMU/EAU/MAU. Acute medical unit, emergency assessment unit, medical assessment unit, the names for the first ward a patient is usually admitted to from ED, usually clinically unwell but not requiring a higher level of care (see below).

- CCU. Coronary care unit, a department for patients who are suffering from cardiac conditions that require a higher level of support or monitoring than can be provided on a normal ward.
- HDU. High dependency unit, a department in which patients require a higher level of care than can be provided on a ward, but don't require intensive care.
- ITU/ICU/Crit Care. Intensive therapy unit/intensive care unit/critical care unit, departments that provide intensive care and life support for the most unwell patients in hospital.
- Cath Lab. A catheterisation laboratory is an examination room in a hospital or clinic with diagnostic imaging equipment used to visualise the arteries of the heart and the chambers of the heart and treat any stenosis or abnormality found.

Acknowledgements

One of my best talents is the ability to surround myself with people who genuinely believe in me. This may sound like a rather insignificant and trivial talent, but I can categorically state that it has proven to be the greatest weapon in my armoury. Without the following people believing in me at the exact time that I needed believing in, neither this doctor nor this book would be here today.

Niki, my long-suffering wife, without whom there would be no story to tell. She gave me the drive and determination to succeed. She sacrificed her dreams so that I could follow mine, and she gave me two wonderful children – a family that keeps me striving for better and gives me something to fight for every single day. This book is as much her story as it is mine. I can never thank her enough for what she has done for me and our children.

Tom and Sue, my parents. I owe them everything, obviously, but more than just being my parents, they are also solid role models who not only encouraged me and my two brothers to aspire to something better in life, but also provided us with the blueprint. My dad built up a business and got us out of Speke, setting this whole journey in motion, whilst my mum went back to university as a mature student and became a nurse in her forties, showing me that it was possible to start again, possible to have a second chance at life.

Thomas Edward Keegan Sr, my grandad and my hero. A Royal Marine through and through, he gave me the answer I so badly needed at the time I so badly needed it. The dedication at the beginning of the book says it all really – little did you know, I owed you so much.

Paula McGuffie (Guff), my sister-in-law. For giving me the initial encouragement and belief to explore a career in Medicine. I'm not sure I would have believed this journey possible, if she hadn't physically pushed me onto the path.

Sergeant Mick (Bastard) Bashford. Sgt Bastard was the spark that lit the embers that became the roaring fire. He challenged me every single day through basic training to become the man I eventually became – I admit I was a bit of a slow burner! He was also responsible for me obtaining the best pair of boots I've ever owned.

Mr May and Mr Gregory. The only two teachers who ever believed in me. To be fair, I never gave the rest much to believe in, but these two saw something in me that not many others did. I hope they are both still alive today, and I hope they read this one day and know they had a major influence on the rest of my life.

Professor Lee 'Bad Homburg' Hemlar. My mate Lee. He read and re-read and read this book again… I think he now knows more about me than I know about myself. Thanks for the encouragement and the feedback throughout this process, I really appreciate it. You helped shape this book into what it is today.

Finally, this is normally where the author thanks the massive team of people who supported them through the publishing process, from their agent down to the tea lady and everyone in between. Unfortunately, I have no agent, not for want of trying, and no traditional publisher. So, after a delay of two years of wasted time and legal wrangling, I have finally managed to regain the rights to my book from a vanity publisher and have chosen to self-publish. As a result, I have put together my own little A-team.

Firstly, I employed the wonderful services of a professional editor, Kat Harvey of Athena Copy, who I cannot recommend highly enough and who has been amazing throughout this final process, a font of knowledge for a literary Neanderthal like myself.

And lastly, but certainly not leastly, I obtained the services of a professional cover artist, Andy Magee, who I would like to thank for designing the front and back covers of the book and for turning my rather amateurish selfie into a real piece of art.

I love you all.

About the Author

Dr Lee-Michael Keegan was born in early 1978 in Speke, a tough, working-class, economically deprived borough of the city of Liverpool, located in the north-west of England.

He attended a local primary school, Alderwood Infants and Juniors before moving to Sudley Junior School in 1987, in the more middle-class borough of Aigburth, Liverpool.

He was a reluctant student. Despite showing lots of early academic promise, he quickly proved he was an unlikely candidate for a high-flying career in Medicine, choosing to spend most of his time outside of school hanging out with street gangs or engaged in sporting activities – boxing for the Golden Gloves ABC in Toxteth Liverpool, representing Liverpool Harriers at 800 m, and playing Sunday league football for several local teams.

He attended Calderstones School, a comprehensive formerly known as Quarry Bank, whose most famous alumni is a certain John Winston Lennon of the little-known rock band The Beatles, eventually leaving with just two C grades to his name at GCSE, after he was permanently excluded prior to his final examinations in 1995.

He immediately enrolled on a plastering youth training scheme (YTS) and again struggled with discipline, lasting barely one year before deciding to join the RAF Regiment as a Specialist Combat Infantryman in May 1996, completing six months of basic training at RAF

Honington before being stationed overseas at RAF Laarbruch, located in Weeze, northern Germany.

He served two active tours of duty whilst in the RAF Regiment, gaining two military campaign medals for serving in Bosnia and Herzegovina and Northern Ireland between 1997 and 1998, before eventually moving back to RAF St Mawgan in Newquay, Cornwall in January 1999. He continued to struggle with discipline throughout his time in the military and was advised that his poor disciplinary record meant he would never achieve promotion. As a result, he decided to take voluntary redundancy from the RAF in May 1999.

He then enrolled on an Access to Art and Design course at Liverpool Community College in September 1999 before being accepted onto the prestigious Fine Art degree at Liverpool John Moores University in 2000. During this period, he met the love of his life and now wife, Niki, belatedly beginning to mature as he started a family.

He left Fine Art in 2002 and started a successful garden maintenance and landscaping company before eventually deciding he was ready to go back to school and start all over again. So began his meteoric academic rise with the retaking of his GCSEs, quickly followed by A levels, in which he gained four A stars in biology, biochemistry, chemistry, and general studies resulting in acceptance onto the six-year Medicine and Surgery degree course at the University of Liverpool in 2008, where he eventually and proudly graduated with honours, finishing in the top ten per cent of his year group, in 2014.

He completed his foundation years at Aintree University Hospital and Liverpool Heart and Chest Hospital (LHCH) and initially decided to follow a career in anaesthetics. However, after helping to organise the junior doctors' strikes of 2015/16 as BMA representative for LHCH, he refused to sign the hated new contract, precluding him from following the more traditional medical training routes. Instead, he took to travelling across the north-west of England as a career locum, completing his medical training whilst avoiding signing the contract.

Since writing this book, he has continued to progress in his career and now works as an acute medical consultant. He currently lives in

Liverpool with his wife, two children, two dogs, and twelve indoor and eight outdoor fish. He continues to keep himself fit and active and boxes at least twice a week, plays five-a-side football, and regularly attends the gym.

He has recently developed a keen interest in functional medicine, championing the removal of ultra processed foods (UPF) from the diet and is the proud owner of the YouTube channel Dr Magnesium Mg2+ (@Dr_Magnesium_Mg2). He can be contacted via his Facebook page Dr Magnesium (@dr.magnesium.2023).

Printed in Great Britain
by Amazon